# JOHN BALDESSARI

# JOHN BALDESSARI

*Coosje van Bruggen*

RIZZOLI
NEW YORK

Published on the occasion of the retrospective exhibition organized
by The Museum of Contemporary Art, 250 South Grand Avenue, Los
Angeles, California 90012

The Museum of Contemporary Art, Los Angeles
March 25–June 17, 1990

San Francisco Museum of Modern Art
July 12–September 9, 1990

Hirshhorn Museum and Sculpture Garden, Washington, D.C.
October 16, 1990–January 6, 1991

Walker Art Center, Minneapolis
February 3–April 28, 1991

Whitney Museum of American Art, New York
July 10–October 13, 1991

Musée d'Art Contemporain de Montréal
November 21, 1991–February 13, 1992

First published in the United States of America
in 1990 by Rizzoli International Publications, Inc.
300 Park Avenue South, New York, NY 10010

Copyright © 1990 Coosje van Bruggen

Library of Congress Cataloging-in-Publication Data
Bruggen, Coosje van
    John Baldessari/Coosje van Bruggen.
        p.    cm.
    Includes bibliographical references and index.
    ISBN 0-8478-1182-4—ISBN 0-8478-1190-5 (pbk.)
        1. Baldessari, John, 1931–   —Criticism and interpretation.
2. Conceptual art—United States.    I. Title.
N6537.B17B78   1990
709'.2—dc20                                89-43561
                                               CIP

The exhibition and this publication have been made possible in part
through the generosity of the Murray and Isabella Rayburn
Foundation; the Lannan Foundation; the National Endowment for
the Arts, a federal agency; Brooke and Carolyn Alexander; and Stuart
T. and Judith E. Spence. Additional support has been provided by
The Projects Council of The Museum of Contemporary Art.

Grateful acknowledgment is made to the following for permission to
quote or excerpt: Ezra Pound, *The Selected Letters of Ezra Pound:
1907–1941*, Copyright © 1950 by Ezra Pound, Reprinted by
permission of New Directions Publishing Corporation, New York;
Charles Baudelaire, *Flowers of Evil: A Selection*, Copyright © 1958 by
New Directions Publishing Corporation, Reprinted by permission of
New Directions Publishing Corporation; Cesare Pavese, *Stories*,
Copyright © 1946, 1953, 1960 by Giulio Einaudi Editore, English
translation copyright © 1946, 1966 by Alma Murch, First published
by the Ecco Press in 1987, Reprinted by permission.

Frontispiece: *Love and Work*, p. 2; *Street (With Two Detached
Observers)*, pp. 8–9; *Imploded House (With Two Observers)*, pp. 66–67;
*Five Male Thoughts (One Frontal)*, pp. 128–29; *If This Then That
(Space Capsule and Man With Hose)*, pp. 232–33. All works created
especially for this publication, 1989.

Designed by Antony Drobinski and Jill Korostoff
Emsworth Design, Inc.

Composition by Rainsford Type, Danbury, Connecticut
Printed and bound by Toppan Printing Company, Tokyo, Japan

# CONTENTS

Foreword and Acknowledgments     *6*
*Richard Koshalek*

Interlude: Between Questions and Answers     *11*

But This Is Not the Moral of the Story...     *69*

The Art of Misleading Interpretation     *131*

Biographical Data     *234*
*Compiled by David Platzker*

Exhibition History     *234*

Bibliography     *243*

Checklist of the Exhibition     *250*

Lenders to the Exhibition     *254*

Index     *255*

Photograph Credits     *256*

# FOREWORD AND ACKNOWLEDGMENTS

The Museum of Contemporary Art is proud to present this long-overdue monograph devoted to the career of John Baldessari. One of the most influential artists to have emerged since the mid-1960s, Baldessari has made an indelible mark on the character of contemporary art and thought. This book provides a comprehensive investigation of Baldessari's extensive oeuvre—from his phototext canvases of the late 1960s to his recent installation projects—and documents the artist's retrospective exhibition at MOCA, which subsequently travels throughout the United States and Canada.

The exhibition presents some ninety pieces by Baldessari, tracing the development of the artist's work—his use of photography and other media, his incorporation of appropriated images and text, and his study of their relationships. Together, the exhibition and book provide welcome opportunity to assess Baldessari's seminal contributions to Conceptual art and their impact on succeeding generations of American and European artists.

Baldessari's work has long been acclaimed and exhibited throughout Europe, but his exposure in the United States—not to mention his native California—has been more limited. His only major survey exhibition in America took place in 1981—nearly a decade ago—at The New Museum of Contemporary Art in New York. Thus, MOCA's presentation is timely and of particular importance given his extraordinary influence on the current generation of artists involved in Conceptual and text-related work.

The success of this book is a tribute to the author, Coosje van Bruggen. Van Bruggen's commitment to the artist's work, her knowledge and insight, and, above all, her independent thinking and personal approach to the subject have resulted in a book that not only situates the artist within contemporary art but also presents an in-depth analysis and unique

perspective on the work. Augmenting van Bruggen's texts are four special projects created by Baldessari for this volume.

The exhibition and catalogue have resulted from the cooperation and assistance of many individuals. First and foremost, of course, is John Baldessari, whose participation and wisdom have been integral to the exhibition and a constant source of inspiration. The lenders to the exhibition have also played a pivotal role by graciously allowing their works to remain in the show for the duration of its tour. MOCA would especially like to thank Ileana Sonnabend, Antonio Homem, Stefano Basilico, Nick Sheidy, and the staff of the Sonnabend Gallery in New York, who generously supplied information and numerous photographic materials. Margo Leavin, Wendy Brandow, Lynn Sharpless, and the staff of Margo Leavin Gallery in Los Angeles also provided generous assistance with the research and inventory of Baldessari's work. Meg Cranston and Cindy Bernard have been a source of constant support for the artist. Thanks should also go to Lori Schafer of The Museum of Modern Art, New York; the staff of the Research and Art Libraries of the University of California, Los Angeles; Lee Kaplan; Frank Kolodny; and the many other institutions and individuals who contributed invaluable assistance and information.

This book has been copublished by MOCA and Rizzoli International Publications, Inc. Our sincere thanks to Rizzoli International President Gianfranco Monacelli and Senior Editor Stephanie Salomon, who, in cooperation with MOCA, worked closely with both artist and author through every phase of this book's realization. This book will remain a valuable resource thanks to the assiduous efforts of David Platzker, who compiled the extensive chronology, exhibition history, bibliography, and caption data. In addition, he made valuable contributions to many aspects of the exhibition's organization. David Frankel provided further support and editorial assistance. The efforts of Antony Drobinski and Jill Korostoff resulted in the outstanding design of this book. Thanks also goes to Laura Stein, who helped to execute the specially created projects.

An exhibition of this size and scope deserves the widest possible audience. Our special thanks to those who have made possible MOCA's organization of an extensive tour: Jack Lane, John Caldwell, and Barbara Levine from the San Francisco Museum of Modern Art; James Demetrion and Ned Rifkin from the Hirshhorn Museum and Sculpture Garden, Washington, D.C.; Martin Friedman, Stephen Fleischman, and Marge Goldwater from the Walker Art Center, Minneapolis; Tom Armstrong and Barbara Haskell from the Whitney Museum of American Art, New York; and Marcel Brisebois and Manon Blanchette from the Musée d'Art Contemporain de Montréal, Canada.

We are deeply grateful to MOCA's Board of Trustees and its Program Committee for their recognition of the importance of this exhibition and their overall guidance and support. Similarly, we thank the entire staff of MOCA for their professional dedication and assistance. Former Chief Curator Mary Jane Jacob acted as principal curator in the initial conception and organization of the exhibition. A critical contribution was made by Alma Ruiz, Exhibitions Coordinator, who has been substantially involved in every stage of the exhibition's organization and tour development. Her tireless care, work, and attention have been of inestimable value to this project. Particular thanks go to Associate Director Sherri Geldin for her role in the overall planning and organization of the exhibition as well as for her guidance in the catalogue negotiations and coordination, for which assistance was provided by Editor Catherine Gudis. Special thanks also go to Director of Development Erica Clark; Director of Education Vas Prabhu; Press Officer Cynthia Campoy; Marketing and Graphics Manager Sylvia Hohri; Exhibition Production Manager John Bowsher and his superb staff; Registrar Mo Shannon; and Controller Jack Wiant.

Finally, this exhibition and publication would not have been possible without the generous financial commitment of the Murray and Isabella Rayburn Foundation; the Lannan Foundation; the National Endowment for the Arts, a federal agency; Brooke and Carolyn Alexander; and Stuart T. and Judith E. Spence. Additional support was provided by The Projects Council of The Museum of Contemporary Art. The artist, museum trustees, staff, and others involved in this project join me in expressing our deepest gratitude.

With this retrospective and its accompanying publication, MOCA chronicles a lasting contribution to the field of contemporary art. There is no doubt that John Baldessari will continue to work and experiment with the same vigor and originality that have marked his entire career. We look forward to being part of the continuing dialogue that he has created within and beyond the art community for the last twenty years.

*Richard Koshalek*
Director
The Museum of Contemporary Art,
Los Angeles

*I'm not going to temper, I don't change, don't want to take the chance of some magic being broken. I like being in my studio, being around all my stuff, magazines, books. This is my existence, this is where I get my power.*

—John Baldessari

# INTERLUDE:
# BETWEEN QUESTIONS
# AND ANSWERS

John Baldessari was born on June 17, 1931, in National City, south of San Diego, California. His mother, Hedvig Jensen, was Danish—the daughter of a shopkeeper in Vejle, Jutland. In the 1920s, as a young woman, she moved to New York, where she worked for several years as a registered nurse at Bellevue Hospital. She met her future husband, Antonio Baldessari, while accompanying a wealthy lady on a trip to California. Antonio was the son of a poor farmer and the youngest of four brothers and two sisters who grew up in a small village high in the Italian Tirol mountains, not far from Trent. He emigrated to America in search of a better livelihood than one gained from delivering mail in return for room and board and an occasional pair of new shoes. He worked first as a coal miner, in Colorado, then settled down in National City, where he set up a succession of small business enterprises.

Because both parents were European immigrants, as a child John Baldessari felt that he did not fit into American society. His lack of an American background allowed him to remain unaware of growing up on the "wrong side of the tracks," but made the initiation of relationships with other children difficult. As he grew, his unusual height caused him to stand out from his peers, keep to himself, and withdraw into a fantasy world of his own.

Baldessari's interest in art can be traced as far back as elementary school and continued during his high school years, though by then he was equally interested in chemistry. At San Diego State College he majored in art, minored in literature, and took some courses in philosophy. After receiving a bachelor of arts degree in 1953, he thought of becoming an artist. But because he had no idea what that entailed, he postponed his artistic aspirations for a year to concentrate on general art history courses

at the University of California, at Berkeley. At that time he began to identify in particular with Dada and Surrealism. There, from September 1954 through the spring of 1955, he tried "to reinvent the wheel," as he put it, by setting up a cross-indexing system in which to record and thus capture everything he had ever read. But he could not keep up with all the information pouring in, and became "literally ill" from the effort. Eventually this obsession with the impossible task of getting everything under control, leaving no loose ends, gave way to the realization that he would have to be satisfied with partial knowledge: "Everybody knows a different world, and only part of it. We communicate only by chance, as nobody knows the whole, only where overlapping takes place." This insight became a point of view that would turn up later in his art in many disguises.

Returning to San Diego State College, Baldessari began to prepare for a master's degree in art, which he received in 1957. That same year he showed one of his paintings, which bore the influences of Cézanne and Matisse, in the "National Orange Show," the annual county fair/art exhibition held in San Bernardino. In a review of the show in the April 1957 issue of *Artnews*, he was mentioned along with others as meriting a blue ribbon. However, it wasn't until he met Rico Lebrun during a summer studio course that Baldessari became convinced that he really should become an artist. He quit his teaching job in a San Diego high school and moved to Los Angeles to study art at the Otis and the Chouinard art institutes. But he soon grew uncomfortable there, feeling he was expected to conform to the then dominant Los Angeles art styles, exemplified by the artists showing at the Ferus Gallery. The gallery, founded in 1957 by curator Walter Hopps and Edward Kienholz, included besides Kienholz such artists as Craig Kauffman, John Altoon, Hassel Smith,

Wallace Berman, Billy Al Bengston, Edward Ruscha, Ed Moses, and Larry Bell.

In the summer of 1959, discouraged by the lack of gallery response to his paintings, Baldessari moved back to San Diego and resigned himself to teaching in the city schools. Shortly after his return, the California Youth Authority offered him a job teaching juvenile delinquents for six weeks at a camp in the mountains: "The only reason I was asked was that I was so big. All the teachers were over 6 foot 4 inches tall." The students rejected most of the courses but asked Baldessari to open up the arts and crafts room at night so that they could work there: "Then I realized how magic and powerful art could be; they valued art more than I did. This moving experience stimulated me to go on, for I was in a kind of identity crisis at the time, and before leaving Los Angeles I had thought of pursuing religious studies at the Princeton Theological Seminary but I was rejected." Thus, despite the feeling that he was "a pariah doing art" and that he "should be doing something more socially useful,"[1] Baldessari tenaciously continued to paint, without much recognition, in a windowless studio at the back of a laundromat owned by his father.

Occasionally Baldessari entered juried exhibitions, participated in group shows, and got involved in special events such as "Jazz at the Art Center #5," one of a series of jazz concerts held on October 13, 1962 at the Art Center in La Jolla, California, for which he created visual effects. For this concert Baldessari designed a backdrop that consisted of four large flesh-colored painting-constructions, hanging from the ceiling of the stage, each of which was divided into a painted X-shaped structure above and a grid of compartments containing gourdlike phallic shapes below. For the intermission, when the musicians went offstage, Baldessari created a 30-minute slide show, juxtaposing words and close-ups

"Jazz at the Art Center #5," at the Art Center, La Jolla, California, October 13, 1962. Painting-constructions by John Baldessari, from left to right: *The Rolly Polly Puppy Mommy Daddy Swank Dude Special, The Brave Little Jolly Jumping Regular Intimate Shocker, The Fraidy Raggedy Ann Bingity-Bangity Bed of Sin Bonus Offer, The Magnificent Sonny the Bunny Torrid Handy Coupon.* All works destroyed in *Cremation Project,* 1970

Selection of slides from the artist's 30-minute slide show on the occasion of "Jazz at the Art Center #5"

of images from magazines, newspapers, and holiday snapshots on a split movie screen. This fragmentary sequence accompanied by music suggested a visual narrative. It was announced in the program as Experiment #1: " 'Surreal Painting from National City.' Poem by John Baldessari."

After his return to San Diego from Los Angeles, Baldessari had turned primarily to landscape painting. Caught up in different styles and confused about what direction to take next, Baldessari—instead of rationally analyzing his art—had decided to respond to his uncertainty spontaneously by driving out every day to the La Jolla cliffs to paint whatever inspired him. The canvases were built up with heavy layers of pigment, which were made tactile by sandwiching little pieces of painted canvas between the layers. By around 1962 the landscape elements dropped out in favor of a far more abstract style only vaguely hinting at its original sources. Baldessari recalls, "While I was doing abstract painting I would drive or walk around and all of a sudden see something in the environment that reminded me of what I was working on." Wanting to hold on to such coincidental finds, he began to take his camera along, photographing any outdoor flat surface—even the backs of trucks—that reminded him of his paintings. Next he began to use these photographic notes as the source material for new paintings, which themselves in turn suggested new photographs, such as the walls of buildings containing bits of billboard

lettering. These stimulated him to include alphabetical characters in his paintings, reminiscent of the undistorted signs of the outside world that Braque and Picasso. had so convincingly applied as clues to objects in their analytical Cubist paintings and collages, which otherwise, at the time, might have seemed quite hermetic.

Other ideas of how to structure surfaces came to Baldessari from observing accumulations of billboard fragments on outdoor walls. He asked a friend, who was a manager of the advertising agency Foster and Kleiser, to supply him with throwaway posters, which

13

*US Mail Marks the X*, 1962
Mixed-media wood construction
22 x 18 in. (55.9 x 45.8 cm)
Collection of Robert Shapazian, Los
Angeles

he picked up in his Volkswagen bus. It was a common practice at the agency to cut up posters too large to mount in one piece; often the image was divided into twenty-four or thirty-six equal parts, without any consideration for their composition. Over a period of time Baldessari assembled a huge number of these disconnected poster fragments in stacks that almost reached to the ceiling of his studio. It took him months of looking at each fragment in order to make a selection. Eventually he mounted the selected sheets, one at a time, on a plywood or Masonite ground. Sometimes he partially painted over a sheet, leaving the tread of a tire or the remainder of a hand; at other times he effaced the images almost entirely in favor of an abstract composition, creating a faint collage effect. The blocked-out sections and obliterated parts of the poster sheets not only disrupted the continuity of the whole image, disorienting the viewer, but also acquired new associations, far more evocative than the figuration remaining from the original advertisements. Accepting the chance effects that resulted from the slicing of the images as part of the composition, Baldessari found himself with areas of negative space that had originally been located between the elements of the poster pictures, but that had been turned into contextless abstractions when the posters were cut up. And by emphasizing these areas with paint, and reversing them into positives, he upset even further the reading of the original advertisement.

*The Back of All the Trucks Passed
While Driving from Los Angeles to
Santa Barbara, California. Sunday 20
January 1963* (details), 1963
Thirty-two 35mm slides
Collection of the artist

Untitled, 1962
Oil on paper; mounted on board
64 x 48 in. (162.6 x 121.9 cm)
Destroyed in *Cremation Project*, 1970

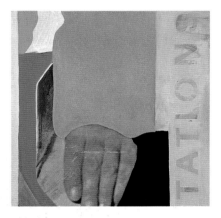

*Standard Hand*, 1962
Oil on paper; mounted on board
38 x 37 in. (96.5 x 94 cm)
Destroyed in *Cremation Project*, 1970

In the early 1960s, then, Baldessari already showed a liking for the principle of reversal, for working against the effect originally intended. This predilection recurs in his composite photoworks of the 1980s as well as in a series of etchings called *Black Dice*, 1982, its title based on a still from the movie of the same name. In a manner similar to the cutting up of the poster sheets, Baldessari arbitrarily divided the 8-by-10-inch movie still twice vertically and twice horizontally, creating nine equal parts. Each part was developed into an etching, to be seen at once individually and as an alienated fragment linked to the original whole. Experimenting with similar issues of control and withdrawal, the artist today randomly sorts through the piles of movie stills he has collected.

I tend to pick out things that are obvious, for instance, ideas that I've used in my last series. And then, while accumulating those photographs, I may find something new I hadn't thought of, and I see it pop up in other places. For instance, I have a new file on sand; first I saw a still with sand lying on the floor of a house, and then, a week or so later, I found something else, and by now I have about ten photographs with sand, and all of a sudden I see a pattern emerge. Next I made an analogy between a telephone and a strand of pearls as a means of communication. A connection between them occurred to me while I looked at a color photograph in *National Geographic*. The pearls, in their turn, I associated with people tied up with chains, so I subtitled my file on sand and pearls "nooses for hangmen." Somehow things are all related in my mind, but then after a while they begin to separate. I create my own dictionary of images, but it's always sliding. Sometimes things will be in one file and at other times in another file, and then I'll have to do cross-referencing. I never go to stock places where they have the stills already arranged in categories. I want to feel like a gold miner, and I don't want the gold given to me.

Source material for *Black Dice*, 1982

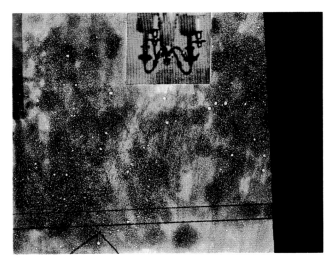

*Black Dice*, 1982
Nine color etchings in aquatint, photo
etching, soft ground, and sugar lift, on
Velin d'Arches paper
16½ x 19¾ in. each (41.9 x 50.2 cm)
Edition of 35 and 10 artist's proofs
Published by Peter Blum Edition, New
York
Courtesy of Blum Edition, New York

18

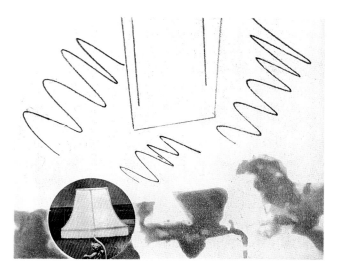

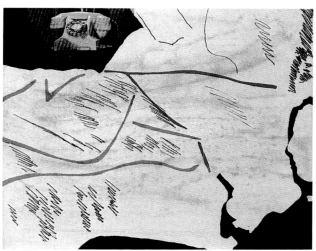

When he sifts through his treasured photographs in the hope of finding that one overlooked, unconscious gesture that will energize his picture, Baldessari feels the same pleasure he did on discovering the transitional areas of negative space in the poster sheets of the early 1960s. "It's like when I am in an airplane cabin and overhear two conversations: one says something and another one says something else. I could not have thought up those phrases on my own, and I respond to it by connecting one to the other, taking both out of their own context, and by making them a part of my imagination." The method of combining two unrelated snippets of conversation or using recycled imagery, or of emphasizing the nondescript area between two separate things, surfaces again and again in Baldessari's art in the form of the contiguity of unrelated images. It is displayed most directly and confrontationally in the '60s poster sheets: some of the 1967 disjunctive phototext paintings, such as *This Is Not To Be Looked At.*; in the '70s conceptual pieces like *Movie Storyboard: Norma's Story*, 1974, or *Blasted Allegories*, 1978; and in the '80s composite photoworks such as *Three Tires with Chinese Man*, 1984, the diptych *Apple*, 1986, or *(Two Chests) For Example*, 1987.

Baldessari's experimentation with billboard materials in the mid-1960s led him to a close examination of their techniques. A poster image is made up of a multitude of small Benday dots, similar to but more prominent than those found in newspaper halftones. In 1965 he began to enlarge and paint these dots, while concurrently becoming more interested in the remnants of cut-up sheets and paper debris lying around the studio. Examining discarded bits of poster sheets under a high-powered magnifying glass, Baldessari, in his urge to get away from traditional painting, began to photograph them for further study. He was in particular attracted by their color scheme whose composition was of a random rather than an aesthetic nature, and by the arbitrary flow of dot patterns on top of the scraps, which, since they no longer served as part of the whole advertising image, had become disconnected from their original function yet continued to have an order and general direction of their own. Inspired by these found scraps, Baldessari transformed the concept into large aluminum cutouts, which could be installed either as an arrangement on the floor or hung as reliefs on the wall. In order to replicate paper, the cutouts were torn, bent, crumpled, or

*This Is Not To Be Looked At.*, 1968
Acrylic and photoemulsion on canvas
59 x 45 in. (149.9 x 114.3 cm)
Collection of Councilman Joel Wachs,
Los Angeles

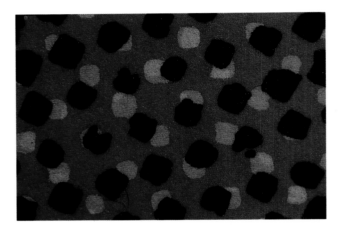

Details of Benday dots from billboard
material

*Three Tires with Chinese Man*, 1984
Black-and-white photographs;
mounted on board
55¼ x 45½ in. overall (140.3 x 115.6
cm)
Courtesy of Margo Leavin Gallery, Los
Angeles

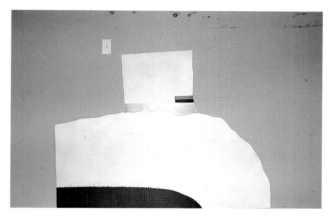

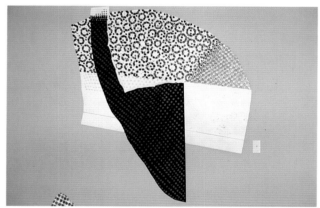

Works from the exhibition and installation "Fragments," at the La Jolla Museum of Art, La Jolla, California, March 30–April 24, 1966 All works destroyed in *Cremation Project*, 1970

flattened and spray-painted white. Solid ground colors, separate or overlapping, and multicolored dot patterns applied with different-sized rubber stamps dipped in acrylic paint, were then layered onto the white surface in many variations. The stamps had been made from "faucet washers attached to wooden sticks." But in working on these capricious forms, Baldessari found that the cutouts began to look more and more like recognizable objects: a combination of three scraps suggested a boat; another cutout implied a faucet, and still another a light bulb or a spout.

In March and April of 1966 Baldessari exhibited both the abstract scraps and the scraps transformed into objects in an installation he titled "Fragments," at the La Jolla Museum of Art (formerly the Art Center in La Jolla). The show made him ask, "When is a part a whole, and when is a whole a part?" In accordance with this theme, he used a double-exposed photograph of himself on the poster for the exhibition. One image showed the artist inside a drawn circle. It recalled a well-known

Detail of poster for "Fragments"

drawing by Leonardo da Vinci, who had such an inclination for mathematical explanations that he rendered a man with arms and legs outstretched as the axis of a circle, illustrating Vitruvius's code of ideal human proportions. In the second image, however, Baldessari—mimicking the Leonardo diagram—happened to appear with one arm longer than the other. He decided to accentuate the accidental outcropping that marred the perfection of the circle and the idea of the body fitting into a preordained geometric form. By incorporating this human flaw into his work, Baldessari undermined the Renaissance ideal of universal man and recalled a more organic way of thinking, such as he admired in the Navajo Indians, who deliberately include mistakes in the weaving of their tapestries.

The summer of 1966 turned out to be one of great discontent for Baldessari. He worked at four part-time jobs and tried unsuccessfully to divide the rest of his time between reading, painting, and taking photographs outdoors. He also took innumerable notes from his readings and pinned them up along with the photographs on his studio walls. This activity began to seem far more appealing than the painstaking translation of photographic details into abstract paintings. He reasoned that since nobody really cared about his work anyway, why not simply do what he enjoyed most. He felt that his paintings had become too elitist, too obscure, and that newspaper photography, magazine illustrations, and text were closer to people's experience than painting, "so," as he noted, "*that* would be the language I was going to use, photographic imagery and words. Actually I remember perversely saying, 'I'm going to give people what they want, and they probably don't want this either!' "

By 1966 Baldessari was using an opaque projector to enlarge the poster sheets and to blow up other kinds of visual material that interested him. That same year he also experimented with such a projector when he taught in an innovative summer program for grade-school children, funded by Dr. Seuss, the children's book writer, at the La Jolla Museum of Art. (The children worked directly on blank 35-mm. slides, which Baldessari later projected for them, at up to 20 feet high.)

In 1967, in a series of three "Art Lessons," Baldessari initiated a dialogue between himself as artist and teacher, a dialogue he still maintains today: "I think when I'm doing art, I'm questioning how to do it." The series began with a mimeographed sheet he had found accidentally on "how to draw things in perspective and how to make them look solid," which had been left in a classroom at the University of California where Baldessari was teaching night school and which he then enlarged with his opaque projector, "just to see if anything could be done with it." He transferred the image to a canvas, intervening very little in it. Similarly, he enlarged a Bible tract compiled from street flyers he had collected. In a third painting, however, for which he had enlarged a sheet with four instructional drawing lessons from a composition book, he painted some parts out and

*Art Lesson,* 1967
Ink and acrylic on canvas
68 x 57 in. (172.7 x 144.8 cm)
Collection of the artist

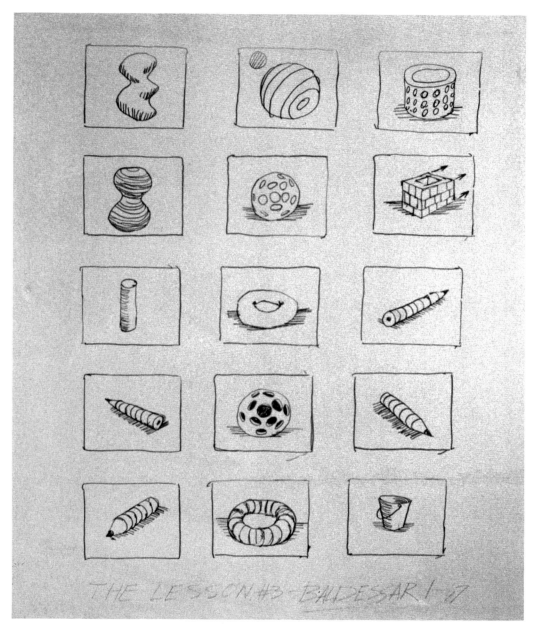

Max Ernst
Illustration from "L'Invention" in Max
Ernst and Paul Eluards's *Répétitions*.
Paris: Au Sans Pareil, 1922. Copyright
© 1989 ARS N.Y./SPADEM.
From the Howard L. and Muriel
Weingrow Collection of Avant-Garde
Art & Literature, Axinn Library,
Hofstra University

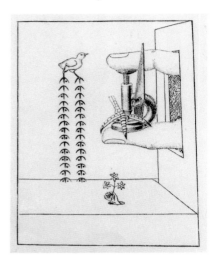

*Suppose It Is True After All? What
Then?*, 1967
Oil on canvas
14½ x 20½ in. (36.8 x 52.1 cm)
Destroyed in *Cremation Project*, 1970

*Art Lesson*, 1967
Oil on canvas
68 x 57 in. (172.7 x 144.8 cm)
Location unknown

emphasized others as he had in the poster sheets. In this *Art Lesson* Baldessari eroded the rules and conventions of drawing, through a streak of irony, in a Dada-Surrealist mode. On one of the four instructional drawing lessons he added the track of a falling apple, mocking the accompanying text that reads "Things falling out of picture." And on another drawing he painted a necktie, illustrating the composition book's rule that "if the road is not drawn in perspective, it will hang out of the painting like a tie."

Baldessari complemented his tie image with typography in the form of a garland, which echoes, though distantly, Apollinaire's poem from *Calligrammes* "La Cravate et la montre" ("The Tie and the Watch"), while the repeatedly dropping apple recalls the chicken tracks in Max Ernst's illustration of Paul Eluard's poem "L'Invention" ("The Invention") 1922. In several later works, Baldessari would graft his ideas onto a Symbolist/Surrealist tradition. Robert Pincus-Witten has pointed out an analogy between the set of photographs *Cigar Smoke To Match Clouds That Are Different (By Sight—Side View)* and . . . *(By Memory—Front View)*, 1972–73 and Man Ray's 1935 photograph *Ce qui nous manque à tous* ("What We All Lack"), which depicts a soap bubble rising from a clay pipe. Ethereal elements, "smoke or bubble have long been considered symbolic of spirit or idea as alternative to state of matter,"[2] Pincus-Witten observes. In Baldessari's *Cigar Smoke To Match Clouds . . . (By Sight . . . )* the flat snapshots containing the clouds function as a sort of window in the studio wall. The smoke rings recall not only Stieglitz's cloud photographs, as Pincus-

Witten notes, but also Magritte's frequent two-dimensional depiction of white clouds against a blue sky, a world without depth the painter described as "no more than a curtain hung in front of me."[3]

Along with a propensity for art-historical references, Baldessari likes to explore and test the conventions of everyday life. Of the cigar smoke photographs, he remarked, "There is also this boring thing, you know, at parties, or a dinner, where someone takes a cigar, and is going to blow a ring, and that sort of thing. So taking that information that's already there in the culture, and pushing it slightly askew, it becomes even more ridiculous. A cloud is amorphous already and then combining it with cigar smoke—that uselessness I like." The six-photograph set *A Cigar Is a Good Smoke*, 1972–73, recalls Magritte's notorious inscription "*Ceci n'est pas une pipe*," in *La Trahison des images*, 1928–39. Combining phrases like "Wood is wood," or "A glass is a glass" (echoing Gertrude Stein's phrase "Rose is a rose is a rose is a rose") with "but a cigar is a good smoke," Baldessari addresses what are his fundamental questions of art and life: "When are things just what they are and when are they different than they are?" And by bringing into play Rudyard Kipling: "And a woman is only a woman, but a good cigar is a smoke," Baldessari substituted the image of woman seen as object with other objects "to see how the phrase would resonate." This piece prefigured a way of thinking—a question—that would run through much of his art: does the quintessence change when objects are replaced with other objects?

*Cigar Smoke To Match Clouds That Are Different (By Sight—Side View)*, 1972–73
Three Type-C prints; mounted on board
14 x 9½ in. each (35.6 x 24.1 cm)
Courtesy of Sonnabend Gallery, New York

A year later, in 1974, while making the *Embed Series*, Baldessari asked himself a related question: "Can I really get someone to believe the messages I have hidden about imagining, dreaming, fantasies, wish, and hope?" The practice of marketing agencies of hiding subliminal messages in television commercials and magazine advertisements, which had become a topic of heated debate during the early '70s, led Baldessari to create the *Embed Series*, in which he "embedded" words into photographic images by means of airbrushing, double exposure, etc. Words and images, without one taking precedence over the other, coexisted separately but together. Whereas in the composite photoworks of the 1980s the effect is of infinite meanings within meanings within meanings without the use of language, like the opening of a Chinese box, in the *Embed Series*, text occurs literally below the surface. In essence, "seeing is believing," and words are spelled out in smokelike messages found in cloud formations, or perhaps cigar dreams?

After the series of "Art Lessons" Baldessari made one more painting, in 1967, derived from a biblical tract: "Suppose it is true after all? What then?" He painted the text in white and black brushstrokes on a heavily built-up red-orange background. But somehow form and content proved unsatisfactory, making the artist question whether his text should function as a subjective decorative element of painting or an objective linguistic sign. After all, someone else could apply the paint, which would allow him to concentrate on the development of ideas instead of on laborious painting.

*A Cigar Is a Good Smoke* (details),
1972–73
Six panels each with one black-and-white
and one color photograph;
colored pencil on board
20 x 24 in. each (50.8 x 61 cm)
Location unknown

*Embed Series: Cigar Dreams (Seeing Is Believing)*, 1974
Three black-and-white photographs
(retouched); mounted on board
20 x 16 in. each (50.8 x 40.6 cm)
International Museum of Photography
at George Eastman House, Rochester,
New York

 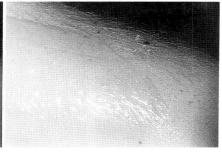

(Early in 1967 Baldessari had concluded his series of poster sheets with a sheet he left untouched by paint—a Polaroid camera advertisement showing someone eating corn on the cob, juxtaposed with what seemed to be a totally abstract pattern created by the cropping of the sheet.) In a subsequent series of text canvases and another of photographically transferred images, also accompanied by painted text, Baldessari allowed himself a far more conceptual approach. In these works the personal touch of the artist's hand was rejected in favor of using a commercial photoemulsion technique for the photographs, and a sign painter was hired to paint the text:

*Embed Series: Oiled Arm (Sinking Boat and Palms)*, 1974
Two black-and-white photographs
(retouched); mounted on board
16¾ x 23⅝ in. each (42.5 x 60 cm)
Collection of Susan and Lewis
Manilow

I think it was about accepting my destiny, and coming to terms with it. At that point of my life I thought all I was going to do was teach in high school, you know, have a family and kids, and do some work for my friends. Probably I was never going to get out of National City, so I was going to show people what it's like, to make art out of where I lived without glamorizing it, and with the idea that truth is beautiful, no matter how ugly it is. I drove around in the car shooting my pictures from the window, because I didn't want to try to make the place more beautiful by setting my camera up with a tripod, getting the right light, and just the right composition. I just wanted it the way it is—it isn't even rural sprawl.

*A Two-Dimensional Surface...*, 1967
Acrylic on canvas
58 x 67 in. (147.3 x 170.2 cm)
Collection of the artist

Untitled, 1967
Mixed-media collage on canvas
43 x 58 in. (109.2 x 147.3 cm)
Destroyed in *Cremation Project*, 1970

# A TWO-DIMENSIONAL SURFACE WITHOUT ANY ARTICULATION IS A DEAD EXPERIENCE

*This was the first text-on-canvas piece I did. I did not like the sign painter's result. The text seemed too "alive." I wanted it to be more "dead."*

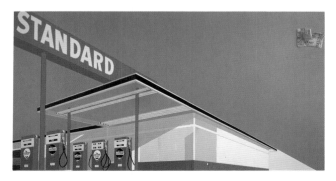

Edward Ruscha
*Standard Station 10¢ Western Being Torn in Half*, 1964
Oil on canvas
65 x 121½ in. (165.1 x 308.6 cm)
Private collection, Fort Worth, Texas

The notion of creating art out of everyday life had been pursued before, by the so-called Pop artists. Baldessari was also inspired by Edward Ruscha and in particular his conceptual treatment of his environment in paintings such as *Standard Station 10¢ Western Being Torn in Half*, 1964, and in his books *Some Los Angeles Apartments*, 1965, and *Every Building on the Sunset Strip*, 1966. The idea of transforming local color, and colloquial expressions into art or poetry had already been anticipated by the great modern poet and physician William Carlos Williams, who, "not after the establishment but speaking straight ahead," used only natural American speech patterns in his poems: "The rhythmical construction of a poem was determined for me by the language as it is spoken. Word of mouth language, not classical English."[4] And Williams also had remarked:

All poets have a tendency to dress up an ordinary person, as Yeats does. It has to be special treatment to be poetic, and I don't acknowledge this at all. I'd rather look at an old woman paring her nails as the essence of the antipoetic.... I wanted to get to the real situation, not human nor aesthetic—almost a philosophic truth which can ignore all human categories.[5]

But instead of making a poetic or philosophical choice of "antiart," Baldessari was driven to his version of "the real situation" solely by despair, by seeing no other way out:

Those places had been that way forever, before I was born, and nobody wanted to live in that area. I remember I was in charge of this lecture series down in this little junior college, south of National City, just before coming to the Mexican border. Some friends of mine in Los Angeles had talked Sam Francis into coming down and speaking; he was even then a fairly big art star. And I remember as I was interviewing him for the students, asking him what he found interesting about this area, him saying, "Well, it's the end of the line. You can't get any further away from the U.S. than this." And that's how I felt. Who'd want to be there? And that's how it felt to make the phototext canvases, which were pushing the limits at the time: I thought, I'm not using paint, it's a photographic process, and so you can't claim that they're paintings. Rauschenberg had done overlaps of paint and screened photographic images, one over the other onto the canvas in a transfer method he had invented himself. But I wanted to be less artful than Rauschenberg and Warhol: this is a photograph, here's a text. That's it. And I thought, because they're done on canvas, they might be equated with art.

The first text and phototext canvases are dated April 26, 1967, the day Baldessari paid the sign painter. He continued making them through 1968. They were all painted on same-size vertical canvases, whose dimensions were determined by the size of the

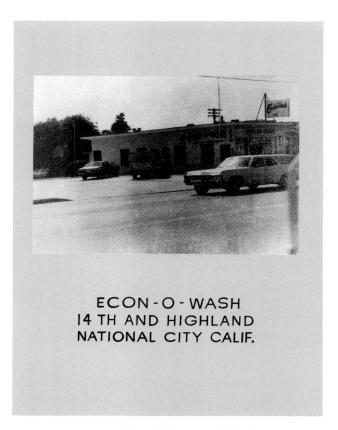

*Econ-O-Wash...*, 1967–68
Acrylic and photoemulsion on canvas
59 x 45 in. (149.9 x 114.3 cm)
Collection of the artist

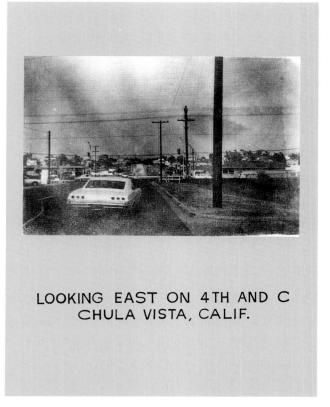

*Looking East on 4th and C...*, 1967–68
Acrylic and photoemulsion on canvas
59 x 45 in. (149.9 x 114.3 cm)
Collection of the artist

RYAN OLDSMOBILE
NATIONAL CITY, CALIF.

*Ryan Oldsmobile...*, 1967–68
Acrylic and photoemulsion on canvas
59 x 45 in. (149.9 x 114.3 cm)
Collection of the artist

WRONG

*Wrong*, 1967
Acrylic and photoemulsion on canvas
59 x 45 in. (149.8 x 114.3 cm)
Los Angeles County Museum of Art;
Contemporary Art Council, New
Talent Purchase Award

door of the artist's Volkswagen bus, which was used to transport them. These canvases can be divided into three categories: those derived from snapshots taken by the artist, those derived from photographs taken by others (primarily by his wife, Carol Wixom), and those taken from other source material, including magazine illustrations, children's books, drawing instruction books, and so forth. The snapshots taken by the artist of the Ryan Oldsmobile salesroom, the Duck Pond Bar, and other buildings in National City are photographed without any attempt at composition. Beneath the images, the names of the places are repeated tautologically, in the characterless, slightly clumsy, but nonmechanical lettering style of the sign painter. Baldessari recalls,

I drove with one hand and pointed the camera out the window with the other, not looking where I was shooting pictures. Then I would stop the car and just write down the location, and that would be it—for instance Econ-O-Wash, 14th and Highland, National City, Cal. or looking east on 4th and C, Chula Vista, Cal. I wanted things the way they were, with ugly wires and telephone poles, without beautification, and with the quality of newspaper photo-reportage, which the photoemulsion images resembled because of their grainy quality.

Living isolated in National City, Baldessari felt liberated from restrictive art theories. There were no social pressures; he had nothing to lose. In the

phototext painting *Wrong*, 1967, as in "Art Lessons," he again played with the rules of so-called correct composition—in this case the rule that one should never take a picture of someone in front of a tree because it will look as if the tree is growing out of the person's head. The original snapshot, taken by Wixom, focuses on the artist in front of a palm tree near their house that seems indeed to grow out of his head. By perversely violating the "rule," Baldessari questioned the validity of the accepted bromides of art education, showing that they had nothing to do with "good" or "bad" art. Recalling Robert Rauschenberg's two almost identical paintings *Factum* I and *Factum* II, both from 1957 and an ironic response to the idea of abstract expressionism

*Kissing Series: Simone Palm Trees
(Near)*, 1975
Two color photographs; mounted on
board
10 x 8 in. each (25.4 x 20.3 cm)
Courtesy of Sonnabend Gallery, New
York

*Watch children at play? They align
things (bottle caps, pebbles, etc.), abut
or tangentialize things, and go through
a gamut of organizational devices.*

*Here a friend tangentializes
("kisses") a palm frond. An art teacher
once told me that two elements in a
design could be either near or overlap,
but it was distracting visually for them
to "kiss."*

*This device allows near and far
objects to exist in the same plane.*

*In* Palm Tree (For Charlemagne)
*parts of trees become a single tree by
alignment and "kissing."*

*The concerns that unite* Wrong, *the*
Kissing Series, *and the* Alignment
Series *are:*

*1. A deliberate rejection and
exploration of conventional
compositional rules.*

*2. Ideas of alignment, touching, and
distance (i.e., when are things together;
when are they apart).*

*3. The anti-compositional device of
focusing on an idea rather than what
is visually pleasing (e.g., rather than a
beautiful photo of a sunset—say, a
photo where the sinking sun must be
perfectly eclipsed by a passing airplane
or bird).*

*Alignment Series: Palm Tree (For
Charlemagne)*, 1975
Type-C prints, black-and-white photograph,
and postcards on board with colored pencil
40 x 26 in. overall (101.6 x 66 cm)
Cincinnati Art Museum, Ohio; gift of
RSM Co.

31

not just stare directly down the road into the middle of the picture for no reason at all.

A similar transposition—taking a photograph from one source and combining it with a text from another—occurs in *This Is Not To Be Looked At.*, 1968. The title is a slightly altered version of Goya's emotive etching from the "Disasters of War" series of 1820. Baldessari complemented the title with a photograph of an *Artforum* magazine cover, featuring a cool Minimalist painting by Frank Stella. In the same way Baldessari set a photograph from a popular composition book, *Art Fundamentals, Theory and Practice*, by Ocvirk, Bone, Stinson, and Wigg, next to a caption from another book called *You Can Draw*, by Adrian Hill. The caption, which instructs the reader on how to draw shadows, became in a slightly modified form the title of Baldessari's work *Place a Book in a Strong Light and This Is What You Will See* (1967–68). At first, photo and text seem matter-of-factly to belong together, but the viewer soon discovers discrepancies between them, giving rise to multiple interpretations.

Gradually Baldessari began to work with more sophisticated quotations, without accompanying photographic images, borrowing from art critics such as Clement Greenberg and Barbara Rose. In *Painting for Kubler*, 1967–68, he paraphrased the following passage from the art historian George Kubler's book *The Shape of Time* in a reaffirmation of the conviction that works are connected to one another in time, that art "does not come out of a void," and to render obsolete that one egomaniacal question so frequently asked in a period in which the emphasis was on the idea alone, "Who did it first?":

The products of prior positions become obsolete or unfashionable. Yet prior positions are part of the invention, because to attain the new position the inventor must reassemble its components by an intuitive insight transcending the preceding positions in the sequence. Of its users or beneficiaries the new position also demands some familiarity with prior positions in order that they may discover the working range of the invention. The technique of invention thus has two distinct phases: the discovery of new positions followed by their amalgamation with the existing body of knowledge.[6]

The text-on-canvas work *Semi-Close-Up of Girl by Geranium (Soft View)*, 1968, was inspired by some lines of stage direction for D. W. Griffith's movie *Intolerance*: "Finishes watering it—examines plant to see if it has any signs of growth, finds slight evidence—smiles—one part is sagging—she runs fingers along it—raises hand over plant to encourage it to grow." The sentence describes a scene lasting a few seconds and tells a concise little story. Baldessari says he was drawn to this text because "it was such an unimportant gesture, and in a sense so dumb, but so beautiful."

THE SPECTATOR IS COMPELLED TO LOOK DIRECTLY DOWN THE ROAD AND INTO THE MIDDLE OF THE PICTURE.

*The Spectator Is Compelled...*,
1967–68
Acrylic and photoemulsion on canvas
59 x 45 in. (149.9 x 114.3 cm)
Collection of Robert Shapazian, Los Angeles

as unrepeatable gestural painting dependent on chance circumstances, and also inspired by the homily "Two wrongs don't make a right," Baldessari planned to create an almost exact duplicate of *Wrong*, but never got around to executing it. In another phototext painting, *The Spectator Is Compelled to Look Directly Down the Road and into the Middle of the Picture*, 1967–68, Baldessari is seen from the back looking down the street in a pose that illustrates the pictorial convention of establishing an eye level. In fact, the composition of the picture is taken from a manual by Ernest R. Norling, *Perspective Made Easy*, which illustrates eye level by showing an artist seen from behind standing on train tracks. The title of Baldessari's work, however, intimates that he or she should ignore any such didactic purpose: why

PLACE A BOOK IN A STRONG
LIGHT AND THIS IS WHAT YOU
WILL SEE.

*Place a Book in a Strong Light...*,
1967–68
Acrylic and photoemulsion on canvas
59 x 45 in. (149.9 x 114.3 cm)
Private collection, courtesy of
Sonnabend Gallery, New York

PAINTING FOR KUBLER

THIS PAINTING OWES ITS EXISTENCE TO
PRIOR PAINTINGS. BY LIKING THIS SOLUTION.
YOU SHOULD NOT BE BLOCKED IN YOUR CONTIN-
UED ACCEPTANCE OF PRIOR INVENTIONS. TO
ATTAIN THIS POSITION. IDEAS OF FORMER
PAINTING HAD TO BE RETHOUGHT IN ORDER TO TRAN-
SCEND FORMER WORK.  TO LIKE THIS PAINTING. YOU
WILL HAVE TO UNDERSTAND PRIOR WORK.  ULTIMATE-
LY THIS WORK WILL AMALGAMATE WITH THE EXISTING
BODY OF KNOWLEDGE.

*Painting for Kubler*, 1967- 68
Acrylic on canvas
68 x 56½ in. (172.7 x 143.5 cm)
Collection of Judy and Stuart Spence,
South Pasadena, California

*A 1968 Painting*, 1968
Acrylic and photoemulsion on canvas
59 x 45 in. (149.9 x 114.3 cm)
Courtesy of Sonnabend Gallery, New
York

A 1968 PAINTING

*I intended to do one of these each year
for the rest of my life. It would be a
history of style/fashion, like saying
"that's a '70s movie." I would also be
able to compare the history of my own
work to this "art of the year" choice in
the style of* Time *magazine's "Man of
the Year" cover. Like an art history
quiz—"students, in what year would
you place this painting if you didn't
know it or the artist?"*

*Strobe Series/Futurist: Girl with Flowers Falling from Her Mouth (For Botticelli) #1*, 1975
Color photograph; mounted on board
13⅜ x 10½ in. (34 x 26.7 cm)
Courtesy of Sonnabend Gallery, New York

SEMI-CLOSE-UP OF GIRL BY GERANIUM
( SOFT VIEW )

FINISHES WATERING IT - EXAMINES PLANT TO
SEE IF IT HAS ANY SIGNS OF GROWTH, FINDS
SLIGHT EVIDENCE - SMILES - ONE PART IS SAG-
GING - SHE RUNS FINGERS ALONG IT - RAISES
HAND OVER PLANT TO ENCOURAGE IT TO GROW.

*Semi-Close-Up of Girl by Geranium (Soft View)*, 1968
Acrylic on canvas
68 x 56½ in. (172.7 x 143.5 cm)
Emanuel Hoffmann-Stiftung, Museum für Gegenwartskunst, Basel

34

*The* Strobe Series, Concerning Diachronic/Synchronic Time: Above, On, Under (with Mermaid), *and* Semi-Close-Up of Girl by Geranium (Soft View) *are all focused on time, that is, a moment drawn out, extended, perhaps "timeless" time, an interlude in which magic might occur.*

*Concerning Diachronic/Synchronic Time: Above, On, Under (with Mermaid),* 1976
Six black-and-white photographs; mounted on board
28¾ x 27¾ in. overall (73 x 70.5 cm)
Courtesy of Sonnabend Gallery, New York

*I wanted the work to be so layered and rich that you would have trouble synthesizing it. I wanted all the intellectual things gone, and at the same time I am asking you to believe the airplane has turned into a seagull and the sub into a mermaid during the time the motorboat is crossing. I am constantly playing the game of changing this or that, visually or verbally. As soon as I see a word, I spell it backwards in my mind. I break it up and put the parts back together to make a new word.*

QUALITY MATERIAL - - -

CAREFUL INSPECTION - -

GOOD WORKMANSHIP.

ALL COMBINED IN AN EFFORT TO
GIVE YOU A PERFECT PAINTING.

*Quality Material—...*, 1967–68
Acrylic on canvas
68 x 56½ in. (172.7 x 143.5 cm)
Collection of Robert Shapazian, Los
Angeles

The decision to use text in art, not decoratively but as information, derived from an attitude Baldessari describes as a sort of "bursting of bubbles." Its stance was "This is what it is. It's not great, it's not bad, it's just what it is, sort of ordinary, like Van Gogh painting a pair of old shoes." Reality for Baldessari simply wasn't glamorous. Art as he had known it didn't seem to share that attitude, but since he did not want to give up art, he was determined that it would draw from his prosaic surroundings, from his daily life and his teaching. The text of a painting about the quality of materials, for instance, originated in a little tag the artist found in the pocket of a new shirt, recommending it as "perfectly made" from "good-quality" fabric. Applying these phrases ironically, he set out to make a "perfect painting, giving people their money's worth."

But, for Baldessari, not just any quotation or any rule of composition would do. From a book on photography, for example, he saved a list of quotations, one of which he intended to match with a snapshot of a street scene in National City:

- One should adapt from a photograph with imagination and not feel obligated to represent the picture exactly as the camera does.
- What the camera has done is to show us what to concentrate upon; and consequently, what to leave out.
- The photographer can change his position, but the result would be another kind of picture.
- For many years now the artist has increasingly welcomed the assistance afforded by the photographer.

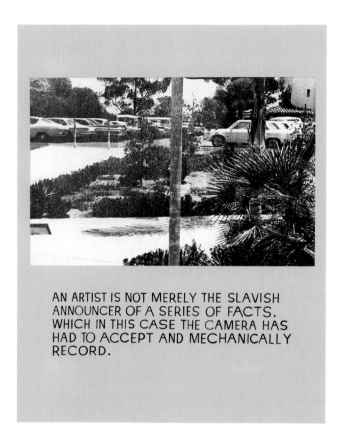

AN ARTIST IS NOT MERELY THE SLAVISH
ANNOUNCER OF A SERIES OF FACTS.
WHICH IN THIS CASE THE CAMERA HAS
HAD TO ACCEPT AND MECHANICALLY
RECORD.

*An Artist Is Not Merely the Slavish
Announcer...*, 1967–68
Acrylic and photoemulsion on canvas
59 x 45 in. (149.9 x 114.3 cm)
Private collection, courtesy of
Sonnabend Gallery, New York

- The practice of basing a painting on what the mechanical eye of the camera records has been greatly overdone.
- Very rarely does a photograph of Nature fulfill all the requirements of a good composition.
- Without design a photograph will be but an announcement.
- In a mere photograph there is a real danger of losing a picture's chief attribute, its design.
- At first glance a photograph will often appear to add up to the conditions of an adequate composition.
- Here is a typical case of a striking photograph that contains elements from which a good composition can be made; as it stands, it cannot be literally copied without asking for trouble.
- Study in expression: the figure conveys to the viewer that this man has something to say.
- Your photograph should convey the mood of your subject.

*Some Rooms*, 1986
Black-and-white photographs with
gouache; mounted on board
96½ x 109½ in. overall (245.1 x 278.1 cm)
The Museum of Contemporary Art, Los
Angeles; gift of the Eli Broad Family
Foundation

*Empty containers for the spectator/*
*voyeur to stare into while being stared*
*at by a center group of faceless people.*
*The rooms are flanked by images of*
*people distanced from but staring at*
*each other.*
   *The vacancy of the rooms and empty*
*gazing stares are anchored by an*
*umbrella pole that serves like the mast*
*of a ship tossing in a storm.*
   *A similar vertical, functioning as a*
*stabilizing element, was used before in*
The Artist Is Not Merely the Slavish
Announcer....

All these excerpts from manuals on photography could be seen as relating to the nondescript snapshot, which has no special characteristics except that it was taken within an American suburban small-town sprawl. But the text that Baldessari selected is undoubtedly the most suited to the image. It reads, "An artist is not merely the slavish announcer of a series of facts, which in this case the camera had to accept and mechanically record." Art has to go beyond pure reportage. It is one thing to present an object or depict a scene without altering it to give it an objective form through verisimilitude. It is another to transform it into art. In this case, text and image, both trivial in their original contexts, escape banality at the very moment of their combination, into either a convincing lie or an enlightening truth—into art.

As Baldessari himself did not do the lettering in the text and phototext canvases, it was all the more important for him to have a "battle plan," to set up boundaries of order and chaos: "For us to see things, the mind has to order information. Otherwise things become just a bunch of retinal stimulation. Complete chaos is hallucination, I guess." The hired sign painter, then, was given some instructions. He was told that he should use the same style of lettering for all the canvases and should apply it simply and straightforwardly without embellishment. The emphasis had to be on information and legibility and not necessarily on art. Black paint on a white surface seemed appropriate for the phototext canvases, while most of the canvases that consisted only of text were done in black on a gray background. Occasionally backgrounds were painted in "landlord colors": peach, pink, or gray-green. The lettering style was in keeping with the primitive photoemulsion images that Baldessari himself transferred to the canvases.

Baldessari had discovered a photoemulsion process that suited him after all kinds of experimentation, including running his canvases through a printing press. He consulted a photo lab in New Jersey about the technique, which sounded very simple, but it actually was quite complex and time-consuming. "When I put the emulsion down, which first had to cook, and tried to brush it on with a camel's-hair brush, it left marks which looked like brushstrokes, too messy and artful." To prevent this, Baldessari began to seal the surfaces with varnish before brushing the emulsion on. The exposures themselves took at least forty-five minutes each. "I just went to take a nap and set an alarm clock in the dark." Next, developer was sprayed on the canvases, which created a soft look. Afterward the artist rinsed it off with a fine spray of water from a garden hose. The procedure of spraying and rinsing was repeated once more with a fixative solution. All this took place in the dark. Once the image was fixed the light could be turned on.

Left to his own devices—in a culturally deprived environment—of how to transfer images permanently onto canvas, Baldessari's only recourse was to turn this process of clumsy experimentation into a

stimulus for his art. Things became less bleak for him when, in 1968, Paul Brach appointed Baldessari an assistant professor in the art department of the University of California at San Diego. According to Baldessari, he was hired because Brach wanted a local artist on the faculty. Other faculty members were Brach's wife, the painter Miriam Schapiro; Newton Harrison, then still a sculptor; and the New York poet and art critic David Antin, from whom Baldessari received his first enthusiastic reception and encouragement to continue his text and phototext paintings. Antin, who ran the university's art gallery, and, to Baldessari's delight, used the gallery funds primarily to invite New York poets to San Diego, also organized the first show on Fluxus there in close collaboration with George Maciunas, the charismatic founder of the movement. Antin passed his lively conversations with the Fluxus members on to Baldessari, who saw Fluxus then "as a continuation of Dada and Surrealism," and in retrospect as "a sort of sloppy proto-conceptual art." Baldessari was introduced to Dick Higgins, and later also met Emmett Williams and Alan Kaprow. He enjoyed their spirit of "anything is possible" and their "why not?" attitude.

*Pure Beauty*, 1967–68
Acrylic on canvas
45⅜ x 45⅜ in. (115.3 x 115.3 cm)
Collection of Ed and Nancy Kienholz

WHAT THIS PAINTING AIMS TO DO.

IT IS ONLY WHEN YOU HAVE BEEN PAINTING FOR
QUITE SOME TIME THAT YOU WILL BEGIN TO RE-
ALIZE THAT YOUR COMPOSITIONS SEEM TO LACK
IMPACT-- THAT THEY ARE TOO ORDINARY.
THAT IS WHEN YOU WILL START TO BREAK ALL THE
SO-CALLED RULES OF COMPOSITION AND TO
THINK IN TERMS OF DESIGN.
THEN YOU CAN DISTORT SHAPES, INVENT FORMS.
AND BE ON YOUR WAY TOWARD BEING A CRE-
ATIVE ARTIST.

*What This Painting Aims To Do.*,
1967–68
Acrylic on canvas
68 x 56½ in. (172.7 x 143.5 cm)
Collection of Mr. and Mrs. Robert J.
Dodds III, Pittsburgh

EXAMINING PICTURES

FIRST OF ALL. WHAT DO PICTURES CONSIST OF ?
WHAT ARE THEY ALL ABOUT ?
THERE IS NO END, IN FACT, TO THE NUMBER OF DIF-
FERENT KINDS OF PICTURES.
NATURALLY ARTISTS FROM TIME TO TIME HAVE
STRUGGLED TO ENLARGE ON THESE LIMITATIONS
AND THE HISTORY OF ART IS A SUCCESSION OF
THEIR SUCCESSES AND FAILURES.SEE THE IM-
PRESSIONISTS. THE CUBISTS.

*Examining Pictures*, 1967–68
Acrylic on canvas
68 x 56½ in. (172.7 x 143.5 cm)
Collection of the artist

It was Antin who, in 1968, got Baldessari his first
Los Angeles show, at the Molly Barnes Gallery. Along
with his text and phototext canvases, Baldessari
showed two illuminated moving-message signs called
"sales casters." Once again he was pushing the limits
of traditional art through the use of a commercial
advertising device. In these works, which looked
even less like art than his earlier text canvases,
Baldessari showed himself fascinated by the
challenge of thinking up new artistic forms to revive
worn out clichés, a concept he was not alone in. In
1967, for example, Bruce Nauman had executed a
neon sign that read *The True Artist Helps the World
by Revealing Mystic Truths.* One sign displayed a text
that Baldessari had found in a composition book:
"Isocephaly—a style of composition characteristic of
the classical period—especially in relation to Greek art
in which the figures in a composition are arranged so
that they are of the same height; as for instance in
a frieze." Another sign displayed a text put together
from bits and pieces in the artist's notebooks:
"Viewpoint: what to put in; what to leave out: the eye
has a tendency to prefer little shapes to big masses. It
also prefers to build an image bit by bit. To the

beginner, a subject such as this presents a baffling
problem."

The Molly Barnes show came at the right moment
for Baldessari; it occurred simultaneously with "The
First Investigation," a show by the New York artist
Joseph Kosuth at a neighboring gallery, the Eugenia
Butler Gallery. Kosuth's work consisted of a number
of definitions of the word "nothing"; the series was
called "Titled (Art as Idea as Idea)." Reviewing both
shows in the December 1968 issue of *Artforum*, Jane
Livingston stated:

JOSEPH KOSUTH, at Gallery 669, in his quest to strip away
from his art everything but the *idea*, has arrived at a series
of dictionary definitions of the word NOTHING, executed
(not by the artist) photographically, in black 4 by 4 foot
panels with white lettering. A few doors away, at the Molly
Barnes Gallery, is an exhibition of paintings by JOHN
BALDESSARI, who, in his way, is also interested in a strict
elimination of "formal" aesthetic encumbrances—as well as
(in answer to Kosuth?) the idea: on one of his black-
lettered-on-grey canvases is written, *Everything is purged
from this painting but art, no ideas have entered this work.*[7]

That Baldessari had made certain text canvases in reaction to Kosuth, as Livingston assumed, was not true. That both shows took place at the same time was a coincidence. Baldessari had never met Kosuth, though he had heard of him through the New York dealer Richard Bellamy. Before Antin arranged for the exhibition at the Molly Barnes Gallery, Baldessari showed his canvases to other galleries in Los Angeles but to no avail. The only art dealer who seemed interested in his work was Nicholas Wilder who had arranged Nauman's first one-man show in 1966. Wilder persuaded Bellamy to take a look at Baldessari's work, but Bellamy also reacted hesitantly, saying, according to Baldessari, "I don't quite know what you are doing, either, but you may like to get to know certain artists in New York." He wrote down a list of names, including Kosuth, Lawrence Weiner, Dan Graham, Mel Bochner, Robert Barry, and Douglas Huebler. This was the first time Baldessari realized that his attitude toward art was shared by other artists.

Shortly after his show, Baldessari visited New York, where he became acquainted with several of the artists on Bellamy's list, in particular Weiner, who, though initially reluctant to let a West Coast artist into his territory, soon became a close friend. Baldessari did not meet Kosuth on that visit. From the latter's essay "Art after Philosophy," published in two parts in *Studio International* in October and November 1969, it is clear that his ideas on conceptual art diverged quite radically from Baldessari's. In Part II of the essay, " 'Conceptual Art' and Recent Art," Kosuth, eager to narrow the arbitrary catchall term "conceptual art," isolated "purely" conceptual art, which excluded any kind of painting. This renunciation was prefigured in some words of Marcel Duchamp, with which Kosuth opened his article: "In France there is an old saying, 'stupid like a painter.' The painter was considered stupid, but the poet and writer very intelligent. I wanted to be intelligent. I had to have the idea of inventing. It is nothing to do what your father did. It is nothing to be another Cézanne. In my visual period there is a little of that stupidity of the painter. All my work in the period before the *Nude* was visual painting. Then I came to the idea. I thought the ideatic formulation a way to get away from influences." Kosuth declared that "*Purely* conceptual art is first seen concurrently in the work of Terry Atkinson and Michael Baldwin in Coventry, England; and with my own work done in New York City, all generally around 1966. On Kawara, a Japanese artist who has been continuously traveling around the world since 1959, has been doing a highly conceptualized kind of art since 1964."

In the same article he stated that "the 'purest' definition of conceptual art would be that it is inquiry into the foundations of the concept 'art,' as it has come to mean." This was Baldessari's intent! But the fact that the text and phototext works were done on stretched canvases seems to have created an ambiguity that caused Kosuth to mention Baldessari

only parenthetically: ("Although the amusing pop paintings of John Baldessari allude to this sort of work by being 'conceptual' cartoons of actual conceptual art, they are not really relevant to this discussion.")[8] From his point of view, Baldessari had preserved the canvas precisely as "the only remaining link to art." Both in their break with and confirmation of traditional painting, the text and phototext canvases defy easy categorization as well as a dogmatic approach, which is typical for Baldessari who insists upon leaving his options open.

By 1969 Baldessari, having established a connection with artists of a kindred spirit in New York, was becoming aware of other conceptual artists in Europe as well, partly through two 1969 exhibitions in which the works of Americans and Europeans were shown side by side, *"Op losse Schroeven,"* (Square Pegs in Round Holes), in Amsterdam, and "When Attitudes Become Form," in Bern. After being invited to participate in a group exhibition, *"Konzeption*—conception," in Leverkusen, West Germany, his first European show, he traveled to Germany in the fall of 1969. In 1970 he had his first one-man show at the Konrad Fischer Gallery in Düsseldorf. The knowledge that he had become part of an international community of like-minded artists made it easier for Baldessari to accept his geographic isolation in San Diego, and his rather odd, unrecognized position in Los Angeles. At the same time he liked living at a safe distance from Los Angeles without much peer pressure, so that he felt free through trial and error to sort out which ideas to keep and which to discard.

## TIPS FOR ARTISTS WHO WANT TO SELL

• GENERALLY SPEAKING, PAINT-
INGS WITH LIGHT COLORS SELL
MORE QUICKLY THAN PAINTINGS
WITH DARK COLORS.

• SUBJECTS THAT SELL WELL:
MADONNA AND CHILD, LANDSCAPES,
FLOWER PAINTINGS, STILL LIFES
(FREE OF MORBID PROPS ___
DEAD BIRDS, ETC.), NUDES, MARINE
PICTURES, ABSTRACTS AND SUR-
REALISM.

• SUBJECT MATTER IS IMPOR-
TANT: IT HAS BEEN SAID THAT PA-
INTINGS WITH COWS AND HENS
IN THEM COLLECT DUST
___ WHILE THE SAME PAINTINGS
WITH BULLS AND ROOSTERS SELL.

*Tips for Artists Who Want To Sell*,
1967–68
Acrylic on canvas
68 x 56½ in. (172.7 x 143.5 cm)
Collection of Robert Shapazian, Los
Angeles

A WORK WITH ONLY ONE PROPERTY.

*A Work with Only One Property.*,
1967–68
Acrylic on canvas
45 x 45 in. (114.3 x 114.3 cm)
The Grinstein Family, Los Angeles

## A PAINTING THAT IS ITS OWN DOCUMENTATION

JUNE 19, 1968 IDEA CONCEIVED AT 10:25 A.M. NATIONAL CITY, CALIF. BY JOHN BALDESSARI JULY 30, CANVAS BUILT AND PREPARED JULY 31, TEXT PREPARED AND EDITED AUGUST I, PAINTING COMMISSIONED AUGUST 3, PAINTING COMPLETED OCTOBER 6, FIRST SHOWING, MOLLY BARNES GALLERY, LOS ANGELES

NOTE
FOR EACH SUBSEQUENT EXHIBITION OF THIS PAINTING, ADD DATE AND LOCATION BELOW. FOR EXTRA SPACE, USE AN ADDITIONAL CANVAS.

NEWPORT HARBOR ART MUSEUM
BALBOA, CALIF. MAY 11 - JUNE 29, 1969
NEWPORT HARBOR ART MUSEUM
NEWPORT BEACH, CA. OCT. 26 - NOV. 24, 1974

THE NEW MUSEUM
NEW YORK, N.Y. MAR. 14, - APR. 28, 1981
STEDELIJK VAN ABBEMUSEUM
EINDHOVEN, MAY 22, - JUNE 21, 1981

*A Painting That Is Its Own Documentation*, 1968–present
Acrylic on canvas
102 x 56½ in. overall (259.1 x 143.5 cm)
Original canvas: 68 x 56½ in. (172.7 x 143.5 cm)
Additional canvas: 34 x 56½ in. (86.4 x 143.5 cm)
Collection of Molly Barnes, Los Angeles

## COMPOSING ON A CANVAS.

STUDY THE COMPOSITION OF PAINTINGS. ASK YOURSELF QUESTIONS WHEN STANDING IN FRONT OF A WELL COMPOSED PICTURE. WHAT FORMAT IS USED ? WHAT IS THE PROPORTION OF HEIGHT TO WIDTH ? WHAT IS THE CENTRAL OBJECT ? WHERE IS IT SITUATED ? HOW IS IT RELATED TO THE FORMAT ? WHAT ARE THE MAIN DIRECTIONAL FORCES ? THE MINOR ONES ? HOW ARE THE SHADES OF DARK AND LIGHT DISTRIBUTED ? WHERE ARE THE DARK SPOTS CONCENTRATED ? THE LIGHT SPOTS ? HOW ARE THE EDGES OF THE PICTURE DRAWN INTO THE PICTURE ITSELF ? ANSWER THESE QUESTIONS FOR YOURSELF WHILE LOOKING AT A FAIRLY UNCOM - PLICATED PICTURE.

*Composing on a Canvas.*, 1967–68
Acrylic on canvas
114 x 108 in. (289.6 x 274.3 cm)
La Jolla Museum of Contemporary Art; gift of the artist

Now that he was no longer producing paintings, Baldessari felt that he should make a grand liberating gesture. He envisioned an act like that of the Japanese artist Hokusai, who, he had read, executed a gigantic drawing by walking for miles on rolls and rolls of paper. Looking out the window on an airplane trip, it suddenly occurred to Baldessari that he was seeing below him not the usual landscape, but the details of a map. Elaborating on this vision, he developed the idea of "actually executing each letter and symbol of the map of California on the corresponding part of the earth. It was an attempt to make the real world match a map, to impose language on nature, and vice versa." The letters imposed on the landscape were intended to be in the same scale as those on an actual map, but reality did not allow for that; as it turned out, the letters were generally too small to be seen from an airplane. Nevertheless, each letter in the word CALIFORNIA was executed, in different sizes and materials, in whatever part of the state corresponded to its position on the map. It was then photographed in color. Looking at the complete set of color photographs of the letters spelling out C-A-L-I-F-O-R-N-I-A together in a row, which form *California Map Project, Part I: California*, 1969, it is difficult to get a sense of the scope of the project as originally executed because each single letter was nothing more than a fragment set in its own stretch of landscape. In contrast to the map, the parts never adjoined, they only alluded to a complete view.

Baldessari started the project in the spring of 1969 with the help of two of his friends, the jazz musician George Nicolaidis and his wife, Judy. They started in the south of the state, at Joshua Tree National Monument, and moved north—spelling out CALIFORNIA backward. First came the last A, which was built in a giant scale out of dry colors, rocks, and

desert wildflower seeds. It was for Baldessari "an exhilarating experience" to stand and work in each part of the state where the letters had been painted on the map: "All that could have been faked, but it wasn't." He brought some of the materials—which included little pieces of red cloth, colored paper, yarn, and dry paint powder—with him. Other materials were found on the sites. As the three moved north, the landscape gradually changed in coloring from brown to green and Baldessari changed his strategy of executing gigantic letters. The artists decided that there was no need for consistency, and thought it would be less boring if they let the geographical situation suggest the materials and the size of the next letters. A telephone pole about 3.6 miles from Newcastle on California Route 193, for example, became the long leg of the L, and the short leg was created by faking a shadow. (The real shadow of the telephone pole was cast to the left, so they sprinkled lamp-black powdered pigment on the ground to the right.) The first A in CALIFORNIA was placed on graffiti-covered rocks found on the road to Paradise near Chico. Eighteen inches tall—in scale with the other inscriptions carved in the rocks—it turned out to be the smallest of the letters. The final letter, the C, located on the northernmost site, at Shasta Lake, was also built out of found material, logs lying around on the banks of the lake.

One night while working on the map piece, Nicolaidis came up with an idea for another collaborative project that could be realized close to home. He proposed making visible the boundary line of the southeast San Diego ghetto, which was at the time not yet indicated on any map. Baldessari suggested making the boundary line out of stickers printed with a dictionary definition of the word "ghetto." While the City Planning Commission denied

*California Map Project, Part I:*
*California*, 1969
Eleven Type-R prints and typewritten
sheet; mounted on board
Prints: 8 x 10 in. each (20.3 x 25.4
cm); text: 8 1/2 x 11 in. (21.6 x 27.9
cm)
Collection of Hubert Burda, Munich

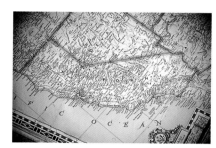

C: Off Jones Valley Road. 9 miles from
   Hiway 299 leading from Redding.
   On Bank of finger of Shasta Lake.
   Materials: found logs.

A: On road to Paradise. 7 miles from
   intersection of Paradise Road and
   Hiway 99 (near Chico).
   Materials: paint on rock.

L: 3.6 miles from Newcastle on
   California 193.
   Materials: telephone pole and
   faked shadow.

I: 5 miles from San Andreas on Hiway
   49. Near Angel's Camp.
   Materials: non-toxic color in creek.

F: Ben Hur Road. South of Mariposa.
   3.4 miles from California 49.
   Materials: scattered bits of red
   cloth.

O: 3.4 miles on Reed Road from
   junction 180. Near Minkler.
   Materials: red yarn.

R: 14 miles north of Kernville in
   Sequoia National Forest. In Kern
   River.
   Materials: found rocks.

N: 4.1 miles from Hiway 395 on Death
   Valley Road. 6 miles on south side
   of road.
   Materials: rocks and dry color.

I: Outside Lucerne: 11.8 miles from
   Lucerne fire station. 2 miles off Old
   Womans Spring Road. Turn at sign
   reading Partin Limestone Products.
   Materials: white dry color (the
   letter is nearly invisible).

A: In Joshua Tree National
   Monument. 15 miles from Twenty-
   Nine Palms Visitors Center on road
   to Cottonwood.
   Materials: dry color, rocks, desert
   wildflower seed.

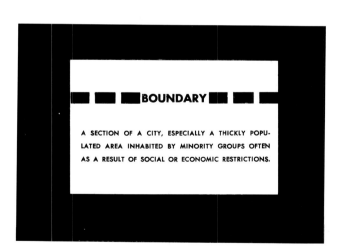

*Ghetto Boundary Project* (detail:
sticker), 1969
Five color photographs and one
adhesive sticker; mounted on board
Photographs: 8 x 10 in. each (20.3 x
25.4); sticker: 2 x 3 in. (2.5 x 7.6 cm)
Los Angeles County Museum of Art;
gift of Jerry Magnin

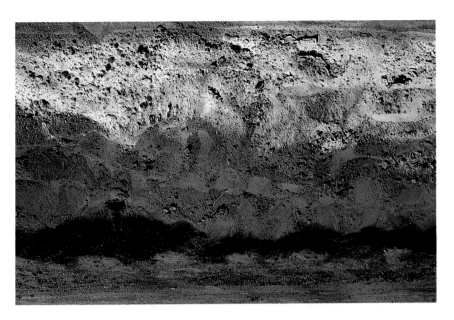

*California—Mexico Boundary Project*
(detail), 1969
Color photograph and typewritten
sheet; mounted on board
Photograph: 8 x 10 in. each (20.3 x
25.4 cm); text: 8½ x 11 in. (21.6 x 27.9
cm)
Courtesy of Sonnabend Gallery, New
York

*California Map Project—Sacramento,
September 15, 1969*, 1969
35mm color slide
Collection of Lawrence Weiner, New
York/Amsterdam

Dennis Oppenheim
*Time Line*, 1968
Parallel lines 1 x 3 feet x 3 miles cut
down the time zone between Fort
Kent, Maine, and Clair, New
Brunswick, on frozen St. John River.
Speed: 35 miles per hour. Execution
time: 10 minutes. Time: U.S.A. 3:15;
Canada 4:15.

the very existence of the ghetto, the artists located 15
miles of its boundaries, and, on April 5, 1969, they
put up about two thousand stickers.

From May 3 until September 1969, Baldessari and
Nicolaidis executed the second part of *California
Map Project*. Like part one, part two also involved
transposing a map detail onto the actual landscape.
Working near the town of Calexico, on the
California/Mexico border, the two artists simulated
"a section of the graded color and dotted line that
indicated an international boundary between
countries on a map." At the same time, Baldessari
executed the third part of the project. The original
map the artists used as a model had a red star
indicating Sacramento as the capital of California.
For this part of the project, a replica of the star was
constructed on the green lawn in front of the State
Capitol Building in Sacramento.

*California Map Project* was a reflection of a
characteristic approach in art toward the American
landscape at the time. It was the heyday of
Earthworks—large-scale outdoor sculptural and
conceptual projects. As early as 1962 the artist Walter
De Maria had conceived of a series of work in the
desert. One of them, *Mile-Long Drawing*, which

consisted of two parallel chalk lines that ran twelve feet apart for an entire mile, was executed in 1968 in the Mojave Desert. In September 1968 Robert Smithson's influential article, "A Sedimentation of the Mind: Earth Projects," had appeared in *Artforum*. And in October 1968, Douglas Huebler had organized a one-day site-sculpture project at Windham College, in Putney, Vermont. Huebler, like Baldessari, was also interested in the relationship of a map to the site it represents. He drew a hexagon on a map of the area and then photographed the actual sites of the five points on the landscape. The photographs were exhibited together with a sample of dirt from each of the points. In the winter of the same year Dennis Oppenheim had executed the three-mile-long *Time Line* along the frozen Saint John River, on the U.S./ Canadian border.

The combination of large letterforms and the California landscape seems to come naturally. Baldessari was not the only artist to combine large letters with images of the California landscape. One has merely to recall Ruscha's painting *Large Trademark with Eight Spotlights*, 1962, or Claes Oldenburg's text accompanying *City as Alphabet*, part of a set of annotated lithographs called "Notes," published by Gemini G.E.L., Los Angeles, in 1968: "Sitting in a car and watching letters silhouetted against the sky has always seemed to me the basic Los Angeles experience. Some of the letters *are* colossal—the M and the T on Pico Boulevard. Another source of the association of letters and landscape is the map of the area one has to consult."

In the summer of 1969, just before his trip north to execute the final (but first) letters of CALIFORNIA with Nicolaidis, Baldessari conceived of a new body of work to follow the phototext canvases, a series entitled *Commissioned Paintings*. For years he had wanted to do something with a group of children's drawings that he had been carefully collecting in boxes. He had begun to make collages out of the drawings and had applied one as a photoemulsion image on canvas, but he had stopped using them when he realized that they were at the same time too much art and not artful enough, which confused the issue of who was the artist. Wishing to sidestep the possibility that the children's spontaneous experience might register as more sophisticated art, he hired adult amateur painters who would not be likely under any circumstance to produce worthwhile art. The amateurs would be technically adept enough to execute a painting, but their choices of subject matter would be so meaningless that Baldessari could easily substitute his own. Becoming the strategist, he devised having a show of paintings without executing them:

If a sign painter could paint my texts, why not ask somebody to paint a picture according to my indications? Every year my father and I used to visit county fairs. Despite the fact that he loved looking at tractors and farm equipment and I hated it, I developed a fondness for Sunday painters there that I shared with David Antin. I'd write down their names on my visits to the fair. Eventually, for

the "Commissioned Paintings" I called some of them up and gave them a dozen slides I just happened to have taken to select from.

The series of slides Baldessari selected all showed George Nicolaidis pointing at various events or objects that caught his eye as he walked through town. The idea came from an outlook on conceptual art attributed to the "Hard Edge" painter Al Held, who is reported to have said, "All conceptual art is just pointing at things." Baldessari took the remark literally, parodying Held's criticism.

Upon completion, between August 8, 1969 and February 14, 1970, the paintings—whose images, like the phototext canvases, had the proportions of a 35-mm. slide—were brought to a sign painter who affixed each artist's name, always following the same formula: "A painting by...." Baldessari wrote of these works:

The entire set was exhibited in galleries in Los Angeles [Eugenia Butler] and New York [Richard Feigen] that dealt in recent modern art. It was important that the paintings were exhibited as a group so that the spectator could practice connoisseurship, for example comparing how the extended forefinger in each was painted. In all, the point was to organize these artists in a different context and provide them with an unhackneyed subject that would attract the attention of a viewer interested in modern art.[9]

To Baldessari, working on this project felt like being a choreographer, who may not dance, or a composer, who may not perform music. He asked the amateurs to render the slide they had selected as faithfully as possible, but he also made small changes in the presentation of the pictures, hoping that through these slight shifts art would emerge:

So much of my thinking at that time was trying to figure out just what I thought art was, you know—choosing this against that, and so on. And I think, yeah, I decided you either believed it was art or you didn't. That's what made it art, and I couldn't have done those works in a big city. In New York I would have felt too much around me of what was proper to do and what wasn't.

The *Commissioned Paintings*, in their focus on "pointing at things" as a process of selection, are an antecedent for later pieces on the theme of choosing, such as *Choosing (A Game for Two Players)*, 1972 (in variations from rhubarb to green beans, garlic, scallions, asparagus, mushrooms, and turnips).

Baldessari, explaining *Choosing (A Game for Two Players): Rhubarb*, wrote:

A participant was asked to choose any three sticks of rhubarb from an available group for whatever reasons he/she might have at the moment. The three chosen sticks of rhubarb were then placed upon a surface to be photographed. I chose one of those three sticks for whatever reasons I might have had, by pointing my finger at the selected one, at which moment a photograph was taken. The chosen stick of rhubarb remained, and two new sticks were added by the same participant. The next choice was made by me, and so on. Each participant developed strategies unknown to the other player as the selection process continued until all the sticks of rhubarb were used.[10]

A PAINTING BY ELMIRE BOURKE

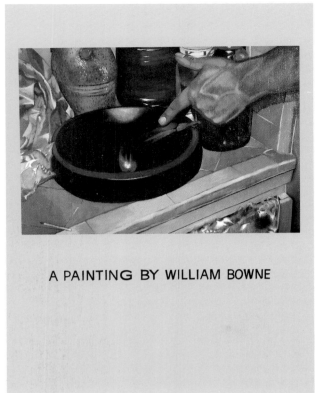

A PAINTING BY WILLIAM BOWNE

A PAINTING BY NANCY CONGER

A PAINTING BY DANTE GUIDO

*Commissioned Paintings*, 1969
Fourteen paintings: oil or acrylic on
canvas
59¼ x 45½ in. each (150.5 x 115.6 cm)
Private collection, courtesy of
Sonnabend Gallery, New York (except
...*A Painting by Sam Jacoby,* location
unknown)

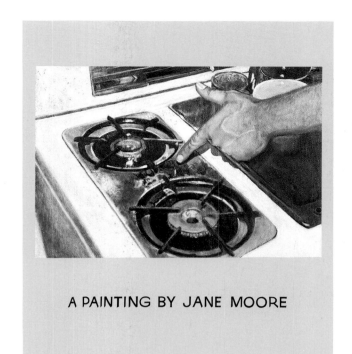

A PAINTING BY JANE MOORE

A PAINTING BY SAM JACOBY

A PAINTING BY HELENE MORRIS

A PAINTING BY PAT NELSON

A PAINTING BY PATRICK X. NIDORF O.S.A.

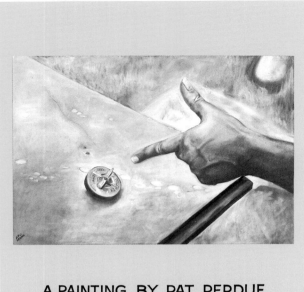

A PAINTING BY PAT PERDUE

A PAINTING BY HILDEGARD REINER

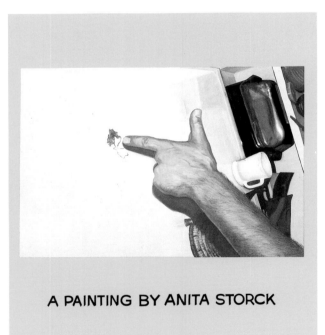

A PAINTING BY ANITA STORCK

**A PAINTING BY EDGAR TRANSUE**

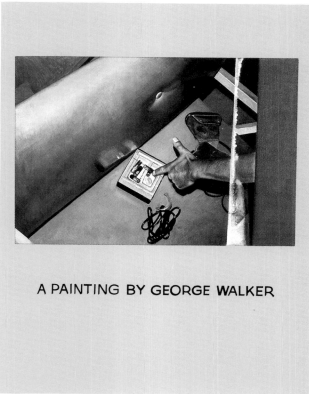

**A PAINTING BY GEORGE WALKER**

*Finger Pointing at Objects* (details),
1969: also source material for
*Commissioned Paintings*
Thirty-six 35 mm slides
Collection of the artist

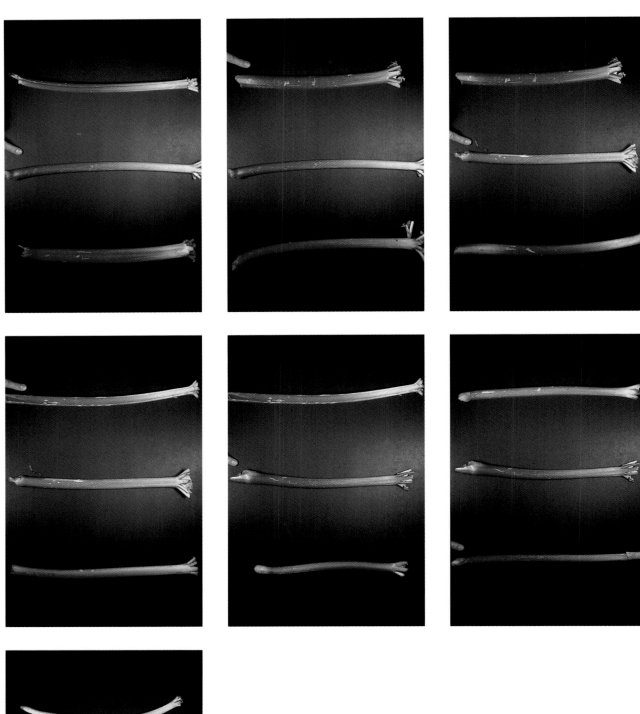

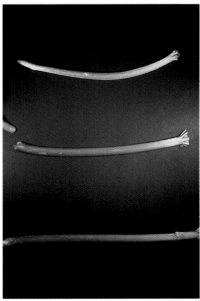

*Choosing (A Game for Two Players): Rhubarb*, 1972
Seven Type-R prints and one typewritten sheet; mounted on board
Prints: 14 x 11 in. each; text: 11 x 8½ in. (35.6 x 27.9 cm; 27.9 x 21.6 cm)
Collection of Angelo Baldassarre, Bari, Italy

*Alignment Series: Arrows Fly Like This,*
*Flowers Grow Like This, Airplanes*
*Park Like This,* 1975
Twenty-four black-and-white
photographs; mounted on board
3½ x 5 in. each (8.9 x 12.7 cm)
Installation dimensions variable
Collection of Massimo Valsecchi,
Milan

This piece, like *Alignment Series: Arrows Fly Like This, Flowers Grow Like This, Airplanes Park Like This*, 1975, has a deceptively simple quality. Baldessari remembers how, as a teacher, he watched small children habitually line up building blocks first one way and then another in all kinds of variations: "If you were to ask them if they were doing art, they would say no. But to me it seemed a very natural kind of art; sophistication had not entered in yet." In *Choosing (A Game for Two Players)* however, Baldessari complicates this kind of simple observation drawn from daily life with a sophisticated concept of "beauty of a composed intricacy of form," as expressed by the eighteenth-century English painter William Hogarth in his *Analysis of Beauty.* From each new trio of vegetables Baldessari chooses

one, and by pointing his finger at it, he changes aesthetic relationships. Furthermore, when all the photographs are lined up in a row, the positioning of the finger establishes a line rising and falling like a mountain skyline, creating what Hogarth, in an inscription of his palette in the famous self-portrait of 1745, called a "line of beauty." Thus the sensuous, erotic overtones of the finger humanize the dryness and dogmatism of the selection process. In *Strobe Series/Futurist: Trying To Get a Straight Line with a Finger,* 1975, the finger in motion has become the "line of beauty." Baldessari's concerns here were "the opportunity to explore sequentiality within the single photograph, to apply a 'What will happen if...' approach, and to explore some of the ideas of Futurism, essentially idioms of movement."

53

In the late summer of 1969, after having finished the series of fourteen "Commissioned Paintings" that now crowded his studio, Baldessari became depressed about the enormous clutter of artwork he had accumulated over the years, as he had hardly ever sold anything. Around that time he was invited to participate in the group exhibition *"Konzeption—conception"* in Leverkusen. For the catalogue entry accompanying the show he sent a series of notes he had just written, including one titled "The world has too much art—I have made too many objects—what

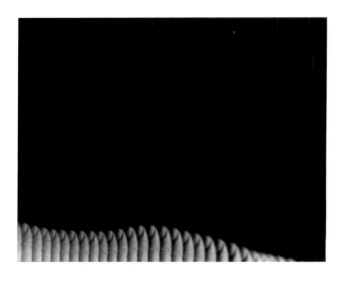 

*Strobe Series/Futurist: Trying To Get a Straight Line with a Finger,* 1975
Four black-and-white photographs; mounted on board
16 x 20 in. each (40.6 x 50.8 cm)
Courtesy of Sonnabend Gallery, New York

to do?" One of the answers to that question reads, "Burn all my paintings, etc., done in past few years. Have them cremated in a mortuary. Pay all fees, receive all documents. Have event recorded at County Recorder's. Send out announcements? Or should it be a private affair? Keep ashes in urn."

Initially his vast studio, a former movie theater built by his father that had closed down because of its location in a poor neighborhood, seemed advantageous because it allowed him to see all his works at once. But after having occupied the space for several years, he realized that it was gradually coming to resemble the set of Ionesco's play *The New Tenant*: "With all my paintings and furniture around me, I was unable to move or to do any art. So I had to figure something out, and the only thing I could do was to make things small. It was that idea that I slowly was being suffocated that made me want to start a house-cleaning."

After a one-day studio exhibition and sale in December 1969, Baldessari decided to make a ritual out of his house-cleaning by having all the works "cremated" and putting the ashes in a book-shaped urn which he put on a shelf. "I have mixed feelings about it now. It should have been a private act, but on the other hand when you diet, you tell it to people, so you know you won't go back on your word. So I made it public, as embarrassing as it was." On August 10, 1970 a notice appeared in the San Diego *Union* stating, "Notice is hereby given that all works of art done by the undersigned between May 1953 and March 1966 in his possession as of July 24, 1970

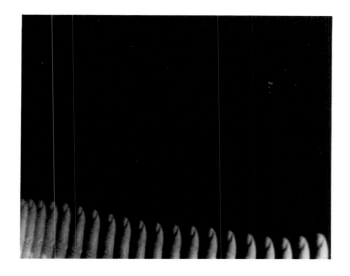 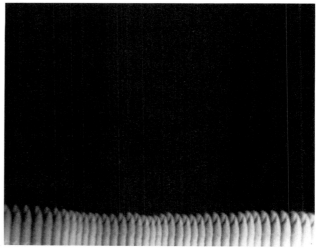

*Line of Force* (details), 1972–73
Thirty-three color photographs;
mounted on board
4 x 5 in. each (10.2 x 12.7 cm)
Installation dimensions variable
Courtesy of Sonnabend Gallery, New
York

*I appropriated this term from some
area of art history—I think Art
Nouveau. Also influenced by Futurism,
cinema, and music. At the time, I was
much involved with flux as a way of
doing art as opposed to conventional
static art. What comes before and after
an image and how can that be
structured.*

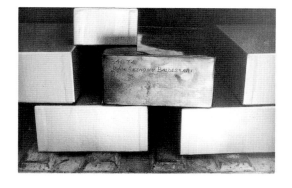

*Cremation Project*, 1970 (details)
Bronze plaque and urn, box of ashes,
six color photographs mounted on
board
Plaque: 9⅛ x 16⅛ in. (23.2 x 40.9 cm);
urn: 10 x 8¼ x 3⅜ in. (25.4 x 20.9 x
8.5); box of ashes: 3½ x 6¼ x 9½ in.
(8.8 x 15.8 x 24.1 cm); photographs:
20¼ x 24¼ in. each (51.4 x 61.5 cm)
Courtesy of Sonnabend Gallery, New
York

were cremated on July 24, 1970 in San Diego, California." Baldessari showed the *Cremation Project* in the "Software" exhibition held at the Jewish Museum in New York, in September 1970. The catalogue heading read, "A Life's Work Goes Up in Flames." The original idea was to install the ashes permanently inside one of the museum's walls. However, a trustee protested, and the urn was installed behind a false wall built only for the duration of the show.

Baldessari had closed a chapter of his life forever by cremating his paintings. In the summer of 1970 he also moved to Santa Monica. Paul Brach had been appointed Dean of the California Institute of the Arts, which was located in Valencia, and invited him to join the faculty. Brach had a special purpose in mind: "John was this low-key, bemused man in a two-bit junior college in San Diego, acting as though he was the absolute center of the international art world....I wanted someone who could open the students up to what critic Harold Rosenberg called the de-definition of art."[11] Baldessari fulfilled that task by initiating a course called "Post-studio Art" (a term he borrowed from Carl Andre) and by importing the kind of culture he had experienced on the East Coast. At the same time he carved out a place for himself:

One of the things I worked for at CalArts was to break the stranglehold of the L.A. aesthetic. I constantly pushed to hire not from L.A. but from New York and Europe—to bring in an alternative aesthetic. *Now* that's a battle that's been won, but you can't believe what it was like. There was only one way to think and that was dictated by the Ferus Gallery. In the 1970s, we were bringing out artists who are known now, but they were formative then: Doug Huebler, Joseph Kosuth, Robert Smithson, Robert Barry, Lawrence Weiner, Daniel Buren, Vito Acconci, Dan Graham, Hans Haacke, Sol LeWitt. Almost all at my invitation. Another thing I did was to tell my students to move to New York.[12]

Baldessari himself has never lived in New York permanently despite several opportunities (one as early as the summer of 1971, when he substituted for Robert Barry at Hunter College, in New York), preferring to come and go regularly without giving up his position of detachment. And since September 1971 he has occupied the same studio at 2001½ Main Street in Santa Monica.

In an interview with his friend Nancy Drew, Baldessari clarified his ideas about teaching "Post-studio Art":

I was hired as a painter and decided when I got there that I wasn't painting and I wasn't much interested in painting as I was into something else. I said I'd like some situation to talk about this information I was involved with and I called it "Post-studio Art" because I didn't want to call it Conceptual art; that was too specific, too constraining. I wanted the course to be a catchall to anyone who wasn't doing straight painting or straight sculpture.[13]

This description of the course also applies to the art. In the early 1970s Baldessari was trying to cut through the traditional categories of painting, sculpture, and photography—as well as through constricting labels such as Minimal and Conceptual.

Predictable artistic doctrines, with no latitude for contradictions, bore him. As he stated, "Boredom—that's something I always fear in myself. I'm interested in boredom, but I know it's a dangerous line to walk. And you know, a lot of times I am boring and banal at the same time; it's an attraction/repulsion thing." However, Baldessari was not trying to escape his times:

It seems at this point that a lot of artists were getting interested in Claude Lévi-Strauss and Wittgenstein. It has always been my feeling that the surge in interest went beyond being just topical, but it offered explanations of other ordering systems in other cultures—how they put units together in whatever syntactical modes. Or it might have been a way out of simply relational art: this red looks nice next to this green, blah, blah, blah....That's one of the reasons I stopped painting. I couldn't spend the rest of my life making different combinations of color. You think back on the old adage "Twenty feet back, all paintings look the same."[14]

The question for Baldessari was how to transform his collections of raw material into art. The method could be perceptual or syntactical, but it always had to be more "cerebral" than "retinal." The focus had to be on art as information. Crucial to this notion was an insight he had gotten from a friend who quit his job in the photo archive of the San Diego Police Department because he found the constant inspection of pictures of traffic accidents, murder cases, and so on "too eerie": "I think that story got me interested in photographs that weren't done to be beautiful, and the whole idea of photographs as document rather than as art began to emerge. I began to look for such situations, which resulted among others in *Police Drawing*, 1971, and *Evidence*, 1970."

Ever since then, from the intricate mind games of the 1970s to the composite photoworks of the 1980s, the artist has left clues or evidence for the spectators to decipher the crime, or the art. But:

The work gets harder and harder because you get more easily dissatisfied and then it becomes so much harder to please each time. You have to make up increasingly sophisticated games to keep yourself occupied. And as you get more sophisticated, you have to think what's going to keep your audience interested. You have to realize that you can't entirely say, "To hell with the bourgeoisie, goodbye cruel world." There's constantly that battle back and forth. The ideal art for me would be complex for myself and simple enough for the public; it would have to satisfy both those needs. I try to make my things look deceptively simple. I think this is the test of any art or literature. If you want to read *Gulliver's Travels* as an adventure story, you can; if you want to read it as an allegory, you can too. Whichever. So Matisse has always been a great model for me. Those things look so easy. Child's play, and you know how many times he redrew them....[15]

I Will Not Make Any More Boring Art *was my response to Nova Scotia College of Art and Design to do an exhibition there, which took place from April 1–April 10, 1971. As there wasn't enough money for me to travel to Nova Scotia I proposed that the students voluntarily write "I will not make any more boring art" on the walls of the gallery, like punishment. To my surprise they covered the walls. In addition a print was also made without my direct supervision, and I also made a 30-minute videotape of the action of my writing the phrase repetitively for the duration of the tape.*

*I Will Not Make Any More Boring Art,*
1971
Lithograph on Arches paper
22⁷⁄₁₆ x 30¹⁄₁₆ in. (57 x 76.4 cm)
Edition of 50
Published by Nova Scotia College of Art and Design, Halifax, Nova Scotia, Canada

*Police Drawing*, 1971
Conté crayon drawing, black-and-
white photograph mounted on board,
and videotape
Drawing: 34 x 19 in. (86.4 x 48.3 cm);
photograph: 8 x 10 in. (20.3 x 25.4
cm); videotape: 30 minutes
Courtesy of Sonnabend Gallery, New
York

*Evidence*, 1970
Bowl with lamp-black powder and
tape
Destroyed

59

Above: The artist's studio in the
vacant movie theater, National City,
California, December, 1969. Below:
Current studio on Main Street, Santa
Monica, California, 1987

Baldessari continues to catch up with the world by keeping himself surrounded with "stuff," magazines, books, etc., which, ironically—as his latest 1989 inventory seems to foreshadow—may bring him once more to the brink of feeling overwhelmed by a surplus of material:

### My Studio

About 3000 square feet. A wood frame stucco building. Vaulted ceiling with four large skylights. I got the place from Bill Wegman when he moved to New York in the early '70s. At the time I thought it too spacious for me. Now there are books, magazines, boxes of photos, file cabinets, etc., etc., everywhere. But it's a working space and not meant to be a feature in *Architectural Digest*. I'm three blocks from the beach and thirty minutes from the airport. I cash checks at Star Liquor across the street and get my laundry done at Security Cleaners next door, and so on. There's a basketball hoop mounted on one beam in the center of the studio. I can't shoot baskets anymore, however—the ball would land on the Xerox machine.

*Color Corrected Studio (With Window)*, 1972–73
Three color photographs on board with paint and colored pencil on board
31½ x 14¾ in. overall (80 x 37.5 cm)
Collection of Susan and Lewis Manilow

*Left:*   A color photograph of a section of my studio.
*Middle:*   The same photograph with color painted additions, i.e., a blue area painted on the wall.
*Right:*   Using the middle photograph as a guide, the same color changes are actually made to the studio. The studio is then re-photographed incorporating the color changes.

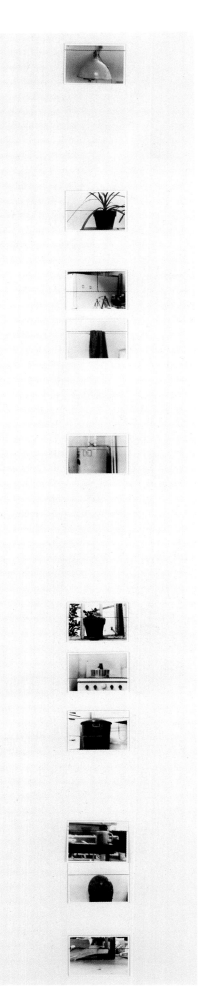

*Alignment Series: Things in My Studio
(By Height)*, 1975
Eleven black-and-white photographs
with ink; mounted on board
3½ x 5 in. each (8.9 x 12.7 cm)
Courtesy of Sonnabend Gallery, New
York

*One way to classify things. An attempt
to get away from "this looks good by
that thing." I like thinking that height
might be the only reason that would
bring these things together. I selected
things in my studio, photographed
them, and noted their height from the
floor. In the piece, they are aligned
vertically using the original
measurements.*

*Measurement Series: Measuring a*
*Chair With a Coffee Cup (Top-Bottom),*
1975
Two black-and white photographs
11 x 13⅞ in. each (27.9 x 35.2 cm)
Courtesy of Sonnabend Gallery, New
York

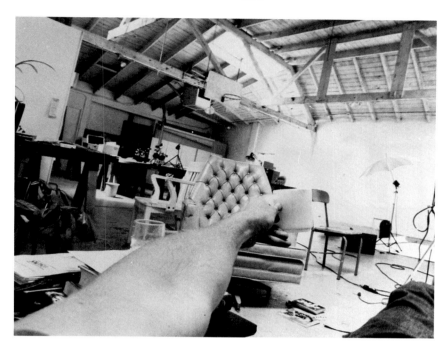

*Car Color Series: All Cars Parked on the West Side of Main Street, Between Bay and Bicknell Streets, Santa Monica, at 1:15 P.M., September 1, 1976*, 1976
Seven Type-C prints on board with pencil
13 x 164 in. overall (33 x 415.6 cm)
Collection of Margo Leavin Gallery, Los Angeles

## NOTES

Unless otherwise noted, all quotations from John Baldessari come from a series of discussions with the author held between September 1987 and April 1989.

1. Quoted in Hunter Drohojowska, "No More Boring Art," *Artnews* 85, no. 1, January 1986, p. 67. Revised and reprinted from " 'I Will Not Make Any More Boring Art': A Profile of John Baldessari," *L.A. Weekly*, July 13–19, 1984.

2. Robert Pincus-Witten, "Blasted Allegories! The Photography of John Baldessari," in *John Baldessari*, New York: The New Museum of Contemporary Art, 1981, p. 56. Exhibition catalogue.

3. René Magritte, quoted in Patrick Waldberg, *Magritte*, Brussels: André de Rache, 1965, p. 91.

4. William Carlos Williams, quoted in *I Wanted to Write a Poem: The Autobiography of the Works of a Poet*, New York: New Directions, 1977, pp. 74–75.

5. William Carlos Williams, quoted in Linda Walshimer Wagner, *Interviews with William Carlos Williams: "Speaking Straight Ahead,"* New York: New Directions, 1966, pp. 60–61.

6. George Kubler, *The Shape of Time*, New Haven and London: Yale University Press, 1962, p. 64.

7. Jane Livingston, exhibition review, *Artforum* VII, no. 4, December 1968, p. 66.

8. Joseph Kosuth, "Art after Philosophy Part II: 'Conceptual Art' and Recent Art," *Studio International* 178, no. 916, November 1969, pp. 160–61.

9. Quoted in *John Baldessari*, Eindhoven: Van Abbemuseum, and Essen: Museum Folkwang, 1981, p. 11. Exhibition catalogue.

10. Ibid., p. 17.

11. Quoted in Hunter Drohojowska, "No More Boring Art," *Artnews* 85, no. 1, January 1986, p. 65.

12. Ibid., pp. 65–66.

13. Quoted in Nancy Drew, "John Baldessari: An Interview," in *John Baldessari*, New York: The New Museum of Contemporary Art, 1981, p. 64. Exhibition catalogue.

14. Ibid., p. 64.

15. Ibid., p. 65.

*I don't lay as much stock by teachin' the elder generation as by teachin' the risin', and if one gang dies without learnin' there is always the next. Keep on remindin' 'em that we ain't bolcheviks, but only the terrifyin' voice of civilization, kulchuh, refinement, aesthetic perception.*

—Ezra Pound
  *letter to Harriet Monroe,
  Rapallo, 27 December 1931,
  from* The Selected Letters of Ezra
  Pound 1907–1941.

# BUT THIS IS
# NOT THE MORAL OF
# THE STORY...

*Once upon a time there was an itinerant artist, a storyteller by the name of J.B. Through analogies and juxtapositions of associative images, he would evoke dream-pictures, in order to discover what he called "memories of the soul." "One man's soul is another man's haddock," he might have added. Anyway, it all began with a black tire rolling down the hill, like a threatening omen. . . .*

From his earliest childhood John Baldessari recalls that he would become much more intrigued when he was taught something through a story than when he was forced to listen to dry didacticisms. Once he became a teacher himself, in 1957, he started to practice the art of storytelling. Somehow it seemed both noncoercive yet at the same time explicit to say something moral about human nature through a story. By concealing his point within a fictitious account Baldessari retains some of the complexities of real life. It is his way of avoiding a rigid, linear manner of pinning down facts, opting instead for the vitality of the unexpected within the chaos and banality of daily life as expressed in a folktale or an ordinary anecdote.

The vehicle of the story suits Baldessari especially well since early on he had realized that he could not concentrate and summarize all of his perceptions into a single piece of art. He would continually think of other related concepts and images that could be substituted. Besides, he felt, the differences and similarities among things could stand out only through comparisons. Baldessari's stories start with a chain of associations, which then tend to transform themselves into a kind of narrative asking for a context. His fascination with the enigma of how a writer works surfaces in a Hollywood joke he likes to tell: A movie producer says to a scriptwriter, "I have a multimillion-dollar idea for a movie." "What is it?" the writer asks. "World War II," comes the reply.

"What about it?" "How should I know," the producer answers, "you're the writer!"

Baldessari has a particular rationale for the use of narrative in his art: "Language seems to me to be a very viable material to use in a creative way. We always think about using forms in some creative way and that seems to me interesting, but no more interesting than using words."[1] For him, the essence of an artwork might be rooted in how to tell a story, just as for Gabriel Garcia Márquez "it always begins with an image, not an idea or a concept. With *Love in the Time of Cholera*, the image was of two old people dancing on a deck of a boat, dancing a bolero."[2] "To detect the birth of a story," in Garcia Márquez's words, might be Baldessari's quest.

One day in 1967, as Baldessari was sitting in the teachers' office of the art department of Southwestern Junior College in Chula Vista, California, telling stories to counter boredom, his imagination was sparked by the accidental discovery of a sound pun, the assonance of "Ing" [res] and "hang," which he then linked to "nail." This illumination led to the writing of a series of "stories," which he paired with complementary photographs, some that he had taken himself from nature and others culled from book and magazine illustrations. These were shown as an installation titled *Ingres and Other Parables* at the Konrad Fischer Gallery in Düsseldorf in 1971, and a year later, they were published in four languages—English, German, French, and Italian—in calendar format by Studio International at the instigation of the art critic and independent curator Barbara Reise. *Ingres and Other Parables* became the artist's first book. The idea of a book pinned up on a wall, open to the page of one's choice, appealed to Baldessari's attraction to "gray" areas. The object is neither fish nor fowl, shifting from art to not quite art, from a book to a lower level of popular material—a calendar. Fabricated out of the artist's experiences and those of his friends, the parables are based on the idea of a textbook for graduate students about what to expect from the art world. In one way or another the parables all hide Baldessari's "parental" guidance, and like stories, they are written in a rhythmic, deceptively simple style. In an interview in 1973, a year after the parables were published, Baldessari said, "When I write, I think about the rhythm a lot, or how the words sound, when I look at a page.... [For the parables] I wrote something, and rewrote it and rewrote it, so it has a certain kind of rhythm. And yet they just seem very offhand."[3]

The "Ingres" parable plays with the question of whether art remains once an artwork is stripped down to an ordinary object—in this case, a nail. The story relates to an entry Baldessari wrote in his journal in 1969: "A work of art, from a work of art, from a work of art, until there is nothing left. A separate artist should be responsible for each version. Condensed function with increasing entropy." The issue here is the so-called dematerialization of art much-discussed topic during the 1960s. The question could be: Where does art reside, in a work's idea or in its materiality? Or, if the tooth of time slowly destroys Ingres's painting, at what point of entropy does art disappear? One tiny nail may well be the answer, but then again, it may not.

In another parable, "The Contract," the pivotal object is a pen. "The pen is on the table," the concluding statement of this tale, and at the same time a common phrase encountered in learning foreign languages, demands an immediate action—to be picked up. But once it is picked up, what then? Baldessari sets up a tension—that of the young artist, torn between having to take risks and make decisions, and being afraid of making the one mistake that will ruin him. For Baldessari, it is precisely that moment of testing one's inventiveness while off balance that can produce art.[4] The question in this case, though, might be, is it attention to detail that distinguishes a genius from an ordinary person? In *Poor Richard's Almanac*, Benjamin Franklin, paraphrasing the seventeenth-century poet George Herbert, notes that a moment of neglect "may breed great mischief...for want of a nail the shoe was lost, for want of a shoe the horse was lost, and for want of

a horse the rider was lost." As Baldessari phrases it, "Is then leaving off the cap of the toothpaste symptomatic of other issues?" How much does chance enter in? In several of the other parables, the right moment passes because one detail is missing.

Timing is crucial to Baldessari, as his current composite photoworks also demonstrate. In these, however, he chooses the moment of anticipation, just before something is about to happen. For instance, in *Lizards to Pianist (With Gold Sphere)*, 1984, a selection of photographic images is stacked, from a vision of "primordial ooze" at the bottom to one of a virtuoso concert pianist at the top, and pushed over to the point of balancing precariously. At any moment, the delicate construction threatens to destroy the wholeness of the sphere within a sphere adjacent to it, to Baldessari "a false idea of perfection anyway." Earlier, in 1981, he had emphasized the "transient nature of the sensual world" by introducing instability in a piece from the *Vanitas Series* by photographing a stack of teetering books next to a flashlight. In this work, the flashlight, replacing the traditional seventeenth-century symbol of passing time—the candle—is about to become annihilated and with it the illumination and knowledge it stands for. "The chase is more interesting," Baldessari states. "I always seem to prefer to keep things open, and I hate to bring things to completion. When doing one work, I am already thinking of the next; I guess I hate answers." The artist prefers questions to solutions, though unpredictable solutions may, at least associatively, provoke new questions.

The theme of letting time pass until it has become too late to act occurs again in the parables "The Great Artist," with its moral of "Art is where you find it," and "The Wait," which ends with the words "Artists come and go." This last sentence recalls T. S. Eliot's line in "The Love Song of J. Alfred Prufrock," "In the room the women come and go/Talking of Michelangelo." The calendar image complementing "The Wait"—a wooden stake fissuring the earth and casting a long shadow, like a makeshift sundial—evokes a similarly melancholic, autumnal mood. It is the end of the day. Is time running out? The story of "The Great Artist," which is accompanied by a photograph of a rock, also suggests gradual erosion caused by time.

*Lizards to Pianist (With Gold Sphere)*,
1984
Black-and-white photographs and
color photograph; mounted on board
108 x 65 in. overall (274.3 x 165.1 cm)
Centro Cultural/Arte Contemporaneo,
Mexico City

## INGRES

This is the story of a little known painting by Ingres. Its first owner took good care of it, but as things go, he eventually had to sell it. Succeeding owners were not so cautious about its welfare and did not take as good care of it as the first owner. That is, the second owner let the painting's condition slip a bit. Maybe it all began by letting it hang crookedly on the wall, not dusting it, maybe it fell to the floor a few times when somebody slammed the door too hard. Anyway the third owner received the Ingres with some scratches (not really tears), and the canvas buckled in one corner – paint fading here and there. Owners that followed had it retouched and so on, but the repairs never matched and the decline had begun. The painting looked pretty sad. But what was important was the documentation – the idea of Ingres; not the substance. And the records were always well-kept. A clear lineage, a good genealogy. It was an Ingres certainly, even though the painting by this time was not much.

The other day it was auctioned off. Time had not been kind to the Ingres. All that was left was one nail. Maybe the nail was of the original, maybe it was used in repairs, or maybe Ingres himself had used it to hang the painting. It was all of the Ingres that remained. In fact, it was believed to be the only Ingres nail ever offered in public sale.

Moral: If you have the idea in your head, the work is as good as done.

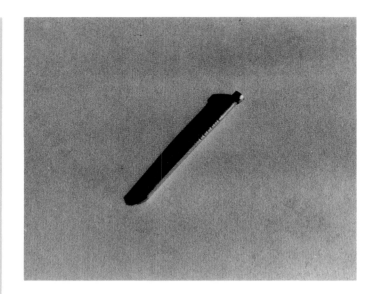

## THE CONTRACT

Once there was an artist who worked very hard. He produced good art, was intelligent, read widely, had insightful opinions, and generally possessed all of those attributes by which talent can be identified.

But the breaks that came to other artists didn't seem to come his way. That is, a large news magazine took pictures of his work but didn't print them. Or just as his work was about to appear on the cover of an art magazine, it would be replaced by the work of another artist. When his name appeared in print, it was usually spelled wrong. Bartenders in the artists' bars didn't argue amongst themselves about the merit of his work. He was not a household word.

But then, one day, the owner of a big gallery called. He wanted to show the artist's work and buy all his back work. Since he was a busy man he asked to meet the artist at the airport. They met and all that was left to do was to sign a contract. The dealer reached for his pen but couldn't find it. The artist didn't have a pen either. They both asked passers-by for the loan of a pen but to no avail. The airplane was due to depart. All that was needed was a pen.

Moral: The pen is on the table.

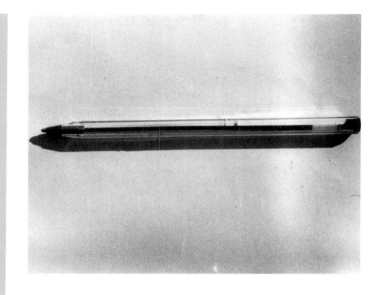

*Ingres and Other Parables* (details), 1971
Ten black-and-white photographs and ten typewritten sheets
Photographs: 8 x 10 in. each; text: 11 x 8½ in. each (20.3 x 25.4; 27.9 x 21.6 cm)
Collection of Angelo Baldassarre, Bari, Italy

## THE WAIT

Once there was an artist who everybody thought was very good. He had a few doubts about this, but it was true – he was smitten with the idea of art. So he painted. And painted. Soon someone said that he should have a show. "Not yet," he said, and went back to work.

He entered his works in local competitions now and then. The local library showed one of his paintings and the art critic of the town paper mentioned his name. A relative said his paintings looked like a linoleum floor and asked if he could draw. He knew that he was slowly becoming an artist.

"You should show your works in a one-man show." "No," he said, "not yet" and went back to work. Fellow art students rose to fame: they sold, they had shows, people talked, they moved to big cities. "Come," they said. "No, not yet," he replied.

Soon his work had authority, had insight, had maturity. Should he show, he thought. No, he answered, though rewards beckoned.

One morning he walked into his studio and it was clear. His work was pivotal, even seminal. The time had come for a show.

He showed and nothing happened.

Moral: Artists come and go.

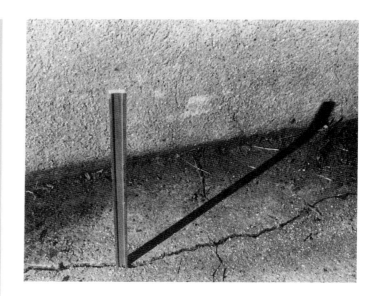

## THE NEON STORY

Once there was an unknown sculptor who was an early worker in neon. The director of a small college gallery who heard him speak of his efforts with this material asked to see his work. Upon seeing the neon sculpture, the director arranged to show the piece in the gallery.

Press announcements were mailed out. On the basis of the announcements, the following occurred:

1. One of America's largest newspapers asked for color photographs to run in the Sunday edition.

2. One of America's largest museums wanted to give a new-talent award to the sculptor.

3. The director of a major gallery in one of America's largest cities offered him a one-man show.

No one had seen any of the artist's work but all had read the press announcement.

Moral: Never underestimate the value of an idea.

## THE BEST WAY TO DO ART

A young artist in art school used to worship the paintings of Cézanne. He looked at and studied all the books he could find on Cézanne and copied all of the reproductions of Cézanne's work he found in the books.

He visited a museum and for the first time saw a real Cézanne painting. He hated it. It was nothing like the Cézannes he had studied in the books. From that time on, he made all of his paintings the sizes of paintings reproduced in books and he painted them in black and white. He also printed captions and explanations on the paintings as in books. Often he just used words.

And one day he realized that very few people went to art galleries and museums but many people looked at books and magazines as he did and they got them through the mail as he did.

Moral: It's difficult to put a painting in a mailbox.

## ART HISTORY

A young artist had just finished art school. He asked his instructor what he should do next. "Go to New York," the instructor replied, "and take slides of your work around to all the galleries and ask them if they will exhibit your work." Which the artist did.

He went to gallery after gallery with his slides. Each director picked up his slides one by one, held each up to the light the better to see it, and squinted his eyes as he looked. "You're too provincial an artist," they all said. "You are not in the mainstream." "We're looking for Art History."

He tried. He moved to New York. He painted tirelessly, seldom sleeping. He went to museum and gallery openings, studio parties, and artists' bars. He talked to every person having anything to do with art; travelled and thought and read constantly about art. He collapsed.

He took his slides around the galleries a second time. "Ah," the gallery directors said this time, "finally you are historical."

Moral: Historical mispronounced sounds like hysterical.

In the parables' text-and-image combinations, neither image nor word takes precedence. One does not mirror or illustrate the other—in fact, they may even point in different directions, while at the same time enriching one another, as in "Art History," in which a rather ordinary, even banal text is juxtaposed with an image of the Egyptian pyramids, producing an effect Baldessari compares to "tying one's tie and thinking about the universe simultaneously." An image conveying a universal sense of destiny is set against a text about the trivial things in life on which we waste our time. The picture alludes to the riddle of the sphinx, or some secret in universal art that happens by itself, and that nobody can completely decipher or appropriate. But on the other hand, does a sophisticated knowledge of art history necessarily stimulate and produce great art? The image of the Egyptian pyramids sets off the story's moral: "Historical mispronounced sounds like hysterical," another sound pun. In "Art History" the durable is contrasted with the fleeting: art is all about fashion; fashion is all about the moment.

The morals of parables such as "The Neon Story" ("Never underestimate the value of an idea"), "The Artist Who Stole Art" ("Art is not in things, it is in the air"), or "Two Artists" ("Time flies, so first things first") reflect the mood of their times. Written in the midst of the Minimal and Conceptual period of the early 1970s, these stories strongly emphasize reason over emotion. But, paradoxically, at the same time they undermine traditional linear Western logic, which assumes that from *a, b,* and *c* follows *d.* The failure of one little detail can make everything go wrong, and reason alone leads nowhere. Baldessari's Zen-like parables depart from the moralistic Christian tradition, in which he was raised, extending from fundamentalist Methodism through his last tie to the church, Episcopalianism, which, despite its more liberal direction, he still found too constricting. This love-hate relationship with Western religion has been part of his work from its beginnings. A journal entry written before 1965 reads, "Make up art fables. Be a good teacher like Jesus." But if there is any messianic quality in Baldessari's teaching, it is buried under a heightened sense of self-irony and wit. The situation becomes even more complex in one of the recent composite photoworks, *Two Stories,* 1987, on the theme of "wanting to believe but not being able to due to doubt." In this work, made up of three columns of photographs, the lefthand column is a satirical portrayal of the life of Jesus Christ through mass-media images. The righthand column consists of assorted still photographs with only a single common element—yellowing grass—and those automatically also are read as a story because it is difficult not to relate this to the Christ story on the left, whose narrative quality is clear. The central column of stills repeats the same partial view of a woman singer accompanied by an accordianist. Only the accordian player's hand and the instrument are visible. The sole change in each photograph is the color of a single accordian key, reinforcing

Baldessari's opinion that "all stories are alike, they may just change in color or mood." The combining of the two ill-fitting stories leaves plenty of room for ambiguous readings but definitely demythologizes the life of Christ, turning it into just one more story. In *Two Stories,* as in *Ingres and Other Parables,* Baldessari operates according to a scheme that is askew and undermines logical expectations. From reading Ludwig Wittgenstein's *Philosophical Investigations* in the mid 1960s, he had become aware that sense can create nonsense, depending on how far a logical argument is pushed. But for the peculiar, nonlinear parables, which seemingly distrust reason by circling around a point of nothingness, he found an even better model in the ideas of John Cage, who as early as 1949, at the Artist's Club on 8th Street in New York City, had given his lecture on nothingness, demonstrating his engagement in and reflections on Zen. Some of Baldessari's remarks reveal a kindred spirit: "I like to participate in teaching but I don't like to lead.... I am teaching best when I can walk out of the room," and "I like being behind the scenes. I think one shouldn't be visible, but yet be visible."[5] One of Cage's stories not only provides an elucidative precedent and context for *Ingres and Other Parables* but also reflects Baldessari's approach to teaching in the early 1970s:

After a long and arduous journey a young Japanese man arrived deep in a forest where the teacher of his choice was living in a small house he had made. When the student arrived, the teacher was sweeping up fallen leaves. Greeting his master, the young man received no greeting in return. And to all his questions, there were no replies. Realizing there was nothing he could do to get the teacher's attention, the student went to another part of the same forest and built himself a house. Years later, when he was sweeping up fallen leaves, he was enlightened. He then dropped everything, ran through the forest to his teacher, and said, "Thank you."[6]

For years Cage has been preparing articles and giving lectures, many of them unusual in form, because, as he has written, "I have employed in them means of composing analogous to my composing means in the field of music."[7] Like Cage, Baldessari draws no hard line between his methods of teaching art and of making art. Each activity is a continuous source of inspiring education for the other. Baldessari would agree with the writer Bernard Malamud that, along with his colleagues, "My other teachers were my students, whom I taught to teach me."[8] When he teaches, Baldessari involves his students through questions and answers, producing new questions while raising issues which he grapples with in his own work. The artist does not try to create Baldessari clones; at the California Institute of the Arts, in Los Angeles, where he has taught for over fifteen years, he usually will not attract students who want to have their ideas confirmed by secure, fixed answers. He sees the ability of the artist as a kind of gift, in a raw state, that the teacher must develop in a pluralistic manner. To him, there are no prescribed notions about where things should end up; art has a life of its own, as mysterious as that may seem. Doing all the right things, Baldessari has discovered, often ends up becoming merely an illustration of art: "I think it is better to push students in a direction where they are not so sure instead of giving them safe answers." For both himself and his students he creates a situation in which, through an imbalance arrived at by questioning, inertia is eliminated. This fight against ignorance, this process of unlearning habitual patterns, favors the exploration of the unknown. As Baldessari describes the experience, "I could reinvent art because I had the freedom through teaching; there was no need to sell work. I remember sitting in my studio nearly in a catatonic state, trying to figure out over and over again what was art and what wasn't art."

Baldessari's notebooks serve as a repository of this attitude, containing, along with notes taken while reading, scraps of disjointed thoughts jotted down, quotations from literature, and shards of conversation overheard in restaurants, classrooms, or on an airplane. Such fragmentary finds, saved from being lost in time, may become useful to the artist later on. When reread, reheard, or rewritten, one of them may surprisingly catch his eye—like an image—somehow proving to be just the right piece to fit the puzzle of a particular moment. Baldessari has compiled many of these notes into lists to be used by his students— however, they are more like threads to be followed rather than rigid guidelines. List making traditionally has been a creative activity for many artists and writers; Ezra Pound pointedly referred to his letters as "laundry lists."

A sample of Baldessari's lists of journal entries appears in his statement "Working Backward" (February 4, 1972), which he introduces as follows:

I usually read a lot and take notes. My work comes out of my notes, although not all my notes come from just reading. I carry a notebook around in my back pocket and usually write down ideas when they come....

1. You can't say that. But I like asking the question. I mean the talk about it can be like a blueprint. Just don't mistake a line for a wall.
2. To generalize is to falsify. Write it 1000 times.
3. That sentence is no more than that.
4. Avoid theorizing; assemble facts.
5. If I say it, is it true?
6. Careful collections of examples rather than a system of classification. Don't look deeply; look on the surface.
7. Art is limitation.
8. Does only art and torture teach?
9. Behind design is the image.
10. Over there is what I didn't do. You might like that, since for every loss, there is progress.
11. Can shadows and reflections dirty our clothes as we walk?
12. Adultery is bad grammar.
13. A wheelchair for the mind. A TV dinner for the eyes.
14. Where are all the stories about the birth of art?
15. Disguises that do not disguise but reveal. A person/ thing disguised disguised.
16. Do we know only the back of the world?
17. What does "I mean it" mean?
18. A zone of silence.
19. "Let shadows be furnished with genitals."
20. Solitary contemplation as hooky.
21. What are those words that can only be spoken?
22. You can't say that.
23. The Greek man was never home or indoors.
24. Is it worth it to teach ants the alphabet?
25. Talk to a cup of coffee.
26. Is it silly to say "I am making art" as I make it?
27. All ideas have their form.
28. Is it impossible to underline in a telegram?
29. Anticipated growths.
30. To a point of beginning rather than end."[9]

Through such interpolations at the margins of his art activity Baldessari pushed against the perimeters of art. Simultaneously he legitimized his notes as a teaching device by sharing them with his students.

At about the same time that Baldessari started keeping lists, he began to use the device of the anecdote as a way to gently ridicule people without criticizing them directly. In this way he could expose the truth without actually telling it. One of the anecdotes circulating at the time involved Jackson Pollock: the artist is said to have once expressed his contempt for collectors by pissing in Peggy Guggenheim's fireplace. This may be true, but then again it may not. The same can be said of a poetic account of Mondrian that Baldessari came across somewhere that stuck in his memory. The story goes that Mondrian used to jest about how, when he walked in the park, his trousers would be stained green by the reflection of the grass. This self-mockery—for he was known for his hatred of secondary hues and organic forms— exposes Mondrian as a personality more imaginative and less rigid than he is usually depicted. And Baldessari is after the beauty and poetry of ordinary, matter-of-fact incidents often overlooked in the turmoil of life. Thus, it was natural that for one of his pieces, he should select not Pollock's abrasive, grandstanding gesture, a pointless kind of bragging, but Mondrian's witty, imagist observation, which lent itself so well to visual transformation. The piece, from 1972–73, was called *The Mondrian Story*. Earlier, he had captured a similar incident of everyday life in the text-on-canvas work *Semi-Close-Up of Girl by Geranium (Soft View)*, 1968.

However, Baldessari's use of film director D. W. Griffith's stage directions for *Intolerance* as a way of story telling does not lead to performance. He prefers natural, simple gestures; theatricality is not present in his artistic vocabulary. Although he approves of performing in class, in early 1973 he still thought that performance as art was a "bogus activity": "I think performance for me is a little bit too hot an activity. I think once it is in a vehicle, say film or writing, somehow it is diffused a little bit. I just like things to be not so important. Performances seem too important. I wouldn't mind performing without anybody knowing about it, without calling attention to it."[10] Television is an acceptable performance medium for Baldessari. In the videotape *Three Feathers and Other Fairy Tales*, 1973, he reads his favorite fairy tales in the tradition of the oral

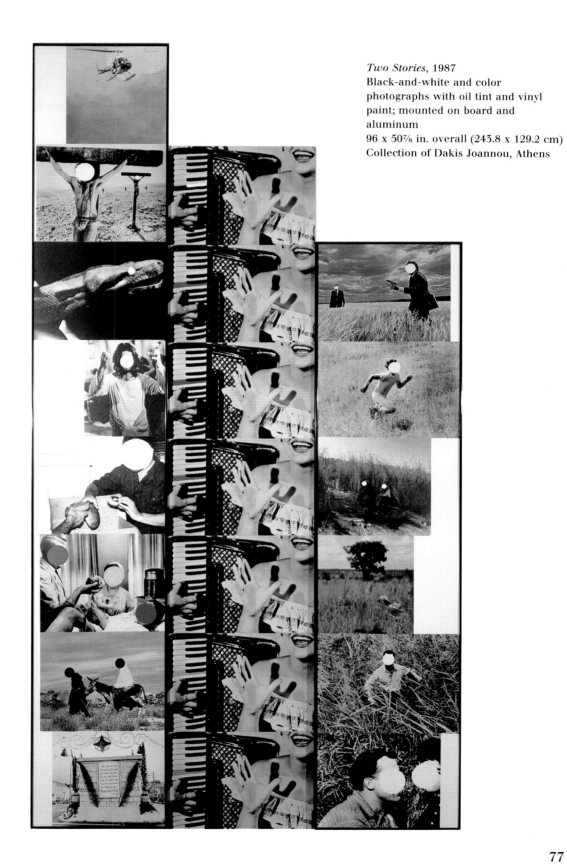

*Two Stories*, 1987
Black-and-white and color
photographs with oil tint and vinyl
paint; mounted on board and
aluminum
96 x 50⅞ in. overall (243.8 x 129.2 cm)
Collection of Dakis Joannou, Athens

*The Mondrian Story*, 1972–73
Two Type-C prints; mounted on board
13 x 20 in. each (33 x 50.8 cm)
Collection of Ida Gianelli, Milan

storyteller. He found a precedent in John Cage's *Indeterminancy: New Aspect of Forms and Instrumental and Electronic Music*, 1959, a two-record set in which Cage, accompanied by electronic music composed by David Tudor, reads several stories of different lengths allotting one minute to each. Sometimes the stories were read very slowly, sometimes very quickly. Baldessari had considered lighting a candle at the beginning of his readings and blowing it out at the end, but decided against this "embroidering" of the tales. Instead, he attempted to turn into art the unadorned activity of storytelling itself—by simply sitting down and reading. Despite being recorded on videotape, *Three Feathers and Other Fairy Tales* focuses attention primarily on the aural rather than on the visual, since the image—that of Baldessari sitting in a chair—never changes. Discrepancies between what is heard and what is seen again become the subject of the videotape *Ed Henderson Suggests Sound Tracks for Photographs*, 1974. A handful of unidentified photographs cut out from *National Geographic* are shown on a television monitor; we hear the artist describing them to a student, Ed Henderson, who is unable to see them. Henderson uses these descriptions as the basis for selecting appropriate sound equivalents for the photographs. His choices are more or less determined by chance—an appealing image or text he finds on the covers of records of sound effects or of stock music for movies he has never listened to before. Henderson gets three tries at each picture. Baldessari directs him by answering his questions about the appropriateness of his choices, and eventually picks what he considers the best solution of the three—the same way he chose rhubarb stalks in *Choosing (A Game for Two Players)*, 1972. Sometimes a mood evoked by a musical selection enhances the picture; at other times a humorous incident will occur, such as when a silly-sounding beep is matched with the image of a snake lying in front of an automobile. As in many of the parables, in this tape Baldessari also questions the process of

decision making: "given this information, this is what I have chosen, this is the way I would act, not in an autocratic way."

In recording videotapes such as *Three Feathers and Other Fairy Tales*, Baldessari reached a much larger audience than the traditional storyteller. At the same time, because of his isolation in the studio, he was deprived of the storyteller's contact with actively involved listeners. It was impossible for him therefore to measure whether "I was spitting against the wind or not by testing once more what art is." He had similar experiences in some of his other, rather perverse conceptual exercises in futility, among them the 19-minute videotape *Teaching a Plant the Alphabet*, 1972. In this tape Baldessari both logically stretches the hypothesis of being able to communicate with plants, and at the same time pushes it into the realm of the absurd. The piece was his reaction to one of the most influential performances recorded on television in the 1960s,

Videotape still from *Three Feathers and Other Fairy Tales*, 1973
Black-and-white videotape with sound
30 minutes

78

Videotape stills from *Ed Henderson
Suggests Sound Tracks for
Photographs*, 1974
Black-and-white videotape with sound
28 minutes

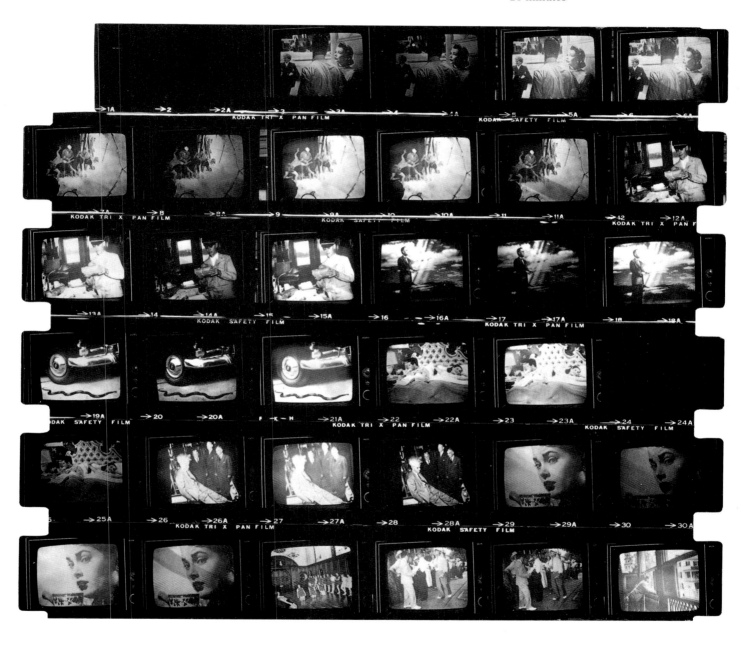

Videotape stills from *Teaching a Plant
the Alphabet*, 1972
Black-and-white videotape with sound
19 minutes

*How to Explain Pictures to a Dead Hare*, an action by
Joseph Beuys that took place on November 26, 1965,
in Düsseldorf, at the opening of the exhibition
"*Joseph Beuys...irgendein Strang*" (Joseph Beuys...
any old noose). Teaching plants the alphabet may
appear to be a deceptively simple action compared to
Beuys's theatrical mysticism of art. Baldessari, in
contrast, is against "art being too important" and
tends to find it in the most ordinary conditions of life.

A similar attitude surfaces in the artist's comments,
in 1973, on a catalog in which Bruce Nauman's art
activities are compared to Marcel Duchamp's:

In the catalog Nauman is talking to a critic and the critic
says, well, what you do best is the way you use your time. I
think what Duchamp meant was—in that respect—that he
just enjoyed living, walking around, eating in restaurants,
talking and that sort of thing but not in any conscious way
as art. Whereas the critic interpreted Nauman's activities in
a very conscious way as art activity.... Duchamp was having
a good time, but having a good time in an incredibly
sophisticated way. That is very disarming, so it is very
successful. And I think it is that attitude in his work of not
caring that is intriguing. It is like he always keeps art a little
bit off balance.[11]

Baldessari's remarks say as much about his own
values as they do about Duchamp: the hidden act
that is uncovered *en passant*, the idea that every
action or non-action in life potentially is art, may be
the drive behind his continuing questioning of the
boundaries between art and life. Two of his language
pieces from 1973 can be seen in this context. *On
Artists' Shoes* runs as follows:

I was at a party once and noticed the following: the hostess
saw that one of the guests was wearing paint-spattered
shoes. "Oh," she exclaimed delightedly, "you must be an
artist!" Whereupon everyone crowded around and a great
fuss was made over him. Unknown to the hostess and the
guests, among them was a very famous film maker.

Moral: You can't tell an artist by his shoes.

The second piece, *Two Questions* poses:

1. What is the story about Picabia picking up a girl while
   driving his car?
2. What is the story about Oldenburg eating a banana?[12]

In *The Pencil Story*, 1972–73, composed of a caption
and two photographs of a pencil, the artist, through
questioning his likes and dislikes about what is and
what is not art, affirms that even the way he
perceives common objects is emotionally conditioned
by his vision of art: "I had this incredible urge to
sharpen this pencil. I wasn't sure, but I thought it had
something to do with art." The sharpened pencil, its
point a pure, untouched graphite cone, becomes the
epitome of perfection in its juxtaposition with the
eroded geometry of the pencil stub, whose dulled
point is the embodiment of unsatisfactory reality.
While *The Pencil Story* is a metaphor for the artist's
struggle for perfection in art, as conditioned by
Western Platonic values, *A Different Kind of Order
(The Thelonious Monk Story)*, 1972–73, demonstrates,
as its title suggests, a different sense of order, which
Baldessari suddenly hit upon while reading a passage
in *The Jazz Life*, by Nat Hentoff. The passage
describes Monk curing his wife Nellie's phobia of

objects hanging crookedly on a wall. Nellie recalls that Monk "nailed a clock to the wall at a very slight angle, just enough to make me furious. We argued about it for two hours, but he wouldn't let me change it. Finally, I got used to it. Now anything can hang at any angle, and it doesn't bother me at all."[13] By slightly twisting the story, or creatively misreading it, Baldessari emphasizes a patriarchal teacher-student relationship in which our conditioned sense of order is questioned:

There's a story about Thelonious Monk going around his apartment and tilting all the pictures hanging on the wall. It was his idea of teaching his wife a different kind of order. When she saw the pictures askew on the wall she would straighten them. And when Monk saw them straight on the wall, he would tilt them. And she would straighten them, and he would tilt them. Until one day his wife left them hanging on the wall tilted.[14]

Baldessari's questioning of conventional concepts also includes the questioning of factors influencing our environment, especially the mass media—television, the movies, newspapers, magazines—which through its non-stop interference in our daily lives seems to condition us more than nature. By delivering a so-called "objective" but actually surrogate reality, it produces the cultural meanings

*The Pencil Story*, 1972–73
Two Type-R prints on board with colored pencil
22 x 27¼ in. overall (55.9 x 69.2 cm)
Collection of Mr. and Mrs. Nicola Bulgari, New York

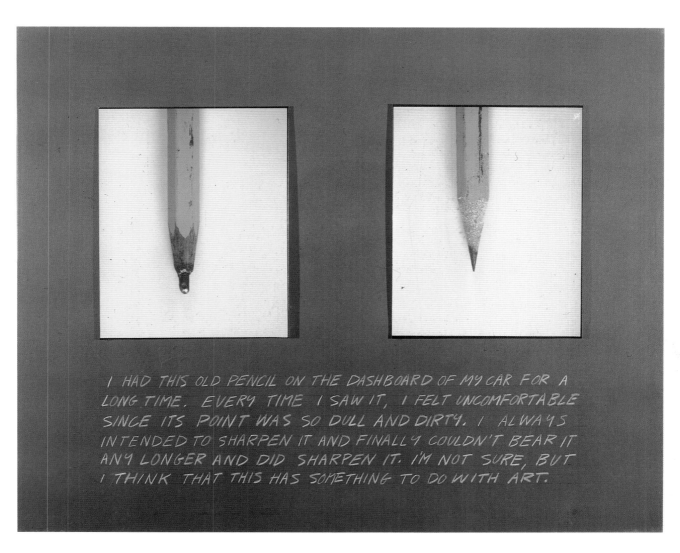

I HAD THIS OLD PENCIL ON THE DASHBOARD OF MY CAR FOR A LONG TIME. EVERY TIME I SAW IT, I FELT UNCOMFORTABLE SINCE ITS POINT WAS SO DULL AND DIRTY. I ALWAYS INTENDED TO SHARPEN IT AND FINALLY COULDN'T BEAR IT ANY LONGER AND DID SHARPEN IT. I'M NOT SURE, BUT I THINK THAT THIS HAS SOMETHING TO DO WITH ART.

*A Different Kind of Order (The Thelonious Monk Story)* (installation and details), 1972–73
Five black-and-white photographs and one typewritten sheet; mounted on board; arrangement variable
Six panels: 11⅝ x 14¹¹⁄₁₆ in. each (29.5 x 29.7 cm)
The Museum of Fine Arts, Houston; Museum Purchase with partial funding provided by the National Endowment for the Arts

that simultaneously preserve and short-circuit traditional criteria and values. In the early 1970s, while he was teaching at the California Institute of the Arts, Baldessari was impressed by the highly advanced music department, and was encouraged by colleagues such as the video artist Nam June Paik, the Fluxus artist Emmett Williams, and the inventor of the "Happening," Allan Kaprow. Having easy access to film equipment, Baldessari tried to analyze filmmaking just as he had set out to understand art, by "taking apart and putting together again," calling the result a film. He was attracted both by the cinematic exploration of time and by the medium's immediacy, so clearly expressed by John Huston, whom James Agee called the "undirectable director": "On paper, all you can do is say something happened, and if you say it well enough the reader believes you. In pictures, if you do it right, *the thing happens right there on the screen*."[15]

*Goodbye to Boats (Sailing In)* (details),
1972–73
Seven Type-C prints; mounted on
board
10 x 6½ in. each (25.4 x 16.5 cm)
Collection of the artist

*A Movie: Directional Piece Where
People Are Looking*, 1972–73
Twenty-eight black-and-white
photographs with acrylic; mounted on
board
3½ x 5 in. each (9 x 12.7 cm)
Installation dimensions variable
Jedermann Collection, N.A.

In order to create a different filmic language, opening up new realities, Baldessari needed to upset the viewer's conditioned responses to cinema. He began to challenge conventions about how to tell a story on screen by proving that a movie does not need to have a story line at all. He already had demonstrated that any sequence of photographic images implies a narrative even if they do not show a development and are inconsistent as to time and space—in works such as *Two Stories; Goodbye to Boats (Sailing In), Goodbye to Boats (Sailing Out), 1972–73; Movie Storyboard: Norma's Story,* 1974; and *Violent Space Series: Six Situations with Guns Aligned (Guns Sequenced Small to Large)*, and *Six Vignetted Portraits of Guns Aligned and Equipoised (Violet),* 1976. Whereas in these pieces a narrative flow is established despite the non-linkage of the photographs, in films such as *Title,* 1973, and *Script,* 1973–77, the lack of a story line blocks almost any movement, producing the effect of a sequence of disparate stills. In taking apart the audience-manipulating constituents of commercial film, such as plot and drama, Baldessari invented his own vocabulary of synesthetic cinema. After studying the way we perceive video and cinema through the reselection and rearrangement of the components of these media, the artist's next step was to declare the stages in that process to be as important as the end result itself. Opposing film's usual linear, hierarchical system of individual parts, which predict and determine the outcome of the whole, Baldessari juxtaposed unrelated components of what seems at first sight completely irrelevant content. All the parts lead in different directions, yet the subject matter is placed in a framework of elegant simplicity, one based on the Minimalist principle "less is more." In *Movie Storyboard . . .*, the framework is the storyboard's functional grid of panels, in *Script* it is the device of repetition: the same action is performed by seven couples, uncovering hidden differences and similarities.[16] The result is more than the sum of the parts. Each segment may fuse into a whole, but at the

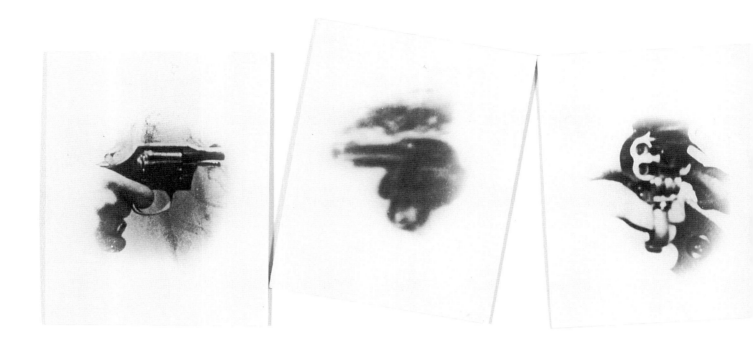

*Violent Space Series: Six Vignetted
Portraits of Guns Aligned and
Equipoised (Violet)*, 1976
Six black-and-white photographs;
mounted on board
14 x 11 in. each (35.6 x 27.9 cm)
Private collection, courtesy of
Sonnabend Gallery, New York

same time it suggests that it is part of another whole,
thus shifting indefinitely into the role of fragment.

In *Title*, which the artist explains "as a primer on
filmmaking," Baldessari "isolates the elements of
cinema." The movie starts with a sequence of shots,
each 30 seconds long, of objects or creatures—a dog,
a man, a chair, a rock—seen first alone, then in
simple relationships (the man to the dog, the dog to
the rock, the rock to the man, the man to the chair,
etc.). A sequence of simple actions follows: a finger
moving, a hand trying to balance a stick that won't
stand up by itself, five peas in a pod being pressed, a
rock hit with a bottle, a hand hammering. Next
comes a section on sound, including both natural and
man-made sounds such as background music and
speech, in varying intensities of loudness, from the
chirp of a cricket to the buzz of a drill to someone
coughing. In the sections on monologue and
dialogue, a student responds to inaudible questions,
and a man and woman read but do not act out the
script of a commercial cowboy movie. Next,
Baldessari demonstrates how film stock reacts to the
six colors of the color wheel, in shots of a red apple,
an orange carrot, a yellow lemon, a green fern, and a
blue-dyed and then a natural purple flower. We also
see both the black-and-white and the color version of
a film scene, in a split image of a woman and child
walking up a street in Venice, California.

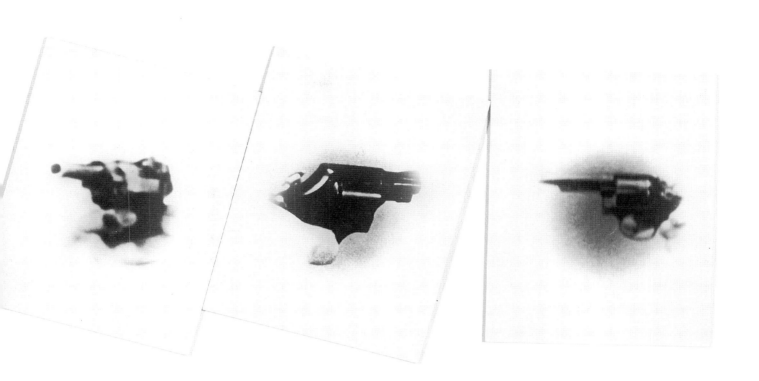

*Violent Space Series: Six Situations
with Guns Aligned (Guns Sequenced
Small to Large)*, 1976
Six black-and-white photographs;
mounted on board
6¹⁵⁄₁₆ x 9⁹⁄₁₆ in. each (17.6 x 24.3 cm)
Courtesy of Sonnabend Gallery, New
York

Left and right: Film stills from *Title*, 1973
16mm black-and-white and color film with sound
25 minutes

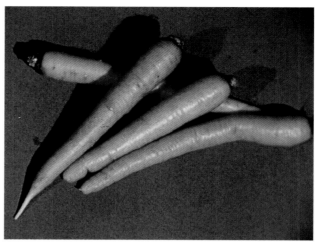

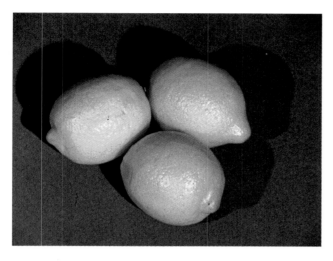

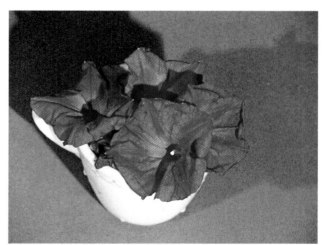

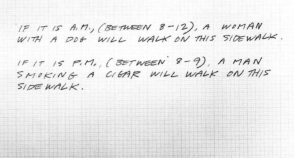

IF IT IS A.M., (BETWEEN 8-12), A WOMAN
WITH A DOG WILL WALK ON THIS SIDEWALK.

IF IT IS P.M., (BETWEEN 8-9), A MAN
SMOKING A CIGAR WILL WALK ON THIS
SIDEWALK.

IF IT IS A.M., THE MAN WHO LIVES
IN THE HOUSE OPPOSITE THIS
WINDOW, WILL WATER HIS GARDEN.

IF IT IS P.M., THE COUPLE LIVING
IN THE APARTMENT NEXT DOOR
WILL PROBABLY ARGUE.

*If It Is A.M.; If It Is P.M.*, 1972–73
Three panels each with graph paper,
one black-and-white photograph, and
ink
14 x 10¼ in. each (35.6 x 26 cm)
Courtesy of Sonnabend Gallery, New
York

(↖) IF IT IS A.M., THE MAN WHO RUNS
THE UPHOLSTERY SHOP ON THE HILL HAS
PROBABLY DONE HIS WORK FOR THE DAY.

(↓) IF IT IS P.M., THE DRIVE-IN MOVIE
WILL OPEN ITS GATES AT 7 O'CLOCK.

The element of timing is represented by two shots of the same duration, again 30 seconds, but psychologically they feel quite different: one, a stationary shot of clouds, seems to last for an eternity, while the second, taken from on top of a tall building of a pedestrian entering the frame from the right and exiting on the left, passes quickly because of its mini-narrative, containing a beginning and an end. (At about the same time Baldessari did another variation on the passing of time in *If It Is A.M.; If It Is P.M.*, 1972–73). In *Title*, a section on camera movement, the camera first dollies from left to right along a wall, picking up and then losing a student; then remains stationary while the student moves from left to right through the field of view; and finally the camera pans, following as the student walks. The concept of time passing returns once again in the section of *Title* dealing with lighting, both natural and artificial, in a stationary, outdoor shot in which the sun passes from dawn to midday to dusk. Baldessari shows in *Title* how lighting affects one's interpretation even when it deals with the same image—such as a woman seen in a three-quarters view, lit first from the left, then from the front, and finally from the right.

For the last part of the film Baldessari excerpted scenes from various movie scripts and instructed two students from the California Institute of the Arts film department to go out and shoot them. He then assembled the scenes in no particular order, subtitling them with their shooting instructions: "Rock, with music background." "Close-up of Holland's face: he is laughing and talking but we hear nothing," and so on. The movie ends where the scenes indicate a narrative is about to begin. *Script*, begun in 1973 (but not completed until 1977, because some of the sound was stolen and had to be redone) is a sort of sequel to *Title*, picking up where it ended: seven pairs of students were given the same seven scenes from different Hollywood movie scripts and instructed to interpret them. Each couple was provided with the same cameraman and soundman (who were also students), but did not see the scenes performed by the other couples. The movie is in four parts: it starts with shots of the texts of each scene, followed by the performances of the whole set of scenes by each couple, then by the repetition of the performances ordered by scene instead of by couple. Part four consists of the artist/producer's selection of the ten best scenes.

In both these films, Baldessari was not so much interested in technical issues such as camera angles (other than the few indications present in the scenes he had selected) as in the degree of control and restraint he was exercising in leaving the camerawork to others, much in the way he had left the painting of phrases for the photo-text canvases up to the Mexican sign painter, and the series of *Commissioned Paintings* to amateur painters. Again he had devised a strategy in advance by defining the overall structure of each film so that it would begin to have a life of its own, and at the same time not obstruct spontaneous acting. In *Title*, the camera was out of Baldessari's hands, handled by his students; in *Script* the actors followed the instructions of the script while taking their own initiative in such matters as telling the cameraman where to locate the lights, and so on. *Title* was shot without retakes in order to preserve a vitality that would be lost by laboring over an idea. The practice recalls a statement by Jean-Luc Godard: "The ideal for me is to obtain right away what will work. If retakes are necessary it falls short of the mark. The immediate is chance. At the the same time it is definitive. What I want is the definitive by chance."[17] In *Script*, several small gestures, and the uncontrolled rising and falling vocal inflections that surface in the nonprofessional acting of the student couples, involuntarily bring out character traits that the couples are unaware of and never intended to show in front of the camera. This creates a personal intimacy, to which the audience subjectively responds. At the same time, the artist structures the movie, a conceptual activity. And the viewer, being able to see different relationships in the same scenes, can objectively question them. A personal cinema is turned into a more universal expression.

SCENE 413: MEDIUM LONG SHOT-QUEEN

(The KING tries to crawl towards her, but dies before
he can do so.)

Film stills from *Script*, 1973–77
16mm black-and-white film with
sound
25 minutes

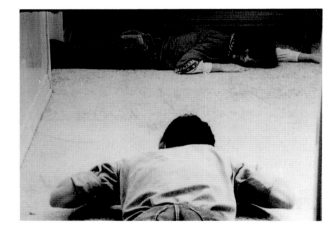

Once one begins to tear at the edges of stories, once traditional narrative is questioned, nothing has to be the way it is: facts, structures, and worlds fall apart, to be infinitely rearranged, redefined, and reinterpreted. In *Story with 24 Versions*, 1974, Baldessari applied a strategy similar to the one he used in *Script*, rearranging the same movie stills with different results. Four black-and-white photographs with their set directions ("He took out a cigarette," "He held the book") are arranged in the twenty-four different sequences possible, each time telling a new tale. In *Movie Storyboard: Norma's Story*, a preparatory stage in movie making, normally discarded, has been turned into an end in itself. This tactic recalls in a way Baldessari's 1966–68 texts-on-canvas, in which he had begun by transforming ideas from his notes into painterly inventions, but in the end had the notes themselves painted by a sign painter, reasoning, "Why can they not be used as they are?" *Movie Storyboard . . .* appeals to the imagination the way a story that is read does, as opposed to a filmed version. Television show stills, including some from *77 Sunset Strip*, are alternated with personal snapshots that were lying around Baldessari's studio—photographs of the San Diego painter Richard Allen Morris, for example. Additionally, excerpts from diverse film scripts are placed side by side with a connecting narrative written by Baldessari himself. Provided with instructions for sound cues and camera angles designed to produce immediate action, the texts mostly complement the pictures, but sometimes, in cases in which suitable images were unavailable, they refer to blank screens. These voids resist the grid, jumping off the page at us. They are comparable to Cage's application of "silences" in his music—intermissions of white noise, never actual soundlessness. As resonances of their accompanying script, these panels, while blank, nevertheless become emotionally colored with their own secret meanings.

*The idea was to use four simple acts (performed with one's hands), pair them with a description of the act (i.e., "He extended his hand"), and to compile them into all the possible scenarios, the result being twenty-four different narratives.*

*It relates to* Norma's Story *in form; however,* Norma's Story *is a relatively sophisticated story while* 24 Versions *is primitive.*

*Story with 24 Versions*, 1974
Twenty-four panels of black-and-white photographs and ink on storyboard layout paper
16¾ x 11⅞ in. each (42.6 x 30.2 cm)
Collection of the artist

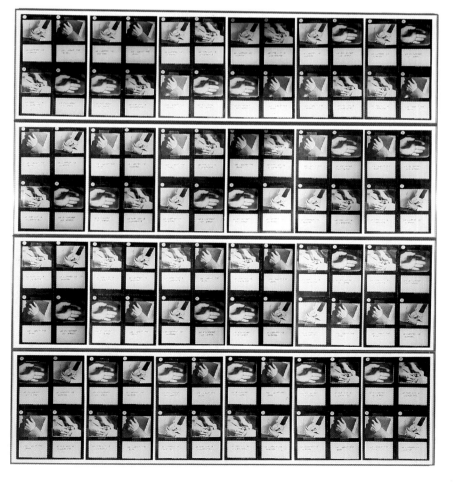

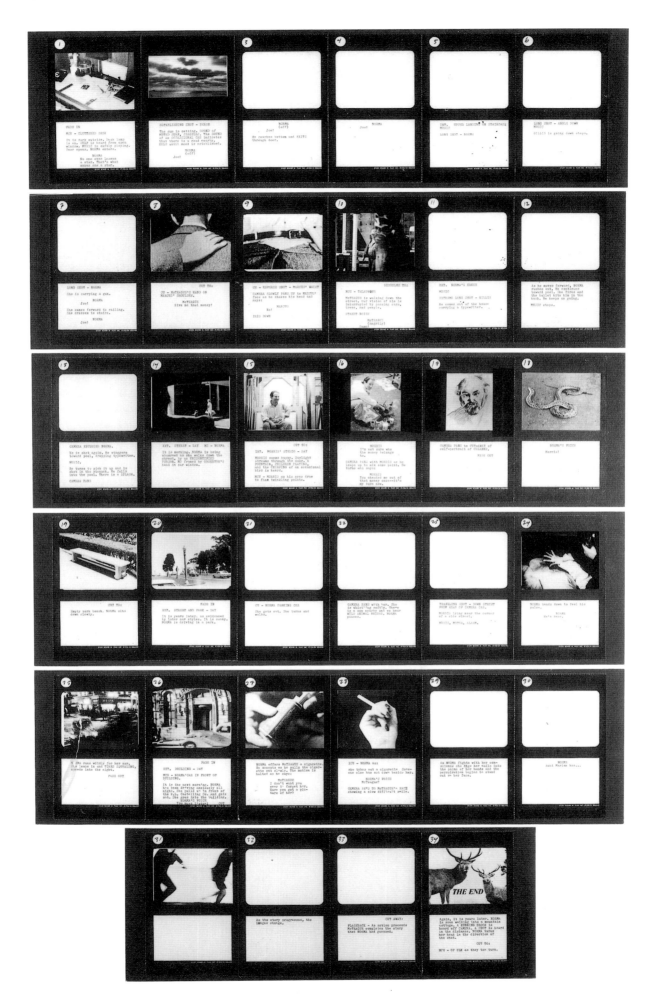

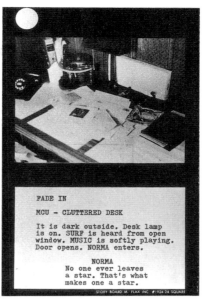

FADE IN

MCU - CLUTTERED DESK

It is dark outside. Desk lamp
is on. SURF is heard from open
window. MUSIC is softly playing.
Door opens. NORMA enters.

                NORMA
        No one ever leaves
    a star. That's what
    makes one a star.

STORY BOARD M. FLAX INC. #1924-24 SQUARE

*Movie Storyboard: Norma's Story,*
1974
Six panels of black-and-white
photographs and ink on storyboard
layout paper
Five: 8½ x 29⅞ in. each (21.6 x 75.9);
one: 8½ x 20¾ in. (21.6 x 52.7 cm)
Courtesy of Sonnabend Gallery, New
York

CU - REVERSE SHOT - MARCUS' WAIST

CAMERA SLOWLY PANS UP to MARCUS'
face as he shakes his head and
says:

                MARCUS
        No!

IRIS DOWN

STORY BOARD M. FLAX INC. #1924-24 SQUARE

                CUT TO:

INT. MORRIS' STUDIO - DAY

MORRIS seems happy. Daylight
streams through the door. A
FOUNTAIN, CHILDREN PLAYING,
and the CHIRPING of an occasional
bird is heard.

MCU - MORRIS as his eyes draw
to fine twinkling points.

STORY BOARD M. FLAX INC. #1924-24 SQUARE

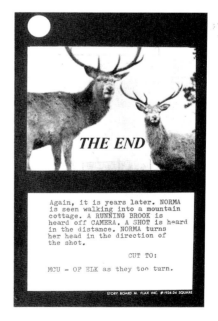

Again, it is years later. NORMA
is seen walking into a mountain
cottage. A RUNNING BROOK is
heard off CAMERA. A SHOT is heard
in the distance. NORMA turns
her head in the direction of
the shot.

                CUT TO:

MCU - OF ELK as they too turn.

STORY BOARD M. FLAX INC. #1924-24 SQUARE

Similarly, in *Violent Space Series: Two Stares Making a Point but Blocked by a Plane (For Malevich)*, 1976, the context of two men standing on a flat roof, both staring at a point above a building's parapet, implies enough to trigger a fantasy about what might be obscured behind the square white plane seen on the left of the image. By injecting an eerie emotional quality into the tabula rasa of the Constructivist white plane, Baldessari was not necessarily trying to reduce Malevich, to take him off his pedestal. Just as he did in *The Mondrian Story*, he simply tried to make Malevich more accessible and human. In this later work, image and title are firmly interlocked: the title states exactly what is going on, adding no information to what we already know from the picture itself. Nothing is taken away from the power of the imagination to fantasize about what is not there.

In combining images with words in *Movie Storyboard: Norma's Story*, Baldessari created a range of relationships, sometimes perfectly matching illustrations to text, sometimes almost disconnecting them. Because of the discrepancies between words

*Violent Space Series: Two Stares Making a Point but Blocked by a Plane (For Malevich)*, 1976
Black-and-white photograph with collage; mounted on board
24⅛ x 36 in. (61.3 x 91.4 cm)
Collection of James Corcoran, Los Angeles

and images, and the holes caused by the interspersed blank panels, which stand mostly for missing images but sometimes also for missing text, bizarre shifts occur in the narrative, touching off the imagination. The process is analogous to the fantasies of a passerby curious about the life going on inside a Modernist skyscraper. In Baldessari's words, "The rigor of reduction is only part of life. More like the truth is that pure, beautifully proportioned rooms are filled up with a bunch of noisy kids." Juxtaposing snapshots from real life with artificially staged movie stills, the reproduction of a Cézanne self-portrait with an image of a snake crawling over the pavement, *Movie Storyboard...* can be seen as the perfect exemplar of the art historian Herbert Read's observation that the four aesthetic modes—realism, surrealism, constructivism, and expressionism—have direct correlations with the four modes of human consciousness: thought, intuition, emotion, and sensation.[18]

Baldessari thinks in terms of both/and rather than either/or. He has a hard time even imagining himself confined to the perfecting of a single theme, executed in one style, embodying universal experience and knowledge. Correspondences and contradictions are integral within one work, and differ from one work to the next, for his art is based on the imperfect human condition. It is in the patching and fixing of missing links, in improvisation and substitution, rather than in the attempt to achieve perfection, that the power of the imagination lies. As Baldessari puts it, "If you don't have an airplane, take a cardboard box." In *Movie Storyboard...* perfectly created scenes are offset with deliberately malfunctioning images and text, causing the work's rigid grid, and any expectation of linear narrative, to break down and thus become open to more erratic experiences that catch one off-guard. Such unplanned side effects, which defy the overall framework, often constitute the essence of Baldessari's art.

One day in 1976, while reading Susanne K. Langer's chapter "The Logic of Signs and Symbols," in *Philosophy In a New Key*, it occurred to Baldessari that he could use the structures of grammar to bring visual components together. Langer states that grammatical structure "ties together several symbols, each with at least a fragmentary connotation of its own, to make one complex term, whose meaning is a special constellation of all the connotations involved. What the special constellation is, depends on the syntactical relations within the complex symbol, or proposition."[19] Baldessari, who calls himself a "frustrated writer, less interested in the form art takes than the meaning an image evokes," began to structure his images so that they syntactically fused writing and visual form. He was particularly inspired by Langer's assertion that *"a proposition is a picture of a structure—the structure of a state of affairs. The unity of a proposition is the same sort of unity that belongs to a picture, which presents one scene, no matter how many items may be distinguishable within it."*[20]

In the artist's book *Brutus Killed Caesar*, 1976, Baldessari takes off from one of Langer's examples of the way relations in language are expressed. The word "killed" connects the two terms "Brutus" and "Caesar." "Where the relation is not symmetrical," Langer notes, "the word-order and the grammatical forms (case, mood, tense, etc.) of the words symbolize its direction. 'Brutus killed Caesar' means something different from 'Caesar killed Brutus,' and 'Killed Caesar Brutus' is not a sentence at all. The word-order partly demonstrates the sense of the structure."[21]

As one leafs through Baldessari's book, two of the three images on each page stay the same: on the left is a younger man, on the right an older one. The image between them—their connecting link, the correlative of the word "killed" in the sentence "Brutus killed Caesar"—depicts the murder weapon, which changes with each page. The first page shows a knife, the second a gun. Both are pointed in no particular direction. The subsequent weapons are presented in an ascending degree of improbability: the eighth page, for example, shows a coat hanger, the ninth a paint-roller, directed toward the older man. The twelfth page, however, shows a banana, directed toward the younger man.[22] Though several of the selected murder weapons—a drill, a saw, a bottle of unnamed liquid—have unpleasant overtones and could somehow lead to death, others seem more bizarre and remote: a golf ball, a clothespin, and the final weapon, thumbtacks.

In a highly imaginative way, Baldessari employs the associative strength of objects, illustrated in the well-known remark that the actor Stanislavski attributed to Chekhov: "If a rifle is seen hanging over a fireplace in the first act, then it should be fired by the third."[23] The alternation of obvious and much less likely murder weapons stretches the fixed meaning of the phrase "Brutus killed Caesar," leaving room for doubt. In *Brutus Killed Caesar* Baldessari lets the principles of grammar determine the order and reading of the three images he has selected for each page. And by creating an ambiguous interplay of the intermediary areas between sign and symbol, between denotation and connotation, he gradually blurs Langer's "logic of terms." Langer states that man uses " 'signs' not only to *indicate* things, but also to *represent* them," and signs that are reminders and "help retain things for later reference" are no longer "*symptoms* of things but *symbols*." In Baldessari's version, the sign value of the consecutive images as correlatives of the word " killed " is gradually subverted as the murder weapons become more and more far-fetched and open to different interpretations, which also threatens to collapse their symbolic value. Thus, with the images about to lose their function as reminders of "killing," it becomes even more difficult to define a special constellation of all connotations involved, making one doubt even the denotations of Brutus and Caesar, already mixed up in a contemporary setting that totally disregards temporal limitations.

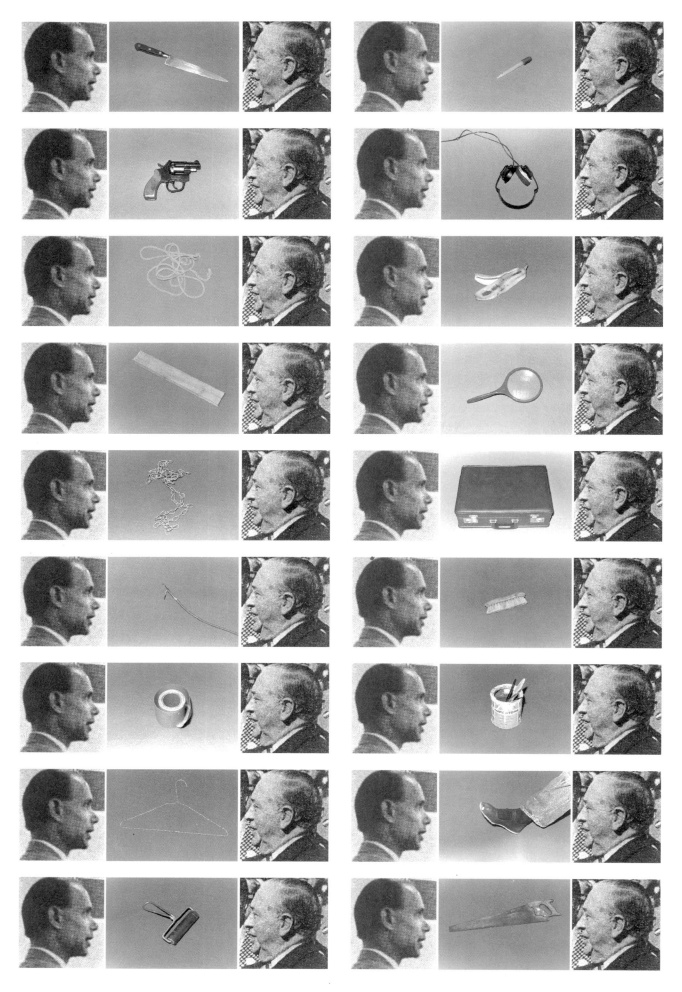

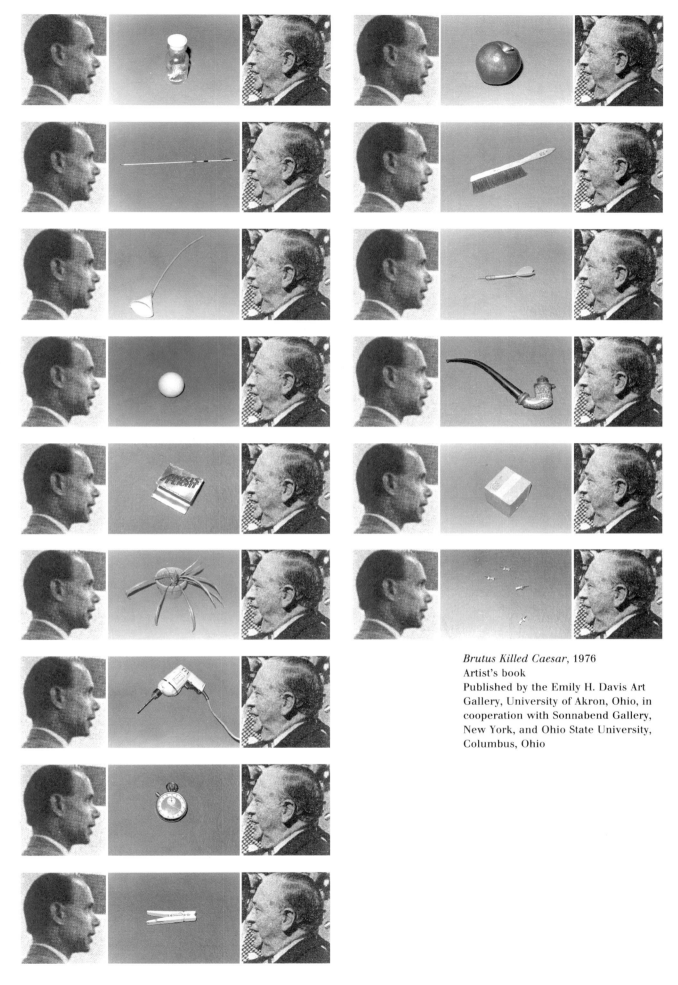

*Brutus Killed Caesar*, 1976
Artist's book
Published by the Emily H. Davis Art
Gallery, University of Akron, Ohio, in
cooperation with Sonnabend Gallery,
New York, and Ohio State University,
Columbus, Ohio

*Imagine This Woman...* (details), 1973
Seven color photographs; mounted on
board
6¾ x 6¼ in. each (17.1 x 15.9 cm)
Collection of the artist

*The text on each reads: "Imagine this
woman exactly as she is, but [\*] instead
of beautiful". [\*] homely*
>                    *unsightly*
>                    *blemished*
>                    *inelegant*
>                    *plain*
>                    *ordinary*
>                    *ugly*
>    *The image of the same woman is
repeated with a single word change
per text.*

With an astounding economy of images, Baldessari elicits an immense range of meanings from the phrase. After trying out the conventional forms that the sentence suggests, he arrives at more imaginative versions that loosen the meaning of the connecting link "killed" to the point of short-circuit, causing the verisimilitude of the proposition to break down. This question of collective acceptance of or rebellion against a given combination of image and text was one he had posited in an earlier work, *Imagine This Woman...*, 1973. A pin-up photograph of a woman is shown seven different times, each time accompanied by a sentence in which one word changes with each repetition: "Imagine this woman exactly as she is but homely rather than beautiful" turns with the next image into "but blemished rather than beautiful," and so forth.

One senses a similar ambiguous mobility in the booklet *A Sentence of Thirteen Parts (With Twelve Alternative Verbs) Ending in FABLE*, 1977. Part of the work is a horizontal foldout of thirteen pictures. On all but one of the images the artist has written nouns or adjectives in yellow, which are to be read syntactically from left to right. The center picture represents the verb, and is intersected by a vertical

Imagine this woman exactly as she is, but blemished instead of beautiful.

foldout of images with alternative verbs written on them. In his rejection of fixed definitions and his preference for constant change and fluidity, Baldessari, in *A Sentence of Thirteen Parts...* reflects the intellectual current of the 1970s, a structuralist attitude rooted in Existentialism. Instead of a single, "authoritarian" interpretation of linguistic signs, he favors the coexistence of pluralistic meanings.

In an inventive way, *A Sentence of Thirteen Parts...* demonstrates Saussure's theory that the linguistic sign is "arbitrary," for there is no natural connection between the signifier and the thing it signifies. The example linguists favor is the arbitrariness of color terms, "which vary greatly from one language to another, even though the colors themselves form a continuum and, being determined naturally by their wave frequency, are universal."[24] The cultural, psychological, and symbolic meanings of colors also differ vastly, as Baldessari demonstrated in his videotape *Six Colorful Stories: From the Emotional Spectrum (Women)*, 1977. In it a sequence of six women unfolds, each with only her head visible in the lower part of the screen, and each set against one of the six colors of the spectrum. Each woman tells a personal story, which is

emotionally "tuned" to the color of her choice— paralleling the way colloquial expressions such as "green with envy, red with anger, yellow with cowardice," etc., must have originated. The tape consists of six segments, respectively titled, "Caught Red Handed (Shelly)"; "Thinking Orange (Deirdre)"; "Catatonic Yellow (Dorit)"; "Green Horn (Ilene)"; "Feeling Blue (Diane)"; and "Apoplectic Violet (Christine)."

*A Sentence of Thirteen Parts (With Twelve Alternative Verbs) Ending in FABLE,* 1977
Artist's book, unfolded
Published by Anatol AV und Filmproduktion, Hamburg, West Germany, 1977

Detail of *A Sentence of Thirteen Parts
(With Twelve Alternative Verbs) Ending
in FABLE*

In an earlier work, *Floating: Color*, 1972, Baldessari had also used the color wheel to arrange colors in a fixed scheme instead of creating relationships between selected colors based on aesthetic reasons only. In the 30-minute film *Six Colorful Inside Jobs*, 1977, the six colors of the spectrum are paired with the days of the week, excluding Sunday. Additionally, it was a performance/installation: for two hours for seven days viewers could witness the activity of painting a room in one of the colors of the color wheel. The room had one door and was constructed without a ceiling, so that a camera above could film it entirely. The film, however, reduces the two-hour period that it took to paint the room each day to five minutes. The performance started out on a Monday with a white room. A house painter entered, painted the walls red, and left as soon as he had finished the job. The overlapping colors—such as orange over red on Tuesday, yellow over orange on Wednesday, and so on—combined with variations in the painting strokes to suggest a state of pixillation, which was

Videotape stills from *Six Colorful Stories: From the Emotional Spectrum (Women)*, 1977
Color videotape with sound
17 minutes

*Floating: Color*, 1972
Six Type-C prints; mounted on board
11 x 14 in. each (27.9 x 35.6 cm)
Collection of Mario Bertolini, Breno,
Italy

augmented by the house painter's speeded-up movements on film.

In *Six Colorful Inside Jobs* a second issue is dealt with, namely the fine line between work, or daily life, and art. The process of house painting is presented as painting, as, in Baldessari's words, "a three-dimensional painting that makes itself, art-as-work/work-as-art, etc." The approach to painting through house painting is firmly rooted in contemporary American art. Frank Stella described it in 1964: "The artist's tools or the traditional artist's brush and maybe even oil paint are all disappearing very quickly. We use mostly commercial paint, and we

generally tend towards larger brushes. In a way, Abstract Expressionism started all this. De Kooning used house painter's brushes and house painter's techniques."[25] This flip-flop between house painting and Painting with a capital *P* could go on endlessly, according to Baldessari: "I used to paint my father's rentals as a kid. There was a fine line between just painting a wall and Painting. Only by pointing out the differences, do I make a change from one to the other. There is something about Sisyphus in this too. It could be a kind of a painter's hell. But essentially it is about work with some small amount of pleasure attached."[26]

Film stills from *Six Colorful Inside
Jobs*, 1977
16mm color film (no sound)
35 minutes

The group of works that make up *Blasted Allegories*, 1978, consists of syntactic sequences of images and words colored according to a system in which visual order is derived from word order and vice versa, synthesizing principles from *Brutus Killed Caesar, A Sentence in Thirteen Parts...*, and *Six Colorful Stories*, the *Word Chain* pieces, and *Violent Space Series*. The title *Blasted Allegories* comes from a letter by Nathaniel Hawthorne to James T. Fields, who wrote in 1854, "Upon my honor, I am not quite sure that I entirely comprehend my own meaning in some of these blasted allegories; but I remember that I always had a meaning—or, at least, thought I had." Baldessari applies this kind of self-examination to himself, and his reliance on allegory connects him directly to Hawthorne. The link is sometimes explicit: his parable "The Great Artist," for example, was inspired by Hawthorne's story "The Great Stone Face," and one inspiration for *Blasted Allegories* was the critic Harry Levin's argument that Hawthorne's gathering of allegories in his American notebooks goes beyond "a handbook of symbols; it is a germinal process for the best of his tales and romances."[27] The same can be said of Baldessari's passion for collecting his own lexicon of images and texts (newspaper and magazine clippings, hundreds of thematically assorted stills from television and obscure movies, excerpts from scripts and articles, quotations from writers he has read over the years), as well as his hastily jotted down, ephemeral thoughts picked up here and there. The latter are the most precious to him, for they induce fresh associations, without which he would feel "amputated."

To create *Blasted Allegories* Baldessari began by assembling a literal "dictionary" of images photographed from commercial television. A series of color filters were used on the camera, which was set to take a photograph every ten minutes. Afterward, each image was inscribed with the first appropriate word Baldessari or his friends could think of, and was filed away in alphabetical order according to color: black-and-white, full color, or one of the six single colors produced by the filters: red, orange, yellow, green, blue, violet. Subsequently, the photographs were assembled in the "sentences" of each work. Despite its visually seductive aspects, *Blasted Allegories* is about the transformational process, the arrangement of a whole series in a permutating group. It is inspired by Claude Lévi-Strauss, who in his book *Structural Anthropology* stated that all myths can be reduced to the formula:

$$Fx(a):Fy(b) \simeq Fx(b):Fa-1(y).\text{"}[28]$$

Curiously enough, the anthropologist never gave elaborate examples or expanded further upon his rather cryptic theorem, and this made it attractive to Baldessari because to him it suggested magic.

For each piece in the series Baldessari invented a "game plan" to avoid a dependence on aesthetic values. He started out with one chain of images with superimposed texts, which, obeying a set of different rules, were subsequently transformed into another chain. In *Blasted Allegories (Colorful Sentence and Purple Patch): Starting with Red Father...*, 1978, for instance, a diagonal red arrow in the top left corner of a grid of photographs indicates the direction in which the work's sentences can be read: horizontally, from left to right, and vertically, from top to bottom. Each sequence of photographs starts with the color red, and continues according to the sequence of the spectrum. As a consequence, the long diagonal of color running from bottom left to top right becomes purple, "sticking out like a sore thumb," in Baldessari's words. The resulting sentences, such as "Father exchanging acrobats indeed harassed grocery," read like newspaper headlines. Another work from the series, *Blasted Allegories (Colorful Sentence): Through (≠ True) Blue to AGOG...*, 1978, has a sequence of blue photographs reading "Agog buddies challenge dream explanation." The pivotal photograph is in full color; a picture of a woman, it is titled "through." Again the emphasis in the work is on process. Normally an artist completing an artwork erases the steps that have been traversed along the way, but the "Blasted Allegories" are nothing more than polished-up notebook sketches, revealing how the artist's mind works. Life and vitality are restored to the work because the viewer is forced to become involved in an unusual associative way of thinking, in this case, something like "Through is not the same as true, triggering the association with blue—depressed (having the blues) loyal (true blue) or slightly risqué (blue movies)—," which in its turn guides the selection of photographs and texts from the blue file, so that blue can be seen as both a state of mind and a color. Baldessari accomplishes a wonderful collision of words and images to form the *Blasted Allegories*, which, exploded into impossibly rich confusions, are also "blasted" in the sense of cursed, often frustrating attempts to untangle them. They almost make one long for rocks without sermons read into them. After all, even Freud is said to have admitted that "sometimes a cigar is just a cigar."

*Blasted Allegories (Colorful Sentence and Purple Patch): Starting with Red Father...*, 1978
Thirty-six Type-C prints on board with colored pencil and tape
30⅝ x 36⅝ in. (77.8 x 93 cm)
The Morton G. Neumann Family Collection, Chicago

*Word Chain: Sunglasses (Ilene's Story),*
1975
Sixty-two 35mm black-and-white
contact prints, one color contact print
on grid paper, and typewritten sheet
Grid paper: 33 x 27 in. (83.8 x 68.6
cm); text: 11 x 8½ in. (27.9 x 21.6 cm)
Collection of Massimo Valsecchi,
Milan

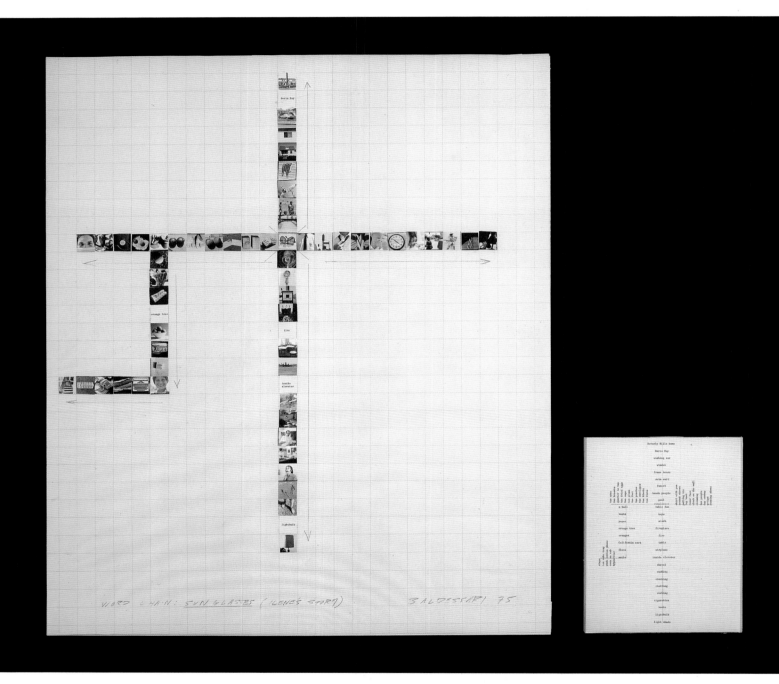

*Violent Space Series: Story Outline (A Story That Ends Up Mostly in Bed),* 1976
Eight black-and-white contact prints with ink; mounted on board
8¼ x 5½ in. (21 x 14 cm)
Courtesy of Sonnabend Gallery, New York

*The* Word Chain *pieces anticipate the* Blasted Allegories *series. The ideas were:*
1. *Associative thought—If I say "peanut butter" one might think "jelly." And from "jelly" might proceed to "doughnut" and so on.*
2. *Words and images as surrogates for each other and vice versa.*

*At the start of each piece there was a pre-determined structure determined by the artist. In* Ilene's Story *it is:*

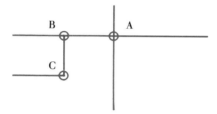

*At each intersection (or perpendicular juncture) I have placed a 35mm contact print (marked a, b, c). At point A there is a photograph of sunglasses, at B a photograph of two blocks and at C a photograph of a smile.*

*An assistant (Ilene) was then asked to construct a story starting with these images using words. So as she began at A moving left, with sunglasses she associated shirt and pen. The length of the story was determined by the length of the lines.*

*Lastly, Ilene was asked to photograph visual equivalents of each work. It is her story; I just provided the outline.*

*It is a story with no beginning and no end. As in life, it is how one reads the information.*

*Two parallel stories, each formed by a different string of events, but each story having the same terminus—bed. Except that* bed *is paired with different images. What is meant by* bed *in one story is not what is meant by* bed *in the second story.*

*The relationships to* Blasted Allegories *are:*
1. *Image and caption are in tandem (one is a surrogate for the other)*
2. *By putting them in a string, a narrative is formed*
3. *What action follows or precedes another action is what makes the story, (i.e., "A gun goes off, a person falls dead " is a different story than "A person falls dead, a gun goes off.")*

*Blasted Allegories (Colorful Sentence):*
$\dfrac{Yellow}{Weigh}$..., 1978
Five Type-C prints and one Polaroid
print on board with colored pencil,
tape, and stickers
27¾ x 40 in. (70.5 x 101.6 cm)
Continental Insurance Companies,
courtesy of Douglas Drake
Gallery, New York

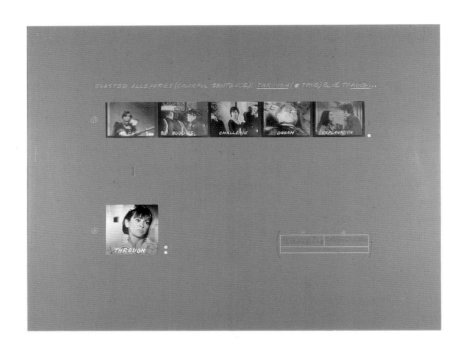

*Blasted Allegories (Colorful Sentence):*
*Through (≠ True) Blue to AGOG...,*
1978
Color photographs on board with
colored pencil
30¾ x 40 in. (78.1 x 101.6 cm)
Courtesy of Sonnabend Gallery, New
York, and Monika Sprüth Galerie,
Cologne, West Germany

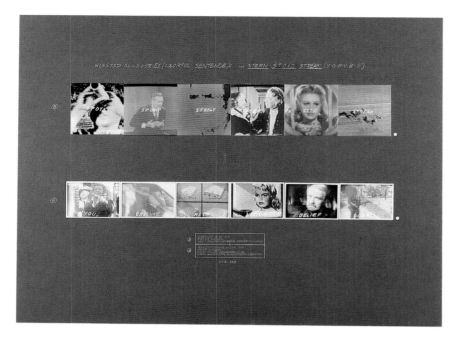

*Blasted Allegories (Colorful Sentence):*
*Stern Stoic Streak (Y.O.R.V.B.G.).*, 1978
Six Type-C prints and six black-and-
white photographs on board with
colored pencil
30½ x 40 in. (77.5 x 101.6 cm)
Lowe Art Museum, University of
Miami, Coral Gables, Florida; Museum
Purchase through a grant from the
National Endowment for the Arts and
Matching Funds

*Blasted Allegories (Colorful Equation):*
*Intertwined with Green Offshoot*
*Intersecting at Pressure Point*, 1978
Eleven color photographs on board
with colored pencil and stickers
30¾ x 40 in. (78.1 x 101.6 cm)
Commodities Corporation,
Princeton, New Jersey

113

*Baudelaire Meets Poe*, 1980
Two black-and-white photographs and
one Type-C print; mounted on board
114 × 114 in. overall (289.6 x 289.6 cm)
Courtesy of Sonnabend Gallery,
New York

From cursed allegories Baldessari moved to the figure of the cursed poet, or *poète maudit*, in *Baudelaire Meets Poe*, 1980, visualizing and symbolizing the moment that Baudelaire discovered some of Edgar Allan Poe's tales in a French translation, in 1846 or 1847. The power of the work of both poets hinges on the antagonism between repulsion and seduction, (*spleen et idéal* in Baudelaire's terms), an opposition that became Baldessari's focus. For both Baudelaire and Poe, the imagination, in Baudelairian terminology, is "the most *scientific* of faculties, because it alone understands the *universal analogy*, or what mystical religion calls *the correspondence*."[29] Correspondences, those hidden relationships between intoxicating perfumes, sounds, and colors, are created by Baldessari between the three photographic images of a snake, a second snake wrapped around a ring, and a leaping frog, while at the same time he contains and isolates these elements each in their own geometric frame on a wall. Thus he implies the state of being alone, a precondition of creativity for both romantic poets. "First the snake," he wrote in 1981, a year after completing his piece, "groveling, sneaking along the ground, lowly, slow moving, inertia, held down by gravity. A flat point of view, like Flatland. Maybe how one feels having a writer's block?"[30] Intuitively, Baldessari symbolizes the poet's desperation over a loss of inspiration, making it evident by the placement of the first snake image in the bottom left corner of the work and of the second image—of a baby snake coiled around a wedding ring on a woman's finger—as "a kind of rebirth," firmly in the center. Symbolic meaning of placement had been essential to Baudelaire in his use of the poetic phrase, for, as he stated in his preface to *Les Fleurs du Mal*, it "can imitate (and in this, it is like the art of music and the science of mathematics) a horizontal line, an ascending or descending vertical line; it can rise straight up to heaven without losing its breath, or go perpendicularly to hell with the velocity of any weight."[31] Baldessari continued his notes on the first snake image with, "Not much happening until [Baudelaire] encounters Poe. But also redolent of indolent voluptuousness, of poetry chained to the earth. Suggestive of the darker regions of the mind, an atmosphere that is infernal. A sign of the demands of the unconscious. I recall that

Baudelaire spoke of his mistress as a '...dancing serpent.'" The artist refers here to Jeanne Duval, for Baudelaire *"la muse malade"* (the sick muse) or *"la Vénus noire"* (the black Venus), the voluptuous goddess dragging her lovers into the abyss.

The image of the baby snake, wrapping itself upward around a jewel, may allude to two couplets of Baudelaire's poem "Le Serpent qui danse" (The Dancing Serpent), devoted to Duval:

> *Tes yeux, où rien ne se révèle*
> *De doux ni d'amer,*
> *Sont deux bijoux froids où se mêle*
> *L'or avec le fer.*
>
> (Your two eyes that neither sweetness
> Nor bitterness hold
> Are two chilly gems mingled of
> Iron and gold.)[32]

and:

> *A te voir marcher en cadence,*
> *Belle d'abandon*
> *On dirait un serpent qui danse*
> *Au bout d'un bâton.*
>
> (When you walk in rhythm, lovely
> With abandonment
> You seem to be swayed by a wand
> A dancing serpent.)

The sensuous, complex central image in *Baudelaire Meets Poe* can be compared to a Baudelairian poetic phrase, extracting beauty from evil. Concerning the third image, Baldessari wrote, "The frog stands for an explosion made at the moment of impact of the two minds meeting. In color, larger than the other two images, and bursting out of, travelling out of the plane of the wall. A metamorphosis as well, changing from snake to frog. Repelling but somehow beautiful, standing for magic. Transubstantiation. The idea reified, made flesh but in a sinister nonsocial fashion."

Detail of *Baudelaire Meets Poe*, 1980

115

*Fugitive Essays (With Caterpillar)*, 1980
Two black-and-white photographs and
one color photograph with pencil;
mounted on board
Black-and-white photographs: 21 x 60½
in. (53.3 x 153.7 cm) 7¾ x 7¾ in. (19.7 x
19.7 cm) 114 x 322 in. overall (289.6 x
817.9 cm); color photograph: 25 x 46 in.
(63.5 x 116.8 cm)
Private collection, courtesy of
Sonnabend Gallery, New York

The essence of *Baudelaire Meets Poe* is the artist's identification with the persistence of both poets, despite rejection and periods of severe depression, in their search for a glimpse of the sublime, for a pure poetic sentiment in the ugly and the evil. In Poe's words, "It is the desire of the moth for the star. It is no more an appreciation of Beauty before us but a wild effort to reach the Beauty above. Inspired by an ecstatic prescience of the glories beyond the grave, we struggle, by multiform combinations among the things and thoughts of Time, to attain a portion of that loveliness whose very elements, perhaps, appertain to eternity alone."[33] Baldessari, however, is interested solely in what drives the artist, and avoids explicit references. He was well aware that the images he selected, even when structurally intensified by their arrangement in geometric forms on the wall, could not in the end become equated with the more visionary phantasms of either poet. They remain instead in the banal realm of the horror movie (like the several films made of Poe tales starring Vincent Price). Precisely through the suggestion of a poetic concept rather than a specific poem, Baldessari achieves a radiating, concealed power of his own, despite the fact that the images of the snakes and the frog are raw material, only slightly transformed and stylized.

Similar to his use of Langer's phrase "Brutus killed Caesar," Baldessari employs Baudelaire's interest in Poe primarily as a device, a means to structure his composition spatially in separate parts. In this respect the artist's approach seems more akin to what William Carlos Williams, reflecting on his own development, had defined as his aesthetic position, than to any *poète maudit*: "I was tremendously involved in an appreciation of Cézanne. He was a designer. He put it down on the canvas so that there would be a meaning without saying anything at all. Just the relation of the parts to themselves. In considering a poem, I don't care whether it's finished or not; if it's put down with a good relation to the parts, it becomes a poem. And the meaning of the poem can be grasped by attention to the design."[34]

The *Fugitive Essays*, 1980, elaborate further on the themes of *Baudelaire Meets Poe*: beauty arising from evil, and the loneliness of the modern poet/artist seen as a permanent human condition. The French saying *laid comme une chenille*—"ugly as a caterpillar" (ugly as sin)—could be their motto. These works are simultaneously visual poems on escape and a discourse on Nietzsche's division of

human nature into a measured Apollonian and an unbound Dionysian duality, which Baldessari compares to the contrasting literary currents of the Fugitives (a group of Southern poets and critics of the 1920s) and the Imagists. Baldessari wrote in 1980 that the essays are on the one hand "a tribute to the Fugitive Poets, 'Deliberate Exiles' and 'Weary Nomads,' as regionalists, traditionalists, and classicists and their quarrel with emotion in art," and on the other, "to the Imagists, representing the present alive revolutionary impulse, the unexpressed possibilities." In the installation *Fugitive Essays (With Caterpillar)*, the two opposing directions of the Apollonian and the Dionysian coexist, separated by a neutral center zone. Baldessari started out with a photography-salon image of a female torso. Set to the left on the wall, at eye level, it represents a naturalistic, nonartistic existence in which artistic impulses do not rise above a critical, empirical level. Next he positioned a classical triangle in full color, its subject matter, a woman's red purse, composed in the preordained format of a triangle, in the center of the wall, toward the floor. This geometric form embodies for Baldessari the eternal phenomenon of Apollonianism, associated with "spaciousness, reason, peacefulness, control, and passivity." To offset the calm symmetry, he set a black-and-white movie still of a caterpillar on the upper right of the wall, to symbolize "foreboding, anxiety, the chaotic, and irrationality." The close cropping of the image evokes a feeling of claustrophobia, enhancing the sense of uneasiness. The irregular shape of the caterpillar determines the shape of the frame, reinforcing the appearance of an unpleasant phenomenon pushing down from the top corner of the room in a diagonal to the opposite, bottom corner.

On the one hand the caterpillar—a sort of primordial being, the incarnation of repulsive unattractiveness—annihilates the Apollonian delight in beautiful forms. On the other, in the triangle, beauty triumphs over the Dionysian suffering inherent in life. The conjunction of the two together both prevents the Apollonian from becoming too logical and schematic and saves the Dionysian from the danger of self-destructive madness. Nietzsche asked, "How can the ugly and unharmonious, the substance of tragic myth, excite aesthetic pleasure?" "Musical dissonance" was his answer, opening the possibility of breaking an Apollonian unity of linguistic and visual forms in favor of a harmony of

118

*Pier 18* (detail), 1971
Variable number black-and-white
photographs
8 x 10 in. each (20.3 x 25.4 cm)
Collection of the artist

opposites. The standard caterpillar story is that this
repulsive creature, in a creative explosion of energy,
turns into a radiantly beautiful butterfly, but for
Baldessari it is the beast itself that is beautiful.

The idea of a gestalt determining the form of the
frame is again explored in the book *Close-Cropped
Tales*, 1981. Starting out with "A Three-Sided Tale"
and ending with "An Eight-Sided Tale," Baldessari
increases the number of angles of perception as well
as the number of sides with each subsequent image
in the book. The shape of the first, three-sided image,
a detail of a movie still, is determined by the shape of
the subject of its focus, a rooster. The triangularly cut
image is positioned in the same relation to the
horizon as in the original movie still. As an
unintended side effect, the triangular form picks up
and emphasizes objects or incidents in the
background of the still that in full frame would not
have attracted attention—a man's head sticking out
above the blankets, for instance. These elements take
on a new meaning in relation to the rooster. The
effect recalls pieces Baldessari did in 1971, starting
with a photographic piece for "Pier 18," a group
show exhibited at the Museum of Modern Art in New
York. Meeting the photographer Harry Shunk on the
deserted pier, Baldessari asked Shunk to photograph
a ball he was bouncing, and to try to keep the ball in
the middle of each frame. Forced to follow the ball,
the photographer was prevented from creating a
perfect composition, so that objects in the
background captured by chance produced
unpredictable and surprising effects.

*Close-Cropped Tales* (details), 1981
Artist's book
Published by CEPA Gallery and
Albright-Knox Art Gallery, Buffalo,
New York, 1981

120

The associations of the first image of "A Three-Sided Tale" range from the rooster as sexual symbol to the time of day, apparently early in the morning. The next image in the book shows a contrasting but equally arresting image of a fedora on a table. This picture too is shaped around its subject, resulting in a much flatter triangle, which includes a gesturing hand holding a cigarette caught at the top of the image. One might ask whether the hat is lying on the table by chance, or whether it is the object of some investigation, as in one of Baldessari's earliest videotapes, *Folding Hat*, 1970. The tape shows the artist folding a hat, a creative, hypnotic activity, since the hat is capable of innumerable changes and permutations while staying constant in its shape. The hat reminded Baldessari of a statement by the French painter Amédée Ozenfant: "What would our art be like if the works we produce with so much difficulty were to have the duration of a hat, say?"[55] The image of a hat folded in a certain way can signal a specific message as well. And combined with the image of a male hand holding a cigarette in a characteristic manner, the hat may bring to mind a case history described by Sigmund Freud in his *Interpretation of Dreams*. In this story of a young woman who suffered from agoraphobia, a hat folded in a peculiar shape, "its middle piece...bent upwards and its side pieces hung downwards," plays a significant role. To Freud there was "no doubt that the hat was a male genital organ," though other cases had shown him that a hat can also stand for female genitals.

Videotape stills from *Folding Hat: Version 1*, 1970
Black-and-white videotape with sound
30 minutes

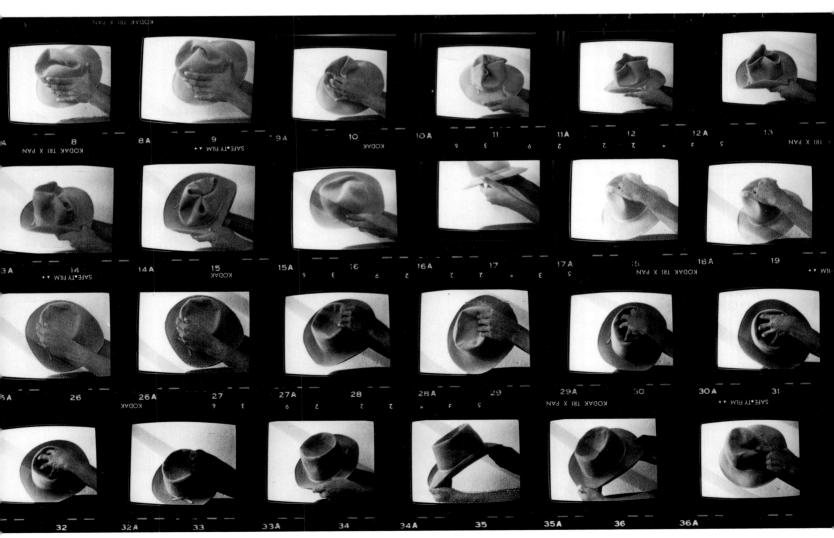

Taking these two interpretations of "A Three-Sided Tale" as an example, it becomes clear that Baldessari selects his images precisely because of their ambivalent potential as dream symbols, undermining fixed notions and always leaving an opening for fresh "guesses." None of the *Close-Cropped Tales* allows any one conclusion. For similar reasons, in *Shape Derived from Subject (Snake): Used as a Framing Device to Produce New Photographs*, 1981, Baldessari again complicates a single reading, this time by rejecting the conventional procedure of framing an image in a square or rectangle: "Imagine the camera viewfinder scissor-like, excising what the mind's eye rejects and retaining what it selects." Baldessari questions the conventional rectangular frame in photography just as Donald Judd had objected to the acceptance of neutral limits in traditional painting, instead of realizing that the canvas is a definite form. Judd, in his article "Specific Objects," written in 1966, had pointed out that "the main thing wrong with painting is that it is a rectangular plane placed flat against the wall. A rectangle is a shape itself, it is obviously the whole shape, it determines and limits whatever is on or inside of it."[56] Baldessari, made aware of the edges of paintings by Barnett Newman, Judd, and Frank Stella, among others, adds his own conceptual twist to the prevailing format of the photograph. While Stella, for instance, in his shaped canvases, emphasizes the perimeter of the plane through the pattern of lines inside it, Baldessari, in *Shape Derived from Subject (Snake)...*, lets the content of the movie still—a man's hand holding a boa constrictor—determine the work's contours. It is as if an unusual camera viewfinder, overtly phallic in its field of vision, had determined the frame for new photographic subjects, upsetting a neutral reading of their peripheries. According to Baldessari, "It is a Procrustean viewfinder and its shape may have as much content/meaning as any it might capture in its net."

The questioning of conventions and limitations in art, such as the window-frame effect in painting or photography, is fundamental to John Baldessari's approach. He is more attracted by contradictions in tradition than by innovative formalism. In his vision, flashes of the mind oppose linear certainties, constructing an alternative that fuses metaphor with the antimetaphorical aesthetic of Minimalism into "What you see is what you don't get." How Baldessari formulates his questions reflects the mood of his time; it not only shows his angle of perception and his feelings and ideas about his subject, but also constitutes his style. And from art he has moved on to life. Questioning how to capture the world impromptu, through hints and implications, through minute details spotted "with the corner of the eyes," as Thoreau so poetically put it, is undoubtedly a questioning directed toward knowledge of the self. And there is always room for the next deviation, distortion, or perversion, as in *Shape Derived from Subject (Snake)...*, in which Baldessari deliberately arrived at "a shape so difficult that it can exclude more picture possibilities than it allows. One that is like a dominant gene imprinting future generations. The problem of the edge affecting what is inside, but with a vengeance.

"It is a Cinderella shoe not looking for Cinderella. Too perfect a solution, but a device to find something possibly more interesting. What if her shoe fit someone else?"

Opposite and following pages: *Shape Derived from Subject (Snake): Used as a Framing Device to Produce New Photographs*, 1981
Nine black-and-white photographs; mounted on board
56 x 44 in. each (142.2 x 111.8 cm)
Installation dimensions variable
Courtesy of Sonnabend Gallery, New York

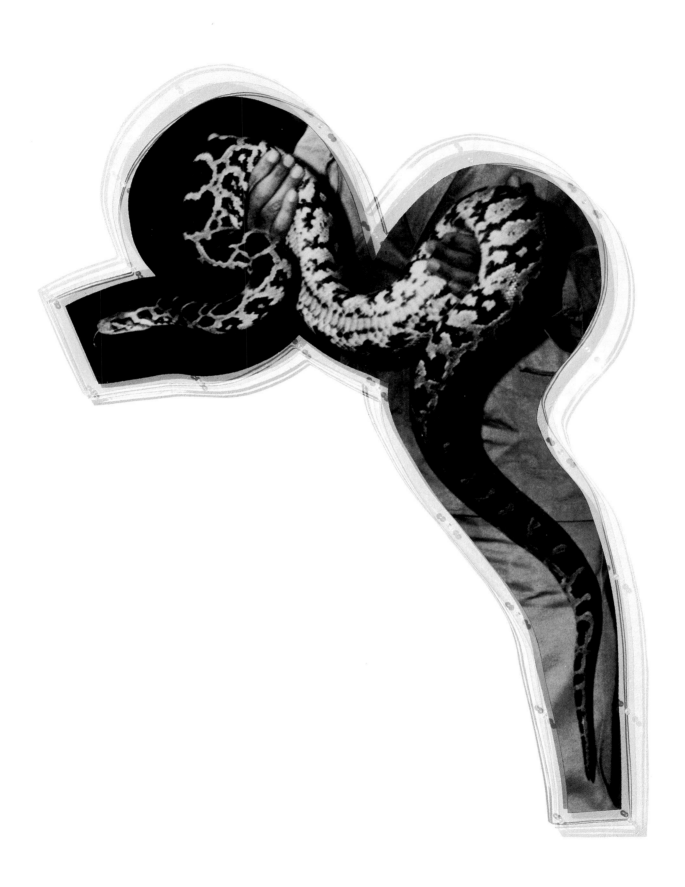

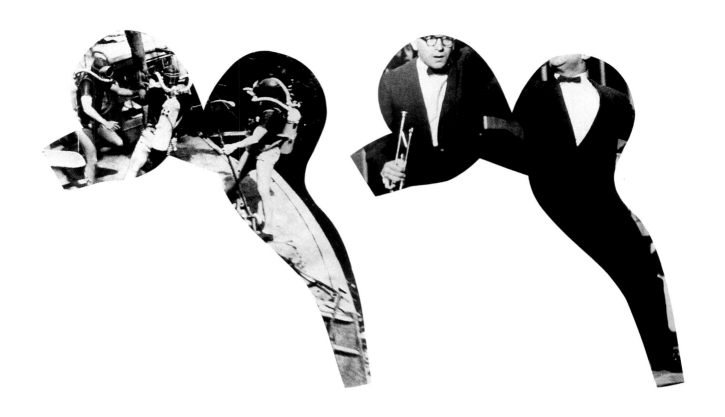

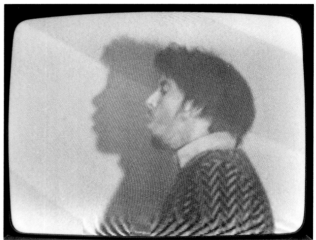

Videotape stills from the action *How Various People Spit Out Beans* in *How We Do Art Now*, 1973
Black-and-white videotape with sound
30 minutes overall

NOTES

1. Moira Roth, "A Conversation with John Baldessari," held in Santa Monica, California, on January 6, 1973, unpublished manuscript, p. 1.
2. Marlise Simons, "García Márquez on Love, Plagues, and Politics," *The New York Times Book Review*, February 21, 1988, p. 23.
3. Roth, p. 2.
4. In *A New Sense of Order: The Art Teacher Story*, 1972–73, Baldessari produced a work based on a story of how a friend, who taught painting, had all his students stand in front of their easels balancing on one foot only, in the conviction that by keeping them off balance a new sense of order would emerge in their paintings.
5. Roth, p. 8.
6. John Cage, *Silence: Lectures and Writings by John Cage*, Middletown, Conn.: Wesleyan University Press, 1973, p. 85.
7. Ibid., p. ix.
8. Bernard Malamud, "Reflections of a Writer: Long Work, Short Life," *The New York Times Book Review*, March 20, 1988, p. 18.
9. Published in *John Baldessari, Frances Barth, Richard Jackson, Barbara Munger, Gary Stephan*, Houston, Texas: Contemporary Arts Museum, 1972, pp. 10–11. Exhibition catalogue.
10. Roth, p. 15.
11. Roth, pp. 15–16.
12. Baldessari's second question refers to *Pastry Case with Sundaes, Bananas, Baked Potatoes (in process of being consumed)*, 1965, for which Claes Oldenburg cast a plaster banana and bit off pieces while it was still wet. "The banana got smaller and smaller, and it tasted terrible," Oldenburg recalls, "but I wanted to re-create the bite." *Two Questions* and *On Artists' Shoes* were published in *Duerle 11/7/73*, the exhibition catalogue for a show held at Museum Dhondt-Dhaenens, Deurle, Belgium, organized by Galerie MTL, Brussels, in 1973.
13. Nat Hentoff, *The Jazz Life*, New York: Dial Press, 1961. Reprinted, New York: Da Capo Press, 1978, p. 203.
14. Quoted in *John Baldessari*, Eindhoven: Van Abbemuseum, and Essen: Museum Folkwang, 1981, p. 19. Exhibition catalogue.
15. James Agee, *Agee on Film*, New York: McDowell, Obolensky, Inc., 1958, p. 326.
16. Repetition of the same action by different people, or comparison of the same objects for a long time, makes variations appear in things that had seemed to be exactly alike. Baldessari uses this effect in, for example, his videotape *How We Do Art Now*, 1973, in the five-minute action *How Various People Spit Out Beans*, which examines physical convulsions as body motion; and in *The Way We Do Art Now and Other Sacred Tales*, 1973, in the two-minute-ten-second action *Examining Three 8d Nails*, in which one so-called identical nail differs in minute detail from the next.
17. Quoted in Gene Youngblood, *Expanded Cinema*, New York: E. P. Dutton & Co., Inc., 1970, p. 80.
18. Ibid., p. 111.
19. Susanne K. Langer, *Philosophy in a New Key: A Study in the Symbolism of Reason, Rite, and Art*, Cambridge: Harvard University Press, 1942. Reprinted, 1979, pp. 67–68.
20. Ibid., p. 68.
21. Ibid., p. 74.
22. The ambiguity Baldessari sets up of who killed whom, symbolized by the murder weapon pointed first in one direction, then in another, can be seen as a questioning of the ethical nature of this political murder. A case can be made for Caesar's progressiveness, as a disruptor of the hierarchical system, making Brutus finally the conservative force, restoring order. To choose neither one nor the other reflects Baldessari's own attitude toward politics: "I always have had this cynical attitude about government, that change doesn't necessarily bring betterment but just more of the same." *Brutus Killed Caesar* was published by the Emily H. Davis Art Gallery at the University of Akron, in cooperation with Sonnabend Gallery, New York, and Ohio State University, Columbus.
23. Chekhov used firearms in many of his plays, including *The Seagull* (1896), *Uncle Vanya* (1899), *The Three Sisters* (1901), and *The Cherry Orchard* (1904). Stanislavski played the role of Trigorin in the Moscow Art Theater's production of *The Seagull* in 1898, but he is not a very reliable source of information regarding Chekhov. As Chekhov never wrote the remark down, many variations of it exist. Baldessari is especially interested in those stories or anecdotes that have become common knowledge, are appreciated because of their point, but in time have lost their original source.
24. John Sturrock, *Structuralism and Since From Levi-Strauss to Derrida*, New York: Oxford University Press, 1979, p. 9.
25. Quoted in Bruce Glaser, "Questions to Stella and Judd," in Gregory Battcock, ed., *Minimalism: A Critical Anthology*, New York: E. P. Dutton, Inc., 1968, p. 156.
26. In the idea of making something by saying it is, Baldessari was inspired by Donald Judd's statement, "'Non-art,' 'anti-art,' 'non-art art' and 'anti-art art' are useless. If someone says his work is art, it's art." The remark appears in a statement of Judd's in the catalogue for "Primary Structures: Younger American and British Sculptors," an exhibition at the Jewish Museum, New York, in 1966; Baldessari found it in an article, which used it for a title, by Thomas Meehan, *Horizon* XIII no. 4, Autumn 1971.
27. Harry Levin, *The Power of Blackness: Hawthorne, Poe, Melville*, New York: Alfred A. Knopf, 1970, p. 41.
28. Quoted in Claude Lévi-Strauss, *Structural Anthropology* (translated by Claire Jacobson and Brooke Grundfest Schoepf), New York: Basic Books, 1963, p. 228.
29. Quoted in and translated by Martin Turnell, in Martin Turnell, *Baudelaire: A Study of His Poetry*, New York: New Directions, 1972, p. 27.
30. Quoted in *John Baldessari*, p. 54.
31. From "Three Drafts of a Preface," translated by Jackson Mathews in Charles Baudelaire, *Flowers of Evil: A Selection*, (edited and translated by Marthiel and Jackson Mathews), New York: New Directions, 1958, p. xiii.
32. From "*The Dancing Serpent*" (translated by Barbara Gibbs), in *Flowers of Evil: A Selection*, p. 31.
33. Edgar Allan Poe, *The Complete Tales and Poems*, with an introduction by Harvey Allen, 1938. Reprinted, New York: Modern Library, 1965, p. 894.
34. Quoted in Linda Welshimer Wagner, *Interviews with William Carlos Williams: "Speaking Straight Ahead,"* New York: New Directions, 1976, p. 53.
35. Amédée Ozenfant, *Foundations of Modern Art*, 1931. Reprinted, New York: Dover Publications, Inc., 1952, p. 210.
36. Donald Judd, "Specific Objects," *Arts Yearbook 8*, New York: *Arts* magazine, 1965.

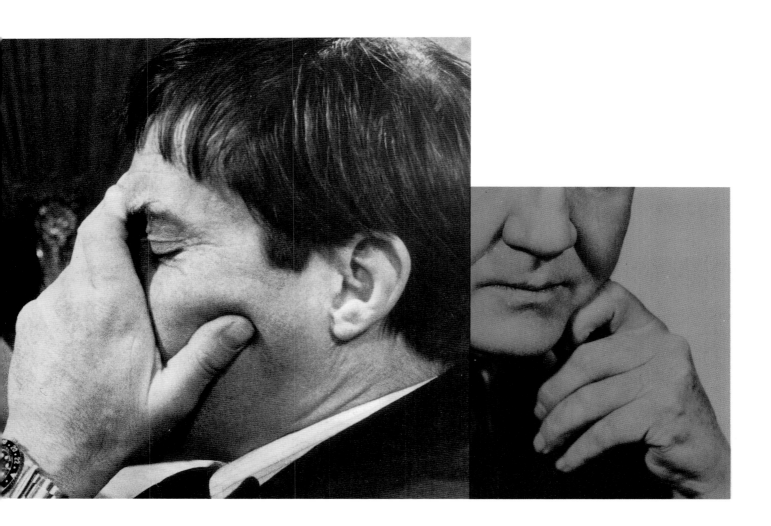

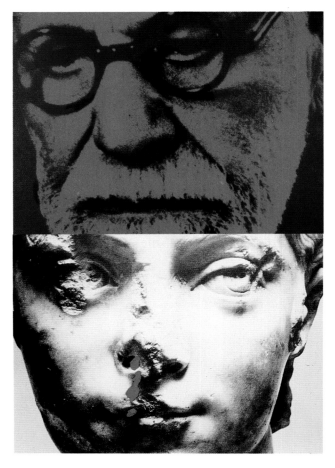

*Emma and Freud*, 1984
Two black-and-white photographs,
acrylic on acetate
24 x 16 in. overall (61 x 40.6 cm)
Courtesy of Galerie Peter Pakesch,
Vienna

*Dreams which are apparently
guileless turn out to be the reverse
of innocent if one takes the trouble
to interpret them; if I may be
permitted the expression, they all
show "the mark of the beast."*

—Sigmund Freud
*The Interpretation of Dreams*

*The style of the twentieth century
. . . expresses but does not
explain. . . . It is a never-ending
revelation of inner life, manifesting
it in moments when the subject of
the story is the link between reality
and imagination.*

—Cesare Pavese
*Stories*

# THE ART OF MISLEADING
# INTERPRETATION

Baldessari's composite photoworks of the 1980s, built up of juxtaposed fragments of movie stills, spontaneously trigger free associations that play unpredictably into our unconscious. In spite of their predetermining titles, and the direction given by the artist's selection, cropping, framing, and rearranging of the material, the movie-still fragments touch a different "personal complex" in each of us. They provide aesthetic pleasure and at the same time release repressed emotions about long-forgotten incidents. By stirring up latent dream thoughts, the composite photoworks inescapably involve us.

Baldessari directs the disparate meanings that emanate from the movie stills into a formal and contextual framework, as fragile and unstable as a tottering stack of building blocks about to fall at any moment into another configuration. Yet these conjunctions of fragments would function as a language, moving from separate components to a whole phrase, if the artist's interventions did not prevent us from completing the sentence. The approach is prefigured in an early language piece, from 1973, the videotape *The Way We Do Art Now and Other Sacred Tales*. In the 48-second segment *A Sentence with Hidden Meaning*, a phrase is presented as a series of close-ups, never as a whole, so that its meaning can only be inferred.

In creating his composite photoworks, Baldessari has gradually shifted from devising imagist games of the mind, in the 1970s, through an iconographical analysis of social codes and mores, in the early 1980s, to an intuitive symbolism using imagery based in the collective unconscious, in the mid and late 1980s:

I was getting more concerned with content over form in art. I thought it would be interesting to zero in on the emotional meaning in the work. I decided to explore it through art history, in still lifes [the *Vanitas Series*, 1981], where a glass of wine or a clock weren't just something to paint; they

meant something. I started with a series called *Virtues and Vices (For Giotto)* [1980]. I liked the idea that one could describe and dissect virtues and vices so exactly back then, whereas now things get so muddy. Could you imagine Dürer doing a study called "Anxiety" or "Repression"? I am beginning to think about my inner feelings, my interior life. I realized that life has something more than a cerebral side. ... There's an emotional side that I'd always kept under wraps. I now have to be laboratory *and* subject.[1]

In July 1984, Baldessari, who by then had entered psychotherapy, stated in an interview, "I've never talked much about my private life. It's that duality again. I can make sense of my art much better than my life. I never wanted to talk about my feelings, but now I see that as a weakness."[2]

These new insights gradually affected the work, first as part of a general interest in human relationships, later in a more sophisticated manner, as Baldessari explored the possibility of both exposing and hiding himself by reflecting on the imperfect human condition of the ego, caught between the superego and the id. Using the spatial terms "above" and "below," the artist managed to layer this Freudian triad with other trinities: the Christian model, lingering on from his parents; the musical triad that he had applied in *Songs: 1 Sky/ Sea/Sand 2 Sky/Iceplant/Grass*, 1973; and the three zones of a Nietzchean system he had used in the *Fugitive Essays*, 1980, consisting of the Apollonian, the Dionysian, and a neutral center zone between the two.

In the composite photoworks images of waitresses, horses, and nurses become representations of the Three Fates, the Three Graces, the Three Furies, or the three stages of life. With their faces blotted out by blue, red, or yellow disks in primary colors, they turn from ordinary figures into symbols. In Baldessari's vocabulary red signals danger, yellow madness, and

blue the platonic ideal of perfection. Often three figures or objects of the same generic type function as footnotes to the main storyline. A photograph of three women and a pair of scales, flanked by a baby (birth), a skeleton (death), and another of a woman holding a strand of a girl's hair (maturity or one of the fates weaving the thread of life), are placed at the margins of an image of a football squad in *Team*, 1987. Three horses competing in a chariot race in *Yellow (With Onlookers)*, and three waitresses sitting apparently in midair, in *Yellow (With Kiss)*, both from 1986, function in the same way. The three lamps contained neatly within a rectangle in *Stalk (With Tire)*, 1986, offset the darkness and chaos of the oceanic id flow in the triangle above the rectangles. In *Earthquake* the shaky balance of building blocks is complemented by three diagonally lined-up billiard balls, a substitution for the Fates. At the mercy of chance, and the forces of nature, the idea of controlling ones's destiny crumbles fast. The three women in *Gift*, 1987, are looking at what may turn out to be Pandora's box; and the trio of gentlemen (graces/Musketeers or thieves?) positioned amid pieces of luggage and mysterious, whited-out canvases in *Bloody Sundae*, 1987—the colored disks over their faces representing their different destinies—reinforce the impression of sex, money, and intrigue in the bedroom scene below.

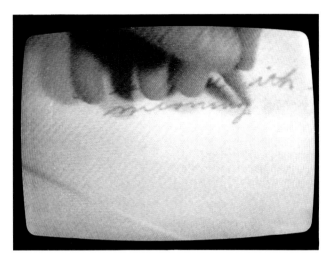

Videotape stills from the segment *A Sentence with Hidden Meaning*, in *The Way We Do Art Now and Other Sacred Tales*, 1973
Black-and-white videotape with sound
30 minutes overall

132

*Team*, 1987
Color and black-and-white
photographs with vinyl paint and
metallic paper; mounted on board
69½ x 88½ in. overall (176.5 x 223.8 cm)
Collection of Mr. and Mrs. William
Wilson III

*Vanitas Series: Warm (Short Depth of Field) Bubbles Descending, Wine Glass/ Key, Watch, Skull,* 1981
One black-and-white photograph and one color photograph; mounted on board
30 x 30 in. each (76.2 x 76.2 cm)
Courtesy of Sonnabend Gallery, New York

*The color segment is meant to be a point of departure. It has many traditional signals of a seventeenth-century Vanitas painting; the color, clutter, and objects signifying transcience, morality, and the five senses. Occasionally a new item displaces a traditional one—a flashlight for a candle, for example.*

*The black-and-white segment is a distillation and emptying—an attempt to construct a modern, relevant Vanitas.*

Installation detail of *Virtues and Vices
(For Giotto)*, 1980
Fourteen black-and-white
photographs; mounted on board
30 x 30 in. each (76.2 x 76.2 cm)
Van Abbemuseum, Eindhoven,
the Netherlands

HOPE

Detail of *Hope* from *Virtues and Vices
(For Giotto)*

*Songs: 1 Sky/Sea/Sand*
        *2 Sky/Iceplant/Grass* 1973,
(installation view)
Variable number color photographs,
chalk, pencil, and one typewritten
sheet
Photographs: 3½ x 5 in. each (8.9 x
12.7 cm); text: 11 x 8½ in. (27.9 x
21.6 cm)
Installation dimensions variable
Collection of the artist

The Songs

*Original plan*: To use certain geographical areas as visual surrogates for musical staffs. For example, one of the areas chosen was a frontal view of the ocean at the beach. Such a view was chosen in that it would easily subdivide into three zones, in this case sky, ocean, sand, and for the purposes of this piece, high, middle, and low (in the sense of a musical register).

Next, a person was given a simple red ball (the musical note) and was asked to throw it high into the air (against this ocean background). With each throw, the person was asked to simultaneously shout "high," "middle," or "low." This notation would be the evidence of a secret melody being composed by that person.

The job of the cameraman was to freeze the ball/note in the proper zone that was called out with each throw. The melody would be limited to the number of frames in a roll of film, or multiples of that number. Thus 36, or 2 x 36, etc.

The resulting photographs would then be numbered in the sequence in which they were taken, and situated on the three-line staff in its proper location.

*The problems*: Of course chance enters in here. A perfect answer to this problem would be the image of the ball appearing in each photo in its proper zone. This photo then would be placed on its proper line, with the line intersecting the ball. There is a small element of time entering into this musical piece in that the ball would not often be centered in the photo but would be skewed to the right or left. So a longer note could be a photo where the ball was skewed to the left.

1. All of the successful shots (or proper notes) are marked with a red (x).
2. A missing photo—so noted on a blank white card and located below the staff. Photo-processor error.
3. Duplicate photos of the same shot. Photo-processor error. The extra photos located below staff.
4. Ball in wrong zone. The photo is located on its proper staff line, the staff line aligned with the zone boundary line; the zone falling below the staff line. These shots are bracketed.
5. No ball appearing in photo. The photo is located on its proper staff line, its bottom edge aligned. These shots are circled.
6. Split zone. In those photos where the shot is clearly not of one zone, the photo is placed in the category of that zone the photo indicates by more than fifty percent.

Perhaps all of the above problem shots can be seen as missing notes, wrong notes, and similar drop-out.

136

*Earthquake*, 1988
Black-and-white photographs with oil
tint, vinyl paint and board; mounted
on board
81½ x 107⅝ in. overall (207 x 107.6 cm)
Collection of Martin and Pam
Mickelson

*Yellow (With Onlookers)*, 1986
Two black-and-white photographs
with vinyl paint; mounted on board
39¾ x 27¼ in. overall (101 x 69.2 cm)
Edelston/Boardroom Collection, New
York

In structure and outline, the sculptural composition of photographs resembles an ice cream sundae. In its piling up of teetering images, the work alludes to Picasso's sculpture *Glass of Absinthe*, 1914, in which a sugar strainer perched on top threatens to throw it off balance. The title *Bloody Sundae* refers also to the riot that broke out after a civil rights march on January 30, 1972, in Londonderry, Northern Ireland, in which thirteen people were killed by British soldiers. The incident, commemorated in the song "Sunday Bloody Sunday," 1983, by the rock group U2, casts an eerie light on Baldessari's piece. But, as in *Blasted Allegories,* the artist also takes the title literally, as a curse upon Sunday—for Baldessari the most boring day of middle-class existence. One theme of this work is the paradox between the uneventful circumstances under which art is made and the exotic, maybe even dangerous function art is supposed to fulfill. As Baldessari says, "I think artists are more sensitive to boredom, and artists are better at finding a way to kill their time, and so they make art. I make art because I can't get enough escape from boredom out of life in general. But *Bloody Sundae* is a false picture, it's just like the movies."

In the piece Baldessari orchestrates many different rectangles like stage flats, producing a theatrical *trompe l'oeil* effect; the balancing of a top-heavy rectangular structure on top of the triangular shape formed by the man and woman lying on the bed in the lower image further increases the sense of imbalance and intrigue. Other details add to the setting of adventure: the man in the top image, whose face is covered by a red disk, for example, holds a gun. Describing his work in general, Baldessari remarks, "There are a lot of recurring things, guns, images about being panicked or being possessive, phallic images obviously." Reversed canvases, shown in the top image, lean against closed trunks that secretly may contain bundles of money or, like Pandora's box, every possible evil. The artist, by deliberately withholding information, makes any authoritative judgment of the situation impossible.

In *Three Red Paintings*, 1988, Baldessari again uses the work of art as a backdrop for a man and woman mixed up in intrigues of sex and violence. Art becomes as exciting an aphrodisiac as the movies. The three still fragments placed together mimic the turbulent narrative of soap operas, but at the same time mirror genuine human interaction—to Baldessari a necessity for the creation of art. The continuity of green and red monochromatic canvases keeps the flow of narration uninterrupted, despite the fact that the frames differ from still to still, which gives the effect of switching channels on television. To Baldessari, *Three Red Paintings* with its orchestration of color, light and dark, and rhythmic development, has something "redeeming" about it, "like seeing a terrible movie but discovering a beautiful set design."

*Bloody Sundae*, 1987
Black-and-white photographs with
vinyl paint; mounted on board
93 x 65½ in. overall (236.2 x 166.4 cm)
Collection of Joseph Rank

Pablo Picasso
*Glass of Absinthe*, 1914
Painted bronze with silver sugar
strainer
8½ x 6½ x 2½ in.
(21.6 x 16.5 x 6.35 cm)
The Museum of Modern Art, New York;
gift of Mrs. Bertram Smith

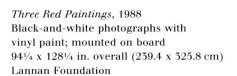

*Three Red Paintings*, 1988
Black-and-white photographs with
vinyl paint; mounted on board
94¼ x 128¼ in. overall (239.4 x 325.8 cm)
Lannan Foundation

Each composite photowork suggests its own code to be deciphered, but at the same time some element always resists "decoding" and escapes into the unknowable. The picture is never complete: "Looking for the truth implies that there is a truth. If we weren't looking for a truth maybe we wouldn't be so frustrated. But I guess we can never get rid of the idea that there must be a secret of some sort. And so I want that to be built in too." Thus in *Planets (Chairs, Observer, White Paper)*, 1987, for example, Baldessari included an image of a group of men staring down intently at a book, as if they had just discovered or witnessed something momentous in it. But perhaps they are simply staring dumbly at a blank piece of paper, or even staring into blankness itself, as if it were some kind of an answer. One cannot help thinking that the key to what is happening lies in whatever action is taking place on that page, but it becomes equally significant that the men, in looking down, have become participants in the events taking place in the stills below.

From early on the role of the spectator had been as important to Baldessari as actions themselves, as for instance in *Action/Reaction (Synchronized): Finger Touching Cactus*, 1975. In *Four Events and Reactions*, 1975, in an almost clinical form of analysis, he used two movie cameras to film concurrently a series of simple actions and the different expressions on a woman's face as she watches these actions—a finger being inserted into a glass of milk, touching a cactus, pushing a plate over the edge of a table, putting out a cigarette. The work consists entirely of a selection of frames that simultaneously record these banal events and the spectator's nuanced reactions.

In *Planets...* the three men looking at the open book, stared at in turn by a fourth man, were originally figures in the same black-and-white movie still, which was then cut into four strips that excluded all material not directly relating to this image. Ultimately, Baldessari based the image on traces in his memory of an old Renaissance engraving depicting three men looking down at a drawing, awed by the theory of perspective.

The principle of four gazes converging at one point is reversed in *Helmsman (With Flaw)*, 1987, in which Baldessari created a "radiation" into multiple points of view by literally extending the spokes of the steering wheel image in the center with strips cut from the same movie still that the wheel appeared in, creating different types of connections. As in *Close-Cropped Tales*, 1981, the cropping and framing comes

*Planets (Chairs, Observer, White Paper)*, 1987
Color and black-and-white photographs with oil tint, vinyl paint, and board; mounted on board and aluminum
100 x 105½ in. overall (254 x 268 cm)
Private collection, Los Angeles

from within the image rather than being imposed from without.

In *Planets...* the strips focusing on the four men in relation to the book caused, at the same time, accidental side effects to appear; a mysterious white sliver standing out from the dark background in one of the strips, for example, turns out to be simply a continuation of the white shirt of a man with a mustache in another strip. As Baldessari points out, "While we're looking at a specific thing, something else is happening over there at the same time, and I'm interested in that something else, which, however, we can't always catch if we try to get it directly."

*If This Then That*, 1988
Black-and-white photographs with
vinyl paint; mounted on board and
plastic
80 1/4 x 67 in. overall (203.8 x 170.2 cm)
PaineWebber Group, Inc., New York

*Looking through both ends of the
telescope:*
*Above: A line of performers, each color-
coded to a personality type, emotional
state, etc.*
*Below: A line of planets paired with
mileage figures (the distance between).
Having said this, I really believe the
work to be about the need for joy and
passion.*

*Helmsman (With Flaw)*, 1987
Black-and-white photographs;
mounted on aluminum
81 x 98 in. overall (205.7 x 248.9 cm)
Collection of Vijak Mahdavi and
Bernardo Nadal-Ginard, Boston

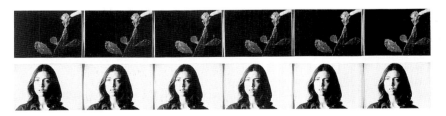

*Action/Reaction (Synchronized): Finger
Touching Cactus*, 1975
Twelve black-and-white photographs;
mounted on board
5 x 7 in. each (12.7 x 17.8 cm)
Collection of the artist

145

Baldessari's comment recalls the writings of Thoreau, the nineteenth-century essayist whose solitary walks in the woods had led to his insight that the power to see things comes about only when one "saunters." According to Thoreau "many an object is not seen, though it falls within the range of our visual ray, because it does not come within the range of our intellectual ray, i.e., we are not looking for it."[3] On the other hand, he would often find, in search of this or that rare plant specimen, that he had discovered another one altogether. Consequently he was convinced that "it is only by a sort of voluntary blindness, and omitting to see, that we know ourselves, as when we see stars with the side of the eye."[4] Baldessari would agree. It is not only the intentions of his mind operating through his eye that makes him select a suggestive image, but also a still may accidentally take on associative power through the awkward displacement of details as a side effect of the cutting. In *Planets...*, for example, cuts through the white handkerchief, and through the chin of one of the men or through the electrical cord of the partly cropped desk lamp, all become connecting links between the strips. Thus the four unframed strips in *Planets...* imply, even in residual form, a rectangle.

In relation to this overall work, the smaller-sized movie-still strips function, however, as an asterisk, but the question arises: which is more important, the text or the footnote? The composite of strips may be collapsed, but it is so powerful as to upset the seemingly stable construct beneath it. Once again the paradox of calculated randomness occurs, for the dynamic change and dramatic action in *Planets...* appears only in this asterisk, at the work's perimeter, distracting one's attention from the static, timeless central image of so-called universal order. This reversal fits in with a human way of seeing. As Baldessari observes:

It's a sort of frustration. I go to any art exhibition, including my own, and it's a big thrill for a moment, but then I see on the other hand just this little piece in this room in this city on this planet, which is spinning around with all these other planets and what about that? When I get wrapped up in all my problems speculating about what the world is about, I never think about the earth spinning around but I wish I could have that alertness, then I might maybe understand something, and I think that's why I always wanted to do a piece about the planets.

Baldessari had first expressed this idea of relativity—that is, that human beings have an inkling of the vastness of the universe but are unable to go beyond their limitations—in *Starry Night Balanced on Triangulated Trouble*, 1984. Extreme distances viewed as through a spyglass—an airplane immersed in water (a sign of man in a primal state), and unreachable galaxies light years away—are compared by Baldessari to the last words Humphrey Bogart speaks to Ingrid Bergman as he walks her to the airplane at the end of the movie *Casablanca*: "I'm no good at being noble, but it doesn't take much sense to see that the problems of three little people don't amount to a hill of beans in this crazy world."

That humanity is, generally speaking, too involved in making itself the measure of things, too caught up in its own concept of order, is reflected in our ideas of "up" and "down," for instance, based on our sensation of walking erect on the earth. However, if we focused on the planets the way Buckminster Fuller did in *The Bear Island Story*, we might grasp the implications of his remark that "all scientists agree that there are no regions of the universe which are uniquely up or down... none of the perpendiculars to a sphere are parallel to one another." Aviators have a less parochial sense of the globe when they say that they " 'come *in* for a landing' and go *out* to fly their courses at greater altitudes in the world surrounding skyocean. *In, Out,* and *Around* are the words that indicate conceptually all our sensing of directional behaviors of physical universe."[5] Aware of this, Baldessari deals with the rotating movements of the planets in terms of in, out, and around in *Planets...* by transforming two of the planetary spheres in the central color photograph. By covering these shapes with large disks of white vinyl paint, he cancels them, turning positive space into negative.

The two men in the images in the side panels, each crippled in his own way—one bound to a wheelchair, the other more literally tied to his seat with rope— are lying on the ground with their chairs tipped over. Baldessari, however, has positioned the stills to show them upright. Both men defy gravity, the very force that keeps the planets in place, for suspended as they are, it is unclear if they are ascending or descending. In this case, however, the "uprightness" of the figures suggesting the social convention of stability is a false security, for neither man is any better off erect than he is supine.

146

*Starry Night Balanced on Triangulated Trouble*, 1984
Black-and-white photographs with oil tint; mounted on board
50¾ x 40 in. overall (128.9 x 101.6 cm)
Collection of Beatrice and Philip Gersh

*High Flight*, 1986
Black-and-white photographs with oil
tint, acrylic and board; mounted on
board
103¼ x 64½ in. overall (262.3 x 163.8
cm)
Courtesy of Margo Leavin Gallery, Los
Angeles

The ambivalence of flying or falling evokes all our twentieth-century insecurities, as well as the wishful thoughts we use to offset them. Freud argued that the common dreams "in which one flies with a feeling of ease or falls in terror"[6] derive from childhood games involving a fast motion that is simultaneously attractive and frightening, such as when a father lifts his baby over his head as if it were flying, or lowers the child quickly, as if it were falling. According to Freud, these sensations return in dreams years later, but without the paternal supporting hands, causing the dreamer's excitement at floating freely to turn into anxiety about falling. Baldessari has re-created the double state of pleasure (flying) and frozen terror (falling) several times, not only in the images of the men tied to their chairs in *Planets...*, but also, for example, in *Upward Fall*, and *High Flight*, both 1986.

*Upward Fall* and *High Flight* immediately evoke "aboveness" through their thin, elongated, vertical Gestalt. Their specific presence is partly a response to the cavernous, high-ceilinged gallery in which these works were first shown: Baldessari did not want his pieces to be "chewed up" by the space. "I realized with these I could go up almost as far as I wanted, and so they contain the tendency of going up even farther. They are about something transcendent, something like the Freudian superego, something above, godlike, the ideal (Platonic in a sense)." "*Almost* as far as I wanted" is precisely the message expressed in *High Flight* through the image of the man who hangs weightlessly as if against the ceiling, like a balloon that has been released but is unable to float up any farther. The frames around the different elements of these works emphasize the separateness of the components, or building blocks, of the composition. At the same time, Baldessari composes within the images, and tries to balance architectural constructs against emotional or psychological subject matter. Sometimes this results in correspondences, comparable to rhymes; at other times collisions of imagery and structure deliberately confuse and distract from a too obvious meaning.

In *High Flight*, the artist used an inverted T form, its ascending force barely grounded in the laterally expansive horizontal bar at the bottom. This small section below, representing the id forces, contains three rectangular building blocks: a central image of female swimmers describing a perfect circle is flanked on both sides by the identical picture of a school of fish, one tinted orange, the other, printed "flopped" and a mirror of its companion, tinted blue. The weightlessness of all three pictures undermines their function as the foundation of the T form. The one stabilizing factor is the man in a diving mask who sits among the swimming fish. As an observer, gazing in particular at a fish that has been singled out from the group by Baldessari's application of a colored dot (blue in the orange group, orange in the blue group), the sitting diver emphasizes the concept of opposites. In Baldessari's system, blue stands for the ideal; orange usually represents the arrival of danger. The symbolism implicit in the binary opposition of the two photographs of fish extends to the women performing a water ballet, so that this central image seems to allude to the complications of sexual/platonic attraction: the women can be read either as angels (blue) or as sirens (dangerous orange).

*Upward Fall*, overtly phallic in shape, has the silhouette of a buttressed rising structure. The ascending force seems at first stabilized by two identical "foundation blocks," their symmetry again achieved by using a photograph and its flopped version together. To accentuate the feeling of sturdiness, Baldessari chose a static photographic image of a cowboy in profile on his horse accompanied by two dogs, who sit facing the camera. The associations that surface run from mantelpiece statuettes to bookends to equestrian statues. The cowboy is a John Wayne type, the perfect conventional embodiment of manly strength and control. The whole piece would appear stable if the rising, elongated rectangle in the center were not just barely anchored to one of the foundation blocks. In relation to the dangerously askew, strutlike supporting image, the rectangle seems about to topple at any moment.

Both *Upward Fall* and *High Flight* express in their upward movement an exasperated aspiration for progress, as the pleasure of flying is short-lived, quickly reversing itself into the anxiety of falling. In *Upward Fall* the fragility of flight is reinforced by the unequal position, size, and content of the two pictorial buttresses, one showing the ephemeral shadow of a ladder, the other an isolated man wandering around in a blue-tinted desert, lending the picture the unreal quality of a fata morgana. And in *High Flight*, pride comes before a fall. The security promised by the superego as father figure, seen in the topmost image in the guise of an aviator, will not last. The yellow dot that replaces one of his eyes signals madness, and his long white scarf flapping out of control in the wind anticipates the fallibility of our century's technological wonders. If the machine breaks down, no hands will support the aviator, and the game of flying will immediately become transformed into the terror of falling.

Falling and flying are treated as a rite of initiation in *Mountain Climber*, 1988. Echoing *Upward Fall* and *High Flight*, Baldessari exaggerated the verticality even further by recklessly hanging a still of a roped mountain climber, contained in a green-tinted rectangle, against the ceiling of the gallery where it was installed, and placing the other elements at the level of the floor. An empty white wall space separates the "green pastoral ease" of the mountain climber above from a black-and-white still of a rope against the sky far below. The effect is dizzying—an elaboration on the representation of the void as a framed white cardboard rectangle employed by Baldessari in *High Flight* in order to stress the fragility of flying. The rope against the sky reaches farther down into a larger rectangular still, where it eventually slants into the hands of a diver under water. The diver carries a flare, colored red by the artist to indicate the id. The stairlike composition of the bottommost elements in *Mountain Climber* ambiguously lead up or down, underlining the contrary directions of climbing and diving. That the ends of the rope are aligned but do not touch, while the top and bottom elements are separated by a large amount of space, gives rise to another ambivalence: are all the elements coming together in one Gestalt, or moving apart into separate pieces?

The two images adjacent to the diver with the red flare in *Mountain Climber* show what seem to be birthday cakes, each confined to its own rectangle. In *High Flight*, which includes stills of a man sucking his thumb and another man blowing out the oversized candles of a cake—and in *Mountain Climber*—Baldessari may be evoking the oral infant state. In *Mountain Climber*, however, the inscription on one cake reading "Good luck Joe," and a candelabra standing next to the other cake holding three candles tinted red, yellow, and blue are connected with the extremes shown in the work—the climber reaching too high in the superego, the diver floating too low in the oceanic id, implying the Icarean hubris of youth.

In *Upward Fall* the Freudian triad of the superego, ego, and id is complemented by the three elements copper, silver, and gold, the symbol of alchemic purification. The usual hierarchical order of preciousness of these metals is disregarded, however, introducing confusion: gold is "above," copper "between," and silver "below." In the work's vertical central column of images, each tinted to suggest a particular metal, three men are seen in three different states of flying or falling. Their movement tends in three different directions: upward, lateral from left to right and slightly upward, and lateral from right to left. The upward movement of the top image is achieved by inverting a still of a man falling off a balcony so that he seems to levitate. The central image is derived from a photograph of a stunt man leaping from one building to another, and the bottom image is of a diver, with both board and swimming pool cropped out. In its physical floating quality, and in the emphasis on visionary rather than descriptive forms, this composite work based on the traditionally magical number three approaches the picture language of myths and dreams.

The dream state even penetrates the title, *Upward Fall*, which Baldessari derived from the term "failing upward," an expression used in business to describe someone who is promoted in order to be taken out of circulation because he or she is not functioning properly. The words "upward fall" unite antithetical meanings, simultaneously denoting an action and its opposite without preference for either one. If anything, the accent lies on their interdependence: ascending is the twin of descending. The trope is analogous to the compound words that combine opposite meanings in some of the world's oldest languages, including the Egyptian and Semitic tongues. In "The Antithetical Sense of Primal Words," an essay published in 1910, Freud discusses this peculiarity in language, comparing it to the syntax of dreams, which ignores antithesis and contradiction: "The word 'No' does not seem to exist for a dream. Dreams are particularly fond of reducing antitheses to uniformity, or representing them as one and the same thing."[7]

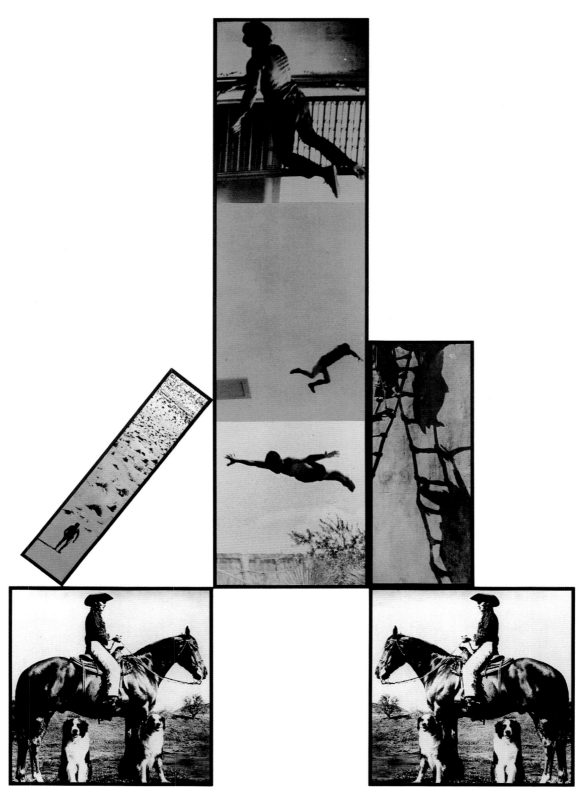

*Upward Fall*, 1986
Black-and-white photographs with oil
tint, and black-and-white photographs
printed on metallic paper; mounted on
board
95 x 68 in. overall (241.3 x 172.7 cm)
Fried, Frank, Harris, Shriver &
Jacobson Art Collection, Los Angeles

*Mountain Climber*, 1988
Black-and-white photographs with oil
tint; mounted on board
Top: 25⅞ x 19⅛ in. (65.7 x 48.6 cm);
bottom: 69¼ x 91½ in. (175.9 x 232.4 cm)
Collection of James and Linda
Burrows, Los Angeles

In both its title and its equation of forms of knife and man—one subject to gravity and the other defying it—*Knife/Dive* also exhibits this fusing of distinct opposites into one, while at the same time, as a diptych, it formally separates them. Two movie stills oppose one another: a diver floating freely in space is offset by a man stabbed in the back with a knife and sprawled over. Baldessari has turned both movie stills around, again achieving a sort of ethereal dream-state that not only defies gravity but also dislodges the original meaning of the photographs. At the upper right the pirate ship from which the diver soars outward has become an unrecognizable, intricate construct. With the back of the murdered man, this shape forms a perfect triangle, suggesting all kinds of associations: the formal lineup of diver and knife, for instance, brings to mind the term "jack-knife dive." A deeper meaning also surfaces, that of the soul leaving the body. (This theme returns later, in a different guise, in *The Soul Returns to the Body*, 1986.) And the image of the departing soul may be a stand-in for the idea of the phoenix rising from the ashes, which in its turn may be a metaphor for the creative act of the artist who lives in the mind alone, unhampered by the burden and limitations of the body. Yet, as Baldessari puts it, "I have this constant dilemma of wanting to soar like a bird but being limited to my own human body. On the other hand, one cannot always be in a poetic trance. Paradoxically, brushing teeth and paying bills are included in life and art as well."

Baldessari applied an arrangement of opposites as a formal device again in the diptych *Eagle/Rodent*, 1984, recalling both the Aesop's fable *The Tortoise and the Hare*, with its moral "Slow and steady wins the race," in which the slow tortoise outsmarts the fast hare, and the story of David and Goliath with its lesson "The meek shall inherit the earth." Similarly, both *Boat and Ship*, 1986, and *Elephant*, 1987, juxtapose large and small. (They could express Baldessari's feelings about being exceptionally tall—six foot six—which makes him not only painfully self-conscious about his own "awkward" physical shape, but also highly aware of its opposite, being tiny.) Imagining what it would be like to be simultaneously in the Sahara and the Arctic, Baldessari combined half of a "hot" and half of a "cold" scene into what appears to be a primordial setting in *Double Landscape*, 1988. Each half is accompanied by an image of the same body of water, but in a further confusion of opposites, the one placed next to the desert is colored an icy blue, while the other, juxtaposed with a snowscape, a warm brown. Among other works that balance opposites are *Landscape*, 1986, which combines an interior and an exterior view; *Gavel*, 1987, showing man's controlling and woman's dependent role in society; *Couple*, 1987, which sets human artificiality and animal instinct side by side; *Small Landscape*, 1986, which combines fleeting water and durable earth; and *4 Types of Chaos/4 Types of Order*, 1984, *Yellow Harmonica (With Turn)*, 1987, and *Roller Coaster*, 1988, which all confront chaos with order.

*Knife/Dive*, 1984
Two black-and-white photographs; mounted on board
60 x 36 in. overall (152.4 x 91.4 cm)
Collection of Peter Blum, New York

153

 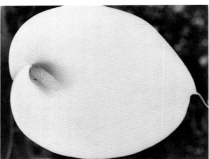

*One of the benefits of sequential work is that of comparisons that can be made within the set. Here instead of an ongoing linear mode, a simple binary system is employed. On/off, yes/no, etc. What do two yeses mean, or two nos. And what does yes/no mean in relation to no/yes. Signals not as solitary but in a syntactical relationship. The reverse of "Just give me a simple yes."*

*Eagle/Rodent*, 1984
Two black-and-white photographs,
mounted on board
24 x 60 in. overall (61 x 152.3 cm)
Private collection, courtesy of
Sonnabend Gallery, New York

*Boat and Ship*, 1986
Two black-and-white photographs;
mounted on board
30½ x 40½ in. overall (77.5 x 102.9 cm)
Collection of Wendy and Richard
Hokin, Darien, Connecticut

*Double Landscape*, 1988
Two black-and-white photographs
with oil tint; mounted on board
26¾ x 98 in. overall (67.9 x 248.9 cm)
Collection of Emily Fisher Landau

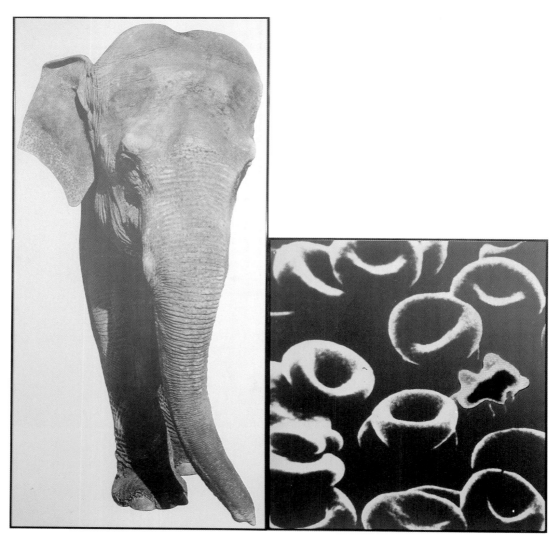

*Elephant*, 1987
Black-and-white photographs with oil
tint; mounted on board
69 x 69½ in. overall (175.3 x 176.5 cm)
Collection of the artist

*Landscape*, 1986
Two black-and-white photographs
62½ x 93 in. overall (158.8 x 236.2 cm)
Collection of Judy and Stuart Spence,
South Pasadena, California

*Couple*, 1987
Three black-and-white photographs
with vinyl paint; mounted on board
71½ x 96½ in. overall (181.6 x 245.1 cm)
Collection of Batsheva and Ronald
Ostrow

*Gavel*, 1987
Two black-and-white photographs
with vinyl paint; mounted on board
48½ x 30¼ in. overall (123.2 x 76.8 cm)
Collection of Ann and Mel Schaffer,
South Orange, New Jersey

*Small Landscape*, 1986
Black-and-white photographs with oil
tint; mounted on board
26½ x 17½ in. overall (67.3 x 44.5 cm)
Federal Reserve Bank of San
Francisco, Los Angeles Branch

158

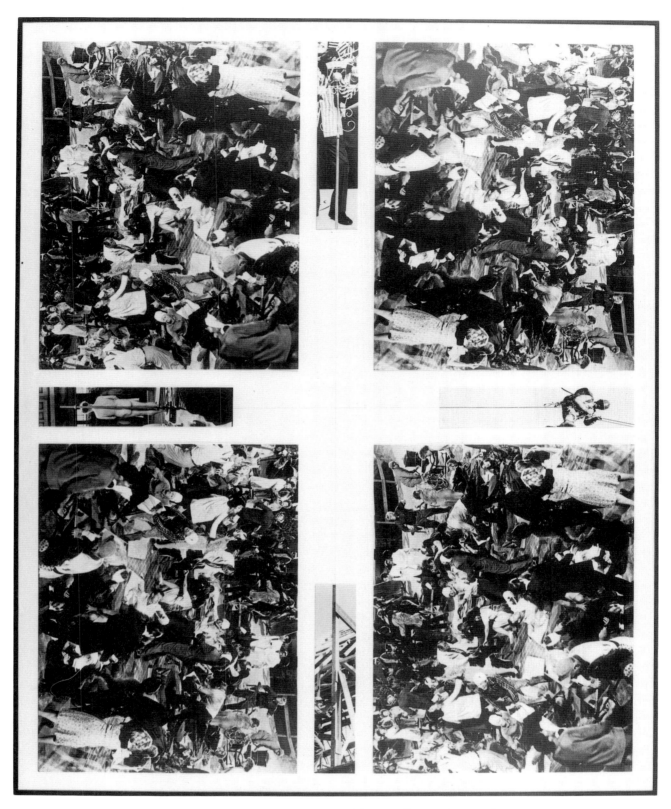

*4 Types of Chaos/4 Types of Order*,
1984
Black-and-white photographs with
pencil on board
74¾ x 59½ in. overall (189.9 x 151.1 cm)
The Capital Group, Inc., Los Angeles

*Roller Coaster*, 1988
Black-and-white photographs with
vinyl paint; mounted on board
48⅜ x 47⅞ in. overall (122.9 x 121.6 cm)
Collection of Rena Bransten

In *Roller Coaster*, 1988, two images are again placed in opposition to one another, this time in a flip-flop situation, that actually uncovers more similarities than differences: the top photograph shows a toy roller coaster, complex circular motion kept in check; in the bottom photograph that same motion has gone awry in an image of jumbled barbed wire. Baldessari found one of the movie stills accidentally, in a trash can on 26th Street, in New York City. Two children, their faces obliterated by yellow disks—a sign, according to Baldessari, for complete randomness—are intrigued by a toy roller coaster, which for the artist represents "destiny in the making. Children learn the game of life from adults, who think they're going somewhere, and in fact are going nowhere, just keeping moving." The overexcitement of the game, bordering on madness, complements literal entanglement. The posts that support the wire have been colored in, and between the red stake of danger and the green stake of freedom, life is in a state of confusion. Baldessari is trying "to give equal time, let's say, to the other side of the story, because we have always this idea that life is orderly, and that anything that is chaotic is disorderly, and an anomaly. I'm saying, well, you know, what if life is pretty much hit or miss, and order is anomaly, and only now and then things make sense? I'm saying to people: Watch out! The most disorderly situation may contain the most order."

160

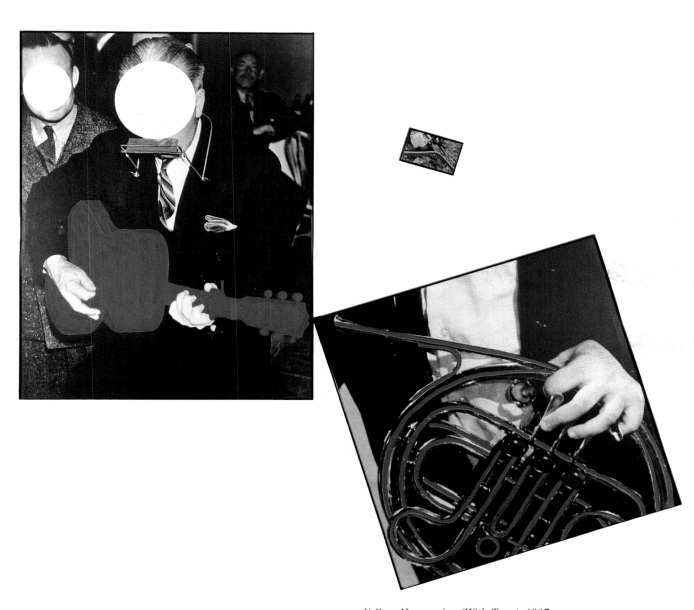

*Yellow Harmonica (With Turn)*, 1987
Black-and-white photographs with
vinyl paint and board; mounted on
board
94½ x 107 in. overall (240 x 271.8 cm)
The Rivendell Collection

Music as a symbol of harmony might be the theme of *Yellow Harmonica (With Turn)* if it were not for a small photograph of a twisted railway track, floating away from the rest of the components, upsetting the order of things. The distorted line of the rail—which, in a black-and-white image, has been colored yellow—amid the rubble of a wrecked train clearly relates to the yellow-tinted harmonica in the mouth of the musician in the neighboring, much larger picture. The musician holds a guitar painted red, a reduced curvilinear shape, which is echoed in the baroque form of the blue-tinted French horn. While it is clear that the practiced fingers of the musicians are controlling their instruments, the harmonica suggests a trap that might hold the musician captive: "I painted the harmonica yellow as something very risky, very chancy, unpredictable, and explosive, that could change very easily the course of destiny." At the very moment when harmony is about to be reached, entropy sets in, all because of that one wrong note, that tiny marginal component, dangerously out of order. Like *Yellow Harmonica (With Turn)*, *Letter* contains an element of chance that interrupts normative stability. The letter, handed down, may turn out to be as weak a link in stolid life as the twisted railroad track. To Baldessari these are "flies in the ointment," and as such are apt metaphors for our age.

The relationship between apartness and togetherness, and the theme of one element creating or disturbing the whole, had been addressed by Baldessari in *Heel*, 1986, made during a period when, having read Elias Canetti's book *Crowds and Power*, he had become fascinated by the meaning of crowds as opposed to individuals. In this work he cropped the center image of a crowd in such a way that several figures at the peripheries seem to drift off. As "strays," they could potentially have turned into independent personalities again, into a man or a woman, had the artist not created a unifying graphic red line to keep them from spreading out any farther, so that they dissolve into the crowd. The red thread brings the crowd to life, determining its pattern, but at the same time contains the disquieting migratory element that threatens to disrupt its cohesiveness. And that calligraphic line, forming both the crowd's strength and its weakness, corresponds with the one vulnerable point in the invincible Achilles, his heel, metaphorically visualized in the stills of wounded men and women positioned around the crowd.

At first glance the movie stills Baldessari selects seem to depict simple, ordinary events, which provide him with a reflection of the world that he can play with in an analytic, dispassionate way. But drama and ambiguity may unexpectedly surface:

The context of the still is removed so that we bring all our emotional baggage to it, what we've seen of life, and on television, and so on. But quite often I find myself imagining things there which I realize later are not there at all. It's about what one brings to it. What is not there is as important as what is there. I like to give a bare amount of information that doesn't asphyxiate the piece. When I fail, I have taken away too much. When I succeed, there's just enough to activate the mind but not enough to provide completeness.

The balance between what is there and what is not there is carried to its extreme in *Columns and Grillwork*, 1988, in which Baldessari allows marginal material—architectural columns and wrought-iron gratings, which would usually constitute a movie still's setting rather than its subject—to become central structuring devices. For him, these static building elements in our environment, designed to create a false impression, are a dressing-up of the world, or the presentation of an impenetrable front to it: "We know that has nothing to do with life at all. It's all a lie. And that's what most architecture is to me, it's trying to present an image." The architectural elements that Baldessari uses are incomplete parts of the overall building, and if they invite one to imagine what that total structure might be, they are also arranged so as to convey instability; the presence of one post and lintel may suggest others, but the actual elements are missing. Adding to the confusion, these columns and ornamental gratings obstruct one's view into the picture. In the only place where escape seems possible, a man with a gun, slightly obscured but still visible, steps into one's line of vision, implying a threat that stops the viewer from wishing to penetrate into deep space. Above, a woman, cropped and shown as a torso with her head covered by a black disk, is as frightening as the proverbial headless horseman. The level of anxiety is raised even more by the vulnerability of the woman off to the right, her bare shoulders just visible and her face erased by a pure white disk.

*Heel*, 1986
Black-and-white photographs with
vinyl paint and oil tint, and one black-
and-white photograph printed on
metallic paper; mounted on board
106½ x 87 in. overall (270.5 x 220.9 cm)
Los Angeles County Museum of Art;
Modern and Contemporary Art
Council Fund

*Kiss/Panic*, 1984
Black-and-white photographs with oil
tint; mounted on board
81 x 72¾ in. overall (205.7 x 184.8 cm)
Collection of Toni and Martin Sosnoff,
New York

*This is a work about the corrosive
effect of sexuality on groups and the
responses that ensue.*

*It is also concerned with the terror of
intimacy and subsequent possessiveness
as an ill result.* Kiss/Panic *explodes in
its defensiveness—as in* Heel, *its center
is unstable.*

*Columns and Grillwork*, 1988
Black-and-white photographs and
vinyl paint; mounted on board and
aluminum
108⅜ x 134¾in. overall (275.3 x 342.3
cm)
Courtesy of Margo Leavin Gallery, Los
Angeles

Baldessari had dealt earlier with the idea of
transience in the face of false monumentality in
*Ingres and Other Parables*, and the theme returns
once more in *Sphinx*, 1988, in which a crumbling
monument of sand is surrounded by images of water:
"We always go for the idea of permanence. We have
to or we'd go crazy, I suppose. We have to believe in
it, even though it is a lie." The fleeting, the changing,
is as attractive to Baldessari as marginal objects
accidentally caught in one's field of perception: "I
have a whole file of photographs labeled 'ephemeral'
that is divided into subcategories such as smoke, fire,
water, feathers, explosions, and so on. I like the idea
of zeroing in on smoke or water and making it more
important than people. Was it Rosso who sculpted
water and smoke? I just love that, for I like to make
ephemeral stuff important. In many of the 1980s
works, ephemeral elements are brought in to upset
and undermine the stereotypical stability of our
'pillars of society.' "

Pushing marginal "stuff" around in *Sailing and
Tennis*, 1987, Baldessari comes close to the bull's-
eye—that rare moment of impact with a promise of
perfection. In this composite photowork innumerable
suggestive contradictions arise, while at the same
time the components are held together in a strong
structural order. The cropping of the figures has
shifted the focal point so sharply to marginal objects
that instead of serving merely as functional
extensions of human beings, these objects are
featured and given a life of their own. Baldessari
chose a quite ordinary color picture of a tennis player
because of the perfect alignment of the stretched
arm, racket, and ball with the line of the wall at the
edge of the court. Beside this central framed
rectangle Baldessari set an image of a toy sailboat,
contained in its own unframed black-and-white strip.
The course of the boat extends the unlikely trajectory
of objects in the tennis picture. Above, a third still is
cropped to outline a ricochet of longing gazes that
create the classical triangle of a woman and two men.

*Sphinx*, 1988
Black-and-white photographs with
vinyl paint; mounted on board
96⅜ x 89 in. overall (244.8 x 226.1 cm)
The Capital Group, Inc., Los Angeles

*Eruption with Clouds Arranged by
Color*, 1984
Black-and-white photograph with oil
tint; mounted on board
66 x 50½ in. (167.6 x 128.3 cm)
The BOC Group, Windlesham, Surrey,
England

Source material for *Sailing and Tennis*, 1987

All the parts of the composition, from this triangle to the extended hand of the woman who sits on the rim of the pool of a park fountain in which the sailboat floats—only her forearm and a part of her skirt are visible—converge in the dynamic central image of the ball about to hit the racket. Yet because of the cropping, room is left for doubt about the image's prevailing vectors: to and fro, far and near. Is the ball being received or returned? In the upper triangle, is the glance of the man at the far right directed toward the woman or toward the other man at the far left, and does this uncertainty extend to the doubtful gender of the tennis player, whose hand alone is visible? And is the graceful figure in black with the sailboat, in an image suggesting a still from Alain Resnais's film *L'Année dernière a Marienbad* (*Last Year at Marienbad*), an anonymous spectator or another glimpse of the woman above? The question, ultimately, is one of control. To Baldessari, "It is all about faith, and faith being so chancy, maybe it is all about chance. I think I have this fascination with predictability and order as opposed to what is sort of up in the air. And usually it is of course something I completely can't anticipate. That chance aspect animates a lot of the work I do, the known versus the unknown."

When Baldessari delivers photographs to the laboratory, with crop marks indicated in acetate crayon, he leaves his options open. "I have made tentative decisions, but I don't always know in advance which battle plan to use. When I finally see the enlargements, I'll most of the time use the tactic I originally planned, but sometimes I'll use an alternative solution." However, the part of the cropping that may seem to the artist coincidental may often be firmly rooted in aesthetic decisions he subconsciously tends to carry out. In fact, all artists' attempts to achieve new strategies may turn out

168

*Sailing and Tennis*, 1987
Color and black-and-white
photographs; mounted on board and
aluminum
90 x 96 in. overall (228.6 x 243.8 cm)
Private collection, courtesy of
Sonnabend Gallery, New York

primarily to be variations or recombinations in the obsessive need to repeat creative acts over and over again, in search of the reconstruction of the idealized self-object, a desire to feel whole again, what psychoanalyst Charles Kligerman points out as "the need to regain a lost paradise—the original bliss of perfection—to overcome the empty feeling of self-depletion and to recover self-esteem. In the metapsychology of the self this would amount to healing the threatened fragmentation and restoring firm self-cohesion through a merger with the self-object—the work of art—and a bid for mirroring approval by the world."[8]

*Sailing and Tennis* contains an unusual number of memory traces of Baldessari's past work. An analogy can be made with a series of earlier pieces about alignment and forced alignment, in which the artist made things that normally would not be lined up appear to be so. Of one such piece, *Aligning Balls*, 1972, the artist remarks, "The floating ball was used as a notation device. The photographs were not aligned with the usual top or bottom edge but by the ball used as a point. There is a proximity to musical notation. The ball repeated in each photograph provides a strong backbone for the apparent randomness of the background/fields in each photograph. Also, each shot is alternatively a photograph of the ball or a photograph of a location or scene."

  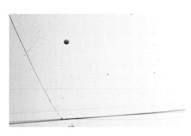 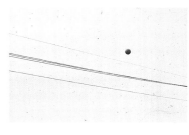

*Aligning Balls*, (details), 1972
Variable number color photographs
and chalk
3½ x 5 in. each (8.9 x 12.7 cm)
Installation dimensions variable
Collection of the artist

Stills from the movie *Title*, 1973
16mm black-and-white and color film
with sound
25 minutes

The principle of ambiguity that occurs through a shift between close-up and distant shots, as in *Aligning Balls*, returns in the curious, compressed space of *Sailing and Tennis*, where a female hand seems simultaneously close to and far from the sailboat, even though the camera has aligned both in the same vertical plane. This in turn recalls a scene in the closing segment of *Title*, 1973, a part of the film that addresses horizontal movement and vertical stasis. On a beach at sunset, a male figure stands facing the camera with his back toward the ocean, while the silhouette of a sailboat appears on the horizon, slowly moving from the right directly toward the man's head. The final cut is made at the moment of eclipse, when sailboat and head are perfectly aligned. In the original movie still that Baldessari selected for the boat image of *Sailing and Tennis*, the stern of another toy sailboat touches the woman's head, in a direct reference to that scene. This part of the picture is cropped out, however, and the focus is instead on the ambiguity of proximity and distance between the woman's hand and the sailboat that was included in Baldessari's image.

The image recalls still other works—*Goodbye to Boats (Sailing In)*, and *Goodbye to Boats (Sailing Out)*, both 1972–73, which were inspired by a photograph of Baldessari's father waving goodbye to a ship sailing to Europe with his mother aboard. Baldessari writes: "The pain and anxiety of the act is counterbalanced by repeating it endlessly, perhaps obliterating the sadness."[9] *Sailing and Tennis*, stressing apartness-togetherness, completes yet another triad: anticipation, in the longing stares between the woman and the two men in the topmost image, and in the triangular configuration pivoting on the ball in midair (an echo of *Throwing Three Balls in the Air to Get an Equilateral Triangle (Best of 36 Tries)*, 1972–73); the moment of contact, in the ball hitting the racket; and separation, symbolized by the little boat sailing away.

*Goodbye to Boats (Sailing Out)*,
(details), 1972–73
Twelve Type-C prints; mounted on board
9¹⁵⁄₁₆ x 6¾ in. each (25.2 x 17.1 cm)
Private collection, courtesy of
Sonnabend Gallery, New York

  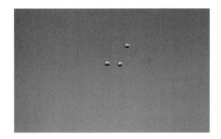

Keeping in mind the concept of "somehow standing for the truth but not really being the truth," Baldessari finds himself controlling the space of the photoworks not only through cropping but also through the kinds of materials he applies to them. Recently, he has begun to tint parts of the black-and-white stills, for example, using oil paint diluted to varying degrees with turpentine. The result is not a fusion of painting and photography but a dualistic effect somewhere between the two. In *Stain*, 1987, for instance, Baldessari took a color photograph as source material for the bottom image, then, perversely, rephotographed it in black-and-white, only to hand color it again in oil tint until its palette approximated that of the original image. Again, the aim—as in the artist's refusal to accept the traditional photographic format—is to break away from a predetermined cliché that one takes for granted. Baldessari purposefully achieves "a color image that looks neither fowl nor fish."

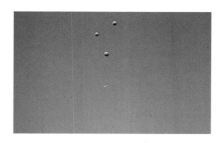 

*Throwing Three Balls in the Air To Get an Equilateral Triangle (Best of 36 Tries)*, 1972–73
Five color photographs; mounted on board
14¼ x 20 in. each (36.2 x 50.8 cm)
Wexner Center for the Visual Arts, Ohio State University, Columbus, Ohio

*Stain*, 1987
Black-and-white photographs with vinyl paint and oil tint; mounted on board
89½ x 57¼ in. overall (227.3 x 145.4 cm)
Courtesy of Sonnabend Gallery, New York

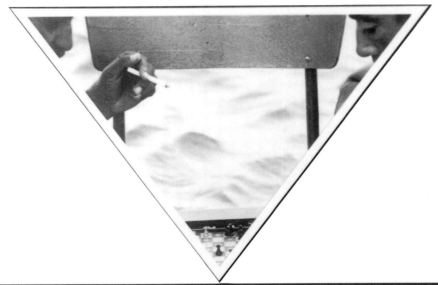

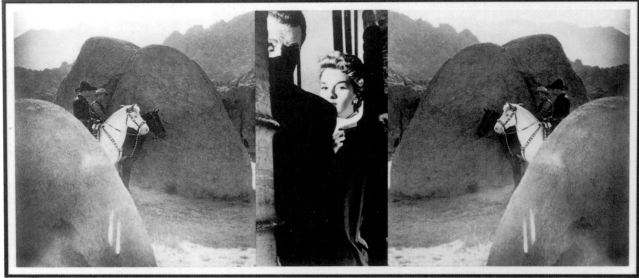

*Black and White Decision*, 1984
Four black-and-white photographs;
mounted on board
64 x 72¾ in. overall (162.6 x 184.8 cm)
The Eli Broad Family Foundation

Admiring the way painters like Caravaggio, Rembrandt, and Goya used chiaroscuro, Baldessari attempts to determine the rhythms of the composite photoworks through lights and darks. In *Black and White Decision*, 1984, he makes optimum use of black-and-white contrasts, employing them symbolically not only in the topmost, triangular image of two chess players, who seem to be determining the fate of a woman staring over the shoulder of a man in the picture below, but also in the stills on either side—the same image, of two riders in a western movie, in one case flopped so that the cowboys seem to face each other. The confrontation of good guy and bad guy is wonderfully commingled, for the black horse carries a cowboy in a light-colored costume and the white horse a cowboy in a black costume, cross-cutting fixed symbolic meanings. The riders are opponents, yet their symmetrical composition provides stability for the man and woman in the center, who seem to wait while their fate is played out, like objects under a microscope.

Baldessari is not averse to Hollywood's dramatic lighting effects, and in fact has sometimes based his selection of subject matter on them, for instance in

*Light and Dark*, 1986, where the light of a bright lamp in one image is juxtaposed with a man's dark eye patch in another, to become a preexisting source of contrast. In *Sailing*, 1986, and *Skateboarder (With Surfer)*, 1987, water and fire fulfill the same function. In *Three Types of Light*, 1984, three movie stills are cropped according to the way that light organizes the elements within the frame: in the bottom image a diagonal bar is created by the reflection of light on a dagger; in the central image an X shape is formed by light shining into the camera from an obscure source; and in the top image a blob of light obscures the face of a man wearing a sombrero, distinguishing itself in its amorphousness from the linearity of the other two light patterns. The accidental appearance of bright light out of nowhere, probably due to a defect in the original print, intrigued Baldessari so much that he simulated the effect in *Two Crowds: Trouble (Excluded): Watching (Included)*, 1986, by pouring bleach around the crowd in one photograph, and on it in another. In *Ancient Wisdom (With Repairs)*, 1987, Baldessari again plays with photographic flaws. The two bottom photographs in this column of three were accidentally stuck together and later pulled apart, marring their surfaces and shapes. The artist enhanced the vaguely erotic fragments left behind by outlining both their negative and their positive contours, resulting in a white shape resembling the head of a vulture and a dark, Picassoid, bull-like form, both in the central image. The top image of a pyramid contains spots caused by water damage, which Baldessari emphasized with bright white vinyl paint.

*Light and Dark*, 1986
Two black-and-white photographs
64¾ x 95⅝ in. overall (164.5 x 242.9 cm)
Private collection, Belgium

*Sailing*, 1986
Two black-and-white photographs
87½ x 54 in. overall (222.3 x 137.2 cm)
Courtesy of Galerie Peter Pakesch,
Vienna

*Three Types of Light*, 1984
Three black-and-white photographs;
mounted on board
78 x 30 in. overall (198.1 x 76.2 cm)
Courtesy of Sonnabend Gallery, New
York

*Ancient Wisdom (With Repairs)*, 1987
Black-and-white photographs with
vinyl paint and oil tint; mounted on
board
84 x 30 in. overall (213.4 x 76.2 cm)
Courtesy of Sonnabend Gallery, New
York

*Pelican in Desert*, 1984
Black-and-white photograph; mounted
on board
24 x 30 in. (61 x 76.2 cm)
Collection of Claes Oldenburg and
Coosje van Bruggen, New York

*In Christian iconography the pelican
picking flesh from its breast to feed its
young is a symbol of Christ. This idea
is paired with the story of Christ in the
desert as a rite of passage.*

*It is about human isolation. The
pelican is gigantic in comparison to the
surrounding elements of the
composition. The bird is seen as a
black two-dimensional shape akin to a
platonic cave—shadow figure. The two
devices are intended to alienate the
pelican and to create a figure in the
tradition of Dr. Frankenstein's monster
or the Elephant Man.*

Baldessari's experimentation with the blocking out of forms from preexisting sources in the stills includes an exploration of shadows, a process he first considered after seeing someone moving through a movie audience cast a shadow across the screen. In *Pelican in Desert*, 1984, he darkened the ephemeral shadow of a pelican with oil tint, giving it more of a physical presence than the bird that cast it. It is related in a way to Freud's idea of dream reversal, a theme that would return in some of Baldessari's later works, such as *Upward Fall* and *Life's Balance*, 1986. The ambiguity caused by the physicality of the ladder's darkened shadow in *Upward Fall*, and by the shadow of the telephone cord in *Life's Balance*, relates to the dream's ability to represent things by their opposites, confusing their reading in a positive or negative sense. In *Two Crowds (With Shape of Reason Missing)*, 1984, Baldessari again transforms positive into negative, using an emphatic cut to remove—and thus make invisible—the reasons for the formation of the crowds. In the resulting holes primal repression surfaces. In 1986, more interested in such blotted-out shapes than in the crowds themselves, the artist made five more works under the title *Crowds (With Shape of Reason Missing)*, which were published in *Zone* magazine; in these

pieces, the reasons for the crowds, the events that brought them together, are painted out in white vinyl paint. Thinking about the appearance of the ensuing shapes and their meaning as a Gestalt, Baldessari was led to those composite works of the later 1980s in which the emphasis is again on certain shapes whited or blacked out. The effect is to reduce the individuality of the figures shown into the anonymity of a generic type. In *White Shape*, 1984, Baldessari demythologizes the heroic artist, namely Jackson Pollock, and in *Double Man and Seal*, 1988, a captain of industry is diminished, as in a Rorschach test, into a black double blob, a representation of a sterile antilife in contrast to the images of wet seals moving around in the oceanic id.

*Life's Balance*, 1986
Black-and-white photographs and
board; mounted on board
97¾ x 68¾ in. overall (248.2 x 174.6 cm)
Collection of Brooke and Carolyn
Alexander, New York

*Two Crowds (With Shape of Reason Missing)*, 1984
Two black-and-white photographs and
board; mounted on board
48 x 30 in. overall (121.9 x 76.2 cm)
Jedermann Collection, N.A.

Source material for *Two Crowds (With Shape of Reason Missing)*

*White Shape*, 1984
Black-and-white photograph with
acrylic; mounted on board
48 x 29 in. (121.9 x 73.7 cm)
Courtesy of G. H. Dalsheimer Gallery,
Baltimore

*Double Man and Seal*, 1988
Black-and-white photographs;
mounted on board
48 x 110¾ in. overall (121.9 x 281.3 cm)
Collection of Bob and Linda Gersh,
Los Angeles

*Thaumatrope Series: Two Gangsters
(One with Scar and Gun)*, 1975
Three black-and-white photographs;
mounted on board
Two: 16 x 20 in. each; one: 5 x 7 in.
(40.6 x 50.8; 12.7 x 17.8 cm)
Graphische Sammlung Staatsgalerie,
Stuttgart

*A thaumatrope is a card with different
pictures on opposite sides which
appear to combine when twirled
rapidly. What appealed to me was the
disjunctiveness of the imagery and the
tension it produces. Two items literally
separate but possessing a gestalt
magnetic attraction. They want to be
together but are not. So one can decide
to unite them in the mind's eye or let
them be bifurcated.*

This rupture of the continuity in the composite photoworks, the breaking up or blotting out of parts of their surfaces, turns out to be inspired by Baldessari's memories of the plaster fillings for missing shards in the Greek vases that he saw on his visits to The Metropolitan Museum of Art in New York, in 1965. (It was in reaction to them that he had blocked out sections of the commercial-billboard images he had collected for his work of the 1960s.) The artist's obsessive merry-go-round need to repeat his creative act in order to feel complete for a moment by a subconscious merging of his identity with that of the work of art here, paradoxically, focuses on the exact opposite of this process: the loss of wholeness. Indefatigably searching for experiences that incorporate unpredictable insights, and involved in a life-long process of gaining fresh knowledge, his imagination was fired precisely by what was missing in the white spaces of the Greek vases. And in gluing together the scattered shards, in emphasizing both the de- and the re-construction of things, Baldessari finds the specific form to fit the theme of apartness-togetherness, to evoke an imperfect human condition rather than the nonhuman stasis of unattainable perfection—death.

This attraction to the unknown, the void, the blocked-out part of the dream, the crack in the whole, returns over and over again in the artist's work. At the same time there is the tension of wanting to provide the missing link, as for instance, in the *Thaumatrope Series*, 1975, or to repair something broken by adding a part to fill the vacancy, which became an assignment for students at Hunter College in New York in the summer of 1970 and which in 1976 was turned into a work. In the *Repair/Retouch Series: An Allegory About Wholeness (Plate and Man with Crutches)*, 1976, as Baldessari wrote, "The raw material was the legless man and the broken dish. In the succeeding photographs a leg and the missing portion of the dish were reconstructed by airbrushing and painting. The act of healing is posited as synonymous with art."[10] (This idea resurfaces in 1988, in the artist's collection of photographs of people wearing bandages.) Baldessari found the perfect combination of wholeness and omission in the blotting out of faces, which he practiced for the first time in *Buildings = Guns = People: Desire, Knowledge, and Hope (With Smog)*, 1985, an installation for the 1985 Carnegie International Exhibition:

I had a big folder lying around in the studio, which I labeled "civic portraits." It's the kind of photograph that tends to be in the middle of the newspaper, not on the front page, about all these people getting awards or pointing to some real estate, you know, in power, winning something....Every time I go to picture places there will always be a profusion of these photographs, and I will always sort of pass them by because they are so ugly; but then I kept thinking I ought to explore why I am so repelled by them, because there is a power there, and I can use it. So I paddled around for years, and I never knew quite how to use them....I would crop them severely, but I felt that I was losing their ugly yet perfect quality. So when I was doing *Buildings = Guns = People: Desire, Knowledge, and Hope (With Smog)*, I think on the one hand I was a little bit worried about using someone's face, as I did not want to get sued, and I didn't know exactly where these photographs were coming from, so I used stickers I had lying around to obliterate the faces; and I felt so good I just kept on doing it.

*Repair/Retouch Series: An Allegory About Wholeness (Plate and Man with Crutches)*, 1976
Four black-and-white photographs; mounted on board
15 x 24 in. overall
(38.1 x 61 cm)
Collection of Gilbert and Lila Silverman, Detroit

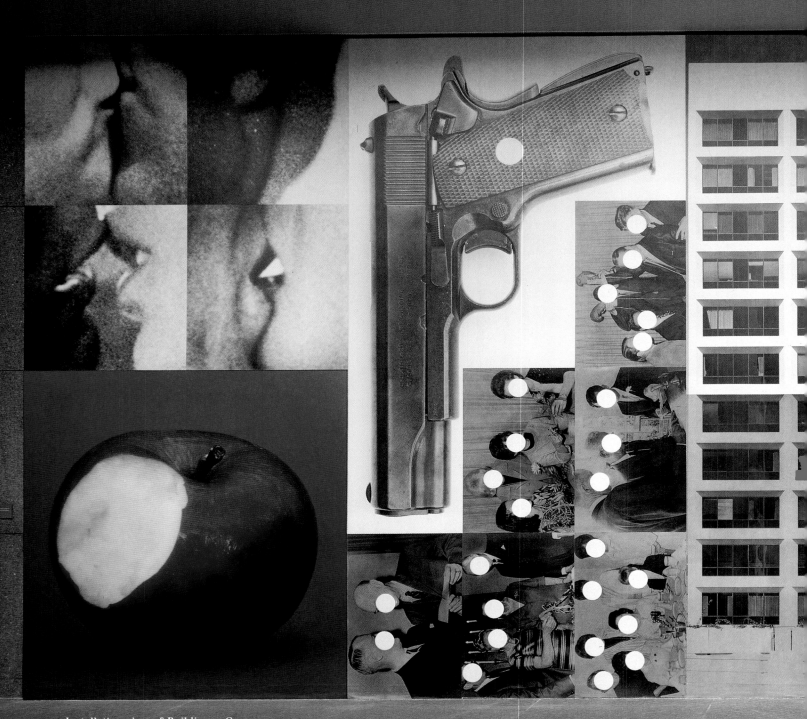

Installation view of *Buildings = Guns
= People: Desire, Knowledge, and Hope
(With Smog)*, 1985
Black-and-white and color
photographs
Installation at The 1985 Carnegie
International, The Carnegie Museum
of Art, Pittsburgh
192 x 450 in. overall (487.7 x 1,143 cm)
The Eli Broad Family Foundation

*Violent Space Series: Nine Feet (Of Victim and Crowd) Arranged by Position in Scene*, 1976
Black-and-white photographs; mounted on board
24⅜ x 36½ in. overall (61.9 x 92.7 cm)
Collection of Robert H. Halff

The blotting out of the faces in *Civic Piece*, 1986, lends it a dreamlike quality—bystanders in our dreams often have no faces. The effect recalls a remark by Hildebrandt that Freud quotes in *The Interpretation of Dreams*, pointing out how in our sleep we can switch the emphasis of our attention from upsetting events to trivial details whose origins are hard to trace: "A family bereavement, which has moved us deeply and under whose immediate shadow we have fallen asleep late at night, is blotted out of our memory till with our first waking moment it returns to it again with disturbing violence. On the other hand, a wart on the forehead of a stranger whom we met in the street and to whom we gave no second thought after passing him *has* a part to play in our dream"[11] By blotting out the faces in *Civic Piece* and later works, Baldessari shifts the emphasis from the identification of individuals to that of generic types. At the same time, the focus of the image moves from its human agents to every other detail initially overlooked—from gavels to trophies to ties to flowers to hairdos, and on and on.

*The complete title explains the piece. What is given is the exclusion of the pertinent information (what emotion is registered on the people's faces, body posture, etc.). What is seen is minimal. Feet in two positional binary signals— down for spectator, up for victim.*

*In later work, crucial information (the face as mirror to the ego) is again missing. It's like a professional killer obliterating the victim's fingerprints.*

*Information is withheld to allow for reader response, and to force the spectator out of conventional modes of perception and information gathering/ interpreting.*

*Civic Piece*, 1986
Black-and-white photographs with oil
tint and gouache; mounted on board
106¾ x 72½ in. overall (271.2 x 184.2 cm)
Collection of Lenore S. and Bernard A.
Greenberg

*Banquet*, 1988
Black-and-white photographs with
vinyl paint; mounted on board
73¼ x 144½ in. overall (186.1 x 367 cm)
Courtesy of Brooke Alexander, New
York

This concentration on attributes rather than on the persons they belong to, begun in the *Vanitas Series* and inventively employed in *Sailing and Tennis*, returns prominently in *Banquet*, 1988. To obtain the image of the man with the red guitar in *Yellow Harmonica (With Turn)*, Baldessari had cropped a larger photograph, cutting out a part of the picture that dealt with a dinner-table setting. Later he became intrigued with the ordinariness of this rejected material, so much in tune with the random, disorderly quality of life, and it inspired him to do a work on this theme. In a sense it reminded him of *The Pencil Story*, 1972–73, his piece showing a sharpened and a dull pencil, although he saw eating as much more fundamental an action than writing. In *Banquet*, Baldessari wanted to combine the representation of a basic need with a powerful emotion. The arrangement of images he devised has a symmetry and order recalling the ritual of official banquets, and at the top a trinity of utensils—spoon, knife, and fork, colored respectively red, yellow, and blue—evokes religious overtones. The artist chose utensils because of their active role; vessels such as plates, cups, and saucers seemed too passive. "It's this idea of choice, for me, and direction, embodied in which one to pick up first. The fork seems a better instrument in terms of selection, but I am also aware that it is a very phallic instrument at the same time. I don't like that so much, but those are the things that come up. Secrets of life might be in very common things." The other images in *Banquet* focus on different table arrangements, or on food itself, and on the gestures of the dinner guests, whose identities are always obscured—their heads are either cropped out or filled in as dark shapes, making the food stand out even more prominently.

In *Civic Piece*, too, Baldessari obliterates the faces of his characters, developing a panoramic landscape with a rhythmic, abstract quality in its lights and darks, highlighted by the white dots. The shape of a rock outcropping in the center of the piece, emphatically colored in green, is echoed by the similar shape of a river, blocked out as a bright white abstract form, in the image below like the missing shard in a Greek vase. These shapes are made the focal point of the composition, breaking up the conventional surface, and enhancing each other as opposites, positive and negative. By coloring the outcropping green rather than a realistic earth tone, Baldessari evokes an "antiworld": "All of a sudden it no longer looked like something that had been

naturally there for eons and eons, but more like a sudden growth form. I wanted it to look very strange, and miraculous and wonderful." In his *Pathetic Fallacy Series*, 1975 (the title is borrowed from John Ruskin), the artist had already ascribed emotional states to inanimate objects, pointing out the absurd flaws in this practice through the literalness of his approach. "Characteristic of this series is a cycle of working that seems to prevail in most of my work, beginning rather ordinarily (*Happy Sky*, and *Happy Landscape; Sad Landscape*), become more adventurous (*Glowering Hair*), and moving to a point where I feel the level of energy is high (*Venial Tongue; Venal Tongue*)."[12] The correspondence between shades of color and human feelings had been the subject of another "pathetic fallacy," *Stoic Peach* and *Injured Yellow*, in which the artist had shown an actress different colors while recording her reactions to them; through double exposure and printing, he then embedded the facial expression in its corresponding color image. Similarly, in the 1980s, he began to introduce color so as to amplify the psychological meaning of the black-and-white movie stills: "Artists can talk about, let's say, an 'angry red,' or a 'peaceful green.' "

Baldessari continued the idea of the *Pathetic Fallacy Series* in the composite photoworks by looking at the habit people have in social situations of making assumptions about others. The comment, for instance, when a newcomer walks into the room may be "Oh, here comes trouble. We don't know at all if that person really is 'trouble'; we may think we know, but actually we just assume." Baldessari explored experiences like these by applying colored disks, signifying different personality types, to the figures in his black-and-white stills, sometimes working in contradiction to an obvious characterization:

Say I'll put yellow on a man, standing for some arbitrary sort of madness, but in fact he might be a nice stable sort of guy, even boring. I'm saying I want you to think of this guy, despite the way he looks, as somebody very chancy and chaotic. Or this letter she is laughing at in *Heel* might be something really upsetting and chaotic, but I want you to think through my color indication of blue that it is very beautiful, idyllic, and safe, something of the platonic ideal we aspire to. Orange I have been using as a sort of wild card.... It can mean whatever I want it to mean, but in the area of danger, for I use it always as an antithesis to blue, the flip side of the coin.

Baldessari's color-code system began with the identification of red as dangerous and its complement, green, as safe or "pastoral.'" The system provided him with a way to translate words and music into visual information as, for example, in *Composition for Violin and Voices (Male)*, a site-specific installation he made for the Centre National d'Art Contemporain in Grenoble, in May 1987. Struck by the immense space of the museum, a former factory, originally designed by the Eiffel studio for the manufacture of conduit pipes and prominently featuring a curved wall, Baldessari at first planned an installation that would "orchestrate" the total space by using old photographs of the factory. He eventually rejected this idea, however, because his lingering association of the conduit pipes with Magritte's notorious sentence *"Ceci n'est pas une pipe"*; he did not want to get involved in art about art. Next, he noticed that the walls were divided into three segments, which made him think of one of his earlier works, *Songs*. This association gave him the idea of using a musical metaphor as a device to orchestrate theatrical emotions as images of stress coded green, blue, and yellow. The device recalled not only *Six Colorful Stories*, which uses color rectangles to express different emotional states and personality types, but also *Violent Space Series: Five Vignetted Portraits of Stress Situations*, 1976, in which the grimacing faces of five people are vignetted and treated like traditional mantelpiece photographs (although tinted violet, as a pun on "violent," instead of sepia).

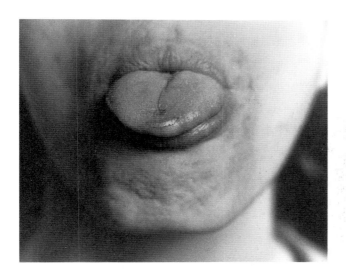

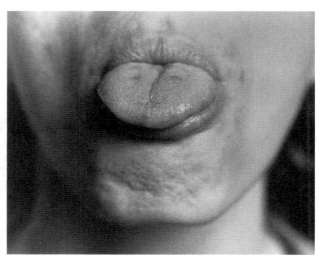

*Pathetic Fallacy Series: Venial Tongue;*
*Venal Tongue*, 1975
Two black-and-white photographs;
mounted on board
16 x 20 in. each (40.6 x 50.8 cm)
Collection of Dr. Jack E. Chachkes,
New York

*Pathetic Fallacy Series: Stoic Peach,*
1975
Type-C print; mounted on board
11 x 11 in. (27.9 x 27.9 cm)
Collection of the artist

*Pathetic Fallacy Series: Injured Yellow,*
1975
Type-C print; mounted on board
11 x 11 in. (27.9 x 27.9 cm)
Collection of the artist

*Two Languages (Begin)*, 1989
Black-and-white photographs with
vinyl paint; mounted on board and
plastic
109 x 115 in. overall (276.9 x 292.1 cm)
Collection of Emily Fisher Landau

*Composition for Violin and Voices
(Male)*, 1987
Black-and-white photographs with
oil tint
Installation at MAGASIN, Centre
National d'Art Contemporain,
Grenoble
Museum of Contemporary Art, Lyons

*Both* Two Languages (Begin) *and*
Composition for Violin and Voices
(Male) *are specifically formed on that
moment* before *the music begins, or in
a wider context, that moment of
decision before an action that excludes
all other actions.*

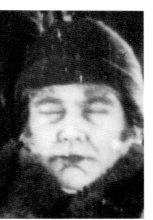

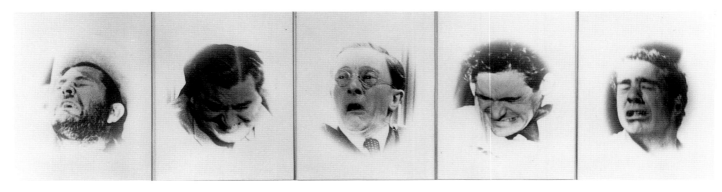

*Violent Space Series: Five Vignetted
Portraits of Stress Situations*, 1976
Five black-and-white photographs;
mounted on board
11 x 13⅞ in. each (27.9 x 35.2 cm)
Collection of Mr. and Mrs. Bing
Wright

For the long walls on either side of the factory
space, Baldessari selected a series of photographs of
male faces expressing a range of emotions from joy
to terror. He tinted some of these photographs, either
to underscore or to contradict the facial expressions
in them—a solacing minister and a bored office
worker, for example, were both colored a crazed
yellow, while a man with a threatening expression on
his face was assigned an idyllic blue. The distances
between the portraits were determined intuitively,
but the arrangement was defined by the figures'
ricocheting glances upward, across, forward, down,
etc. [a method of grouping Baldessari first employed
in *A Movie: Directional Piece (Where People Are
Looking)*, 1972–73]. This series of male faces,
arranged like the pages of a musical score, was
complemented by a picture of a violin, an instrument
associated with schmaltz as well as with sincere
emotions. The violin was hung on a curving wall,
which its curvilinear shape perfectly suited. Its bow,
hung on the wall behind, had been printed in
negative to create a visual tension for the viewer
trying to relate the two parts of the instrument to
each other.

Baldessari had set up a situation of people staring
at one another from a distance in an earlier
installation, for the Vleeshal in Middelburg, in 1985.

To see the work, which was entitled *Space Between
(24 Photographs of Middelburg Residents)*, the viewer
walked between two rows of passport-type
photographs in the former meat-packing hall, which
featured portraits of women on one side and of men
on the other, thus breaking the pattern of gazes
created by the portraits staring at one another across
the hall. An antecedent of this installation was *Man
and Woman with Bridge*, made in 1984 and re-
created, temporarily, as a billboard in downtown
Minneapolis a year later. In that work the preverbal,
instinctive communication between man and woman
is symbolized by a fox crossing a log that bridged two
precipices. In later works such as *Spaces Between*,
1984, *Spaces Between (One Risky)*, 1986, and *Exterior
Views*, 1986, Baldessari omitted the bridge, or
replaced it with a white beam. The subject of spaces
between again becomes a matter of apartness-
togetherness: "People apart, either by attraction or
repulsion. The subject is the space between, the
magnetic field created by the peripheral poles. A way
to scrutinize relationships." What is featured is not
the moment of two people being together—a moment
of arrested motion—but the moment of their implied
intention to be together, injecting new life and
intensity into the stills.

198

*Space Between (24 Photographs of Middelburg Residents)*, 1985
Black-and-white photographs;
mounted on board
Installation at Vleeshal, Middelburg,
the Netherlands

*Man and Woman with Bridge*, 1984
Collage of black-and-white
photographs; mounted on board
14½ x 48 in. overall (36.8 x 121.9 cm)
Collection of Elisabeth and Ealan
Wingate

Installation of the billboard *Man and
Woman with Bridge* in Minneapolis,
May 31–August 31, 1985, as part of the
"Artside Out" exhibition sponsored by
Film in the Cities and First Banks

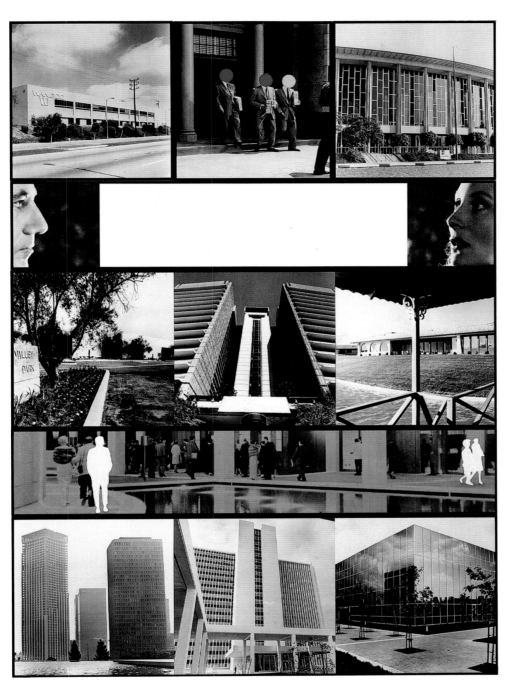

*Exterior Views*, 1986
Black-and-white photographs with oil
tint, acrylic, and board; mounted on
board
101½ x 72½ in. overall (257.8 x 184.2 cm)
The Capital Group, Inc., Los Angeles

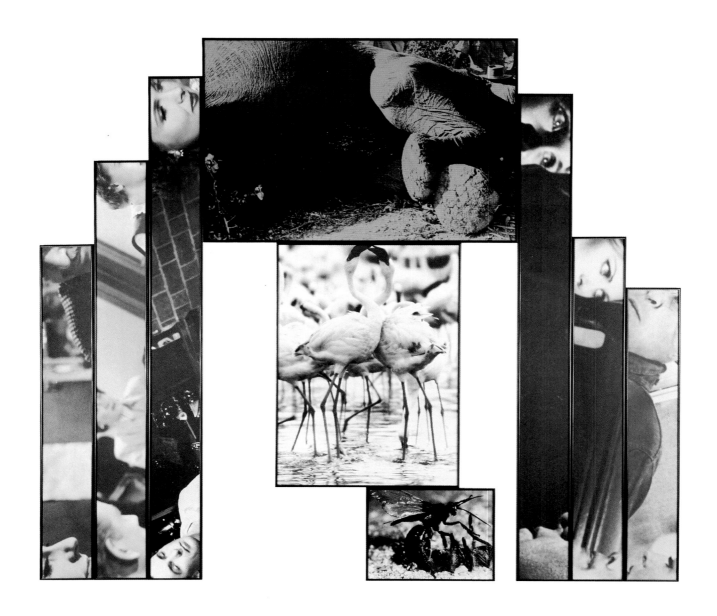

*Elephant Weight (Blue)*, 1986
Black-and-white photographs with oil
tint; mounted on board
64¾ x 73½ in. overall (164.5 x 186.7 cm)
Collection of Isabella del Frate
Rayburn, New York

The theme of human yearnings failing to connect returns in *Elephant Weight (Blue)*, 1986. In the side panels of the piece, men and women gaze at one another, longing to interact but keeping aloof. The isolation of one person in the presence of others is reinforced by the central panel, which comprises three images showing animals secluded within their own worlds. A felled elephant at the top hovers between life and death, confronting the viewer with a sense of loss, while at the same time the blue color that Baldessari has tinted it suggests a Platonic ideal, an attempt by the artist to resurrect the power of myth. In yet another Freudian dream reversal, the lightest supports the heaviest: the reclining elephant presses down on an image of a flock of flamingos, itself supported by two minute winged ants. *Elephant Weight (Blue)* relates to another work of 1986, *Giraffe Weight*, in which a giraffe lying on its back is flanked by two custodians—one coded a safe green and another coded dangerous red, respectively, to represent, in Baldessari's terms "world and antiworld." The vulnerability of the stately animal, off its legs, is accentuated by a rhythmic outline in blue, at once a transcendent arabesque and, in its association with a police outline of a victim drawn on the pavement, a sign of sadness, loss, and death. Yet the ambiguous image also suggests that the giraffe may still be alive. In *Elephant Weight (Blue)* and *Giraffe Weight*, rudimentary, disconnected human contact is pitted against the integral, primal state of noble but endangered animals.

In *Fish and Ram*, 1988, Baldessari zeros in on animals, because that's "where my sympathies lie. You know, I'm cutting out the people." In this work a red line, like the line on a graph, winds through a conventional woman-as-sex-object image—a woman wearing a fur. After coursing through a photograph of a group of stock-market executives, the graph line becomes dynamic, running through a figure wielding a whip as well as his victim being whipped. But this moment of erupting violence—which, accentuated by a yellow disk covering the head of the figure being whipped, threatens to extend into uncontrollable madness—is arrested by yet another image of domesticated, collective male bonding, a photograph of soldiers in formation. As Baldessari remarks, "I'm simplifying with these lines, but also aestheticizing, and I'm playing them against the rigidity of the frame as well. I'm turning a very violent situation into an aesthetic situation. I like that contrast of the beautiful against the violent. And in the surrounding panels I'm talking about a sort of social regimentation." The work contrasts the rational world of man gone amok with the instinctual wisdom of the animals in the work's two topmost color images, a fish and a ram, majestic but subjected to human cruelty—hunted. "I invest animals with the idea of some sort of truth. Animals always seem much wiser than people."

*Giraffe Weight*, 1986
Black-and-white photographs with
acrylic and oil stick; mounted on
board
71¾ x 49¾ in. overall (182.3 x 126.4 cm)
Collection of Thomas and Shirley
Davis

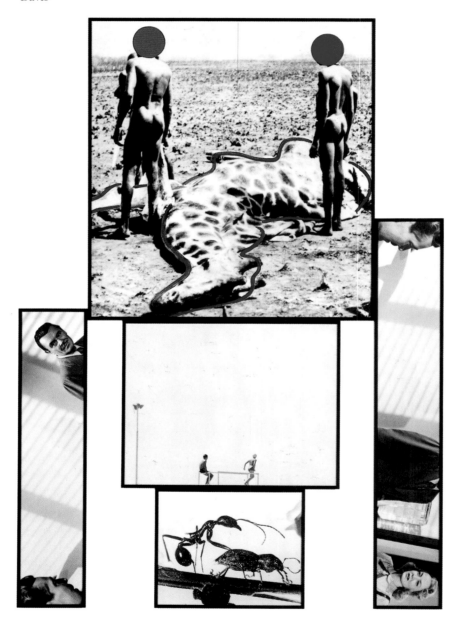

*Fish and Ram*, 1988
Black-and-white and color
photographs with vinyl paint; mounted
on board
109¾ x 144¼ in. overall (278.8 x 366.4 cm)
Museum of Contemporary Art,
Chicago; Museum Purchase with
funds from Gerald S. Elliott and the
National Endowment for the Arts

Baldessari again juxtaposes the organic forces of nature with man's attempt to control it through regimentation. Images of athletes, mythical animals, and herds and crowds in different groupings—from packs of hunters, Indian phalanxes, and columns of soldiers to army parades—appear in works such as *Stroll*, *That Is*, *Ribbon*, and *Lighthouse*, all from 1986; *Bowl (With Two Voices)*, *Inverse (Brackets)*, *Minerva (With Old and New Truths)*, and *Mary*, from 1987; and *Two Fish*, 1988.

*Elephant Weight (Blue)*, *Giraffe Weight*, and *Fish and Ram* all contain memory traces of an intense dream Baldessari had during a flight back from Europe in 1984. He recalls dreaming "I was walking along a path through the darkness of a dense jungle of big trees, with vines hanging down from them. Ahead of me, at the far end of the path, yet close enough to be distinguishable and glistening in the light, appeared a deep blue gorilla. Approaching the animal, I said to myself, 'but that's very strange,' when I realized that its coat wasn't furry but feathery, as shiny and beautiful as the tail of a peacock."

In an interview, Baldessari traced the blue gorilla dream to two previous experiences far apart in time. The more recent event took place in 1967, at a party of the College Art Association that the artist attended: "I recall standing talking to other guests when a woman entered dressed in an exotic and colorful feather coat. I was instantly attracted to her, but the feelings of romance soon turned into disappointment, for I never got to speak to her." The second experience had to do with the artist's father, from whom he felt alienated, owing not only to an age difference of about 50 years but also the sense of cultural divide felt by many American-born children of European parents.

*Stroll*, 1986
Black-and-white photographs with oil tint, vinyl paint, and board; mounted on board
61 x 72½ in. overall (154.9 x 184.2 cm)
Collection of Linda and James Burrows, Los Angeles

*Ribbon*, 1986
Black-and-white photographs with oil
tint and vinyl paint; mounted on board
72¾ x 48½ in. (184.8 x 123.2 cm)
Collection of Ursula Kalish, New York

*That Is*, 1986
Black-and-white photographs with oil
tint, sepia tone, vinyl paint, gouache,
and board; mounted on board;
88½ x 77⅛ in. overall (224.8 x 195.9 cm)
The Carnegie Museum of Art,
Pittsburgh; Patrons Art Fund

*Lighthouse*, 1986
Black-and-white photographs with
vinyl paint; mounted on board
72½ x 47½ in. overall (184.2 x 120.7 cm)
Collection of Bob and Linda Gersh,
Los Angeles

*Minerva (With Old and New Truths)*,
1987
Black-and-white photographs with oil
tint and acrylic; mounted on board
92¼ x 48½ in. overall (234.3 x 123.2 cm)
The Museum of Fine Arts, Houston;
Museum Purchase with funds
provided by Agnes Cullen Arnold
Endowment Fund

*Inverse (Brackets)*, 1987
Black-and-white photographs;
mounted on board
64¼ x 48 in. overall (163.2 x 121.9 cm)
Private collection, courtesy of
Sonnabend Gallery, New York

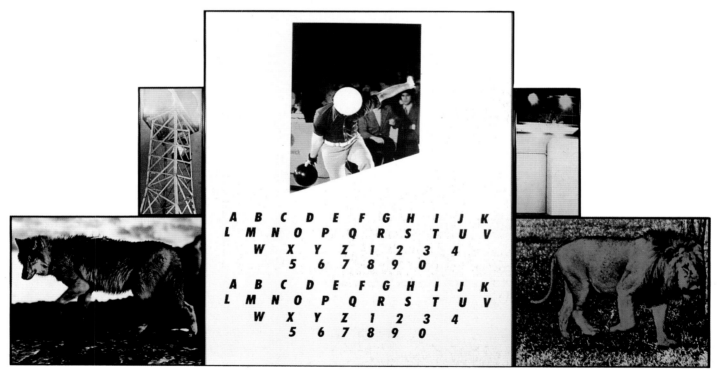

*Bowl (With Two Voices)*, 1987
Black-and-white photographs with oil
tint; mounted on board
57½ x 108⅝ in. overall (146.1 x 275.9 cm)
Collection of Dolores and Herbert
Goldsmith, New York

*Mary*, 1987
Black-and-white and color
photographs with vinyl paint, and
marker; mounted on board
48¼ x 80½ in. overall (122.6 x 204.7 cm)
Private collection, courtesy of
Sonnabend Gallery, New York

*Two Fish*, 1988
Black-and-white and color
photographs with oil tint and vinyl
paint; mounted on board
84¼ x 48½ in. overall (214 x 123.2 cm)
Collection of Laura-Lee W. Woods

Reminiscing about his youth, Baldessari suddenly remembered an exceptional moment when his father, who usually wore old clothes, at the urging of his wife bought a brand new suit. Every Sunday Antonio would wear the new suit to mass, but he covered it up with an old overcoat, so that nobody could see this sign of his new prosperity. To Baldessari this event seemed of importance to the blue gorilla dream, in which the seductive blue creature to which he felt strongly drawn from a distance turned out to be up close a dangerous "gorilla"—also a slang word for a thug, someone who harms other people.

The blue gorilla dream and the recollection it triggered show Baldessari's distrust of appearances. The worn-out may conceal the brand new, cheapness expensiveness, and Beauty the Beast. And to the artist the pursuit of beauty is indissolubly connected to a fear of pain caused by loss of the ideal, a wariness repeatedly suggested in the many composite photoworks depicting men and women longing to communicate but at the same time remote in their insularity. A similar mood is transferred into *Elephant Weight (Blue)*, *Giraffe Weight*, and *Fish and Ram*, in which the artist identifies with the threatened animal species: "Knowing that I stood out from the crowd as a child hurt me. I became an outsider rather than an insider. I was not normal, a too large baby, so the elephant man I understood well." And this sense of personal loss expands into the unspeakable terror of collective loss in *Inventory*, 1987, which embodies the complete estrangement and absence of human ethics by placing side by side a photograph of supermarket commodities and a carload of the stacked, emaciated corpses of concentration camp victims.

*Horizontal Men*, 1984
Black-and-white photographs;
mounted on board
97¼ x 48⅝ in. overall (247 x 123.5 cm)
Frederick R. Weisman Art Foundation

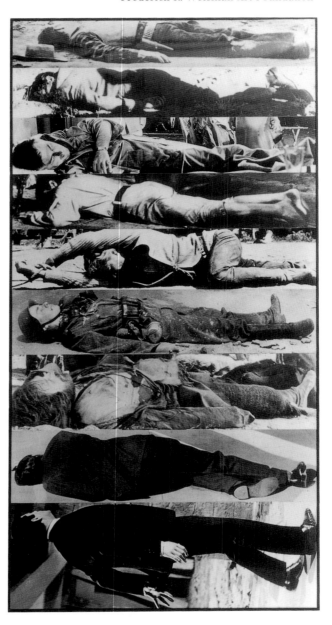

*This work was inspired by seeing images of stacked corpses in Nazi concentration camps. It was the obverse of man vertical—the measure of things. Man horizontal is a vulnerable alternative to man powerful and priapic.*

*Inventory*, 1987
Black-and-white and color
photographs with vinyl paint; mounted
on board and masonite
97 x 97½ in. overall (246.4 x 247.7 cm)
Collection of the artist

*Rolling:Tire*, 1972
Six black-and-white photographs;
mounted on board
Five: 16 x 24 in.; one 6½ x 10 in. (40.6
x 61; 16.5 x 25.4 cm)
Courtesy of Sonnabend Gallery, New
York

"For most of us photography stands for the truth,"
Baldessari has said. "But a good artist can make a
harder truth by manipulating forms or pushing paint
around. It fascinates me how I can manipulate the
truth so easily by the way I juxtapose opposites or
crop the image or take it out of context. When two
forces contend in a photograph, I may favor one side
or the other—the rider or the horse, for example, the
upright mummy in its coffin or the woman standing
in awe next to it. Cropping can make the outcome of
a struggle ambiguous." And it is precisely the
ambiguity between true fiction and unlikely
reportage that Baldessari was after in his first violent
tale, *Rolling: Tire*, 1972, which had as its subject a
black tire rolling down a hill. The work began with a
news story in the *Los Angeles Times* of May 22, 1972,
reporting an event that seemed so curious, so nearly
surreal, that the artist decided to save the clipping:
"A free-rolling truck tire struck and killed a
pedestrian in Delano, according to the California
Highway Patrol. As Francisco Ramirez, 30, drove
north on California 99, a tire came off his truck,
crossed the north and southbound lanes, and hit Don
Edwin Yarbrough, 21, of Denton, Tex. the C.H.P. said.
Yarbrough was reported dead at the scene." This
distressing news account could be an event in a
folktale. In retrospect, Baldessari commented, "We
tend to live too much with our heads. A thing, for
instance a garbage can, has no life. I know that it is
only a receptacle, but I also think of a garbage can as
having a life. Anything around me can be invested
with lifelike characteristics."

Shortly after the appearance of the news story Baldessari took his students, equipped with still and video cameras, on a field trip to assemble "raw material" just outside the California Institute of the Arts. A stick was thrown back and forth, an activity Baldessari recorded by taking snapshots, and later transformed into two works: *Floating: Stick (Two Figures; Two Choices, One Framing)*, 1972, and *Floating: Stick (With Two Figures to Get Various Triangles)*, 1972–73. He recalls that an old car tire found on the site was rolled up a hill and down again by the artist Matt Mullican, at that time one of his students. The conception and staging of such simple actions lead straight back to Baldessari's childhood: as a child, he was already more interested in ordinary subjects than in fanciful events, as when he drew a man on a stepladder, for example, sawing off fronds from a palm tree he had observed on his way to school. But in the case of the tire, this naive playfulness was replaced by a foreboding, sardonic frame of mind. Combining the newspaper clipping with five black-and-white snapshots of the rolling tire, Baldessari loaded the object with psychological meaning, pointing out that what may start out as a perfectly innocent activity can reverse itself, through a dramatic turn of fate, into a lethal accident—a nightmare come true.

**A free-rolling truck tire** struck and killed a pedestrian in Delano, according to the California Highway Patrol. As Francisco Ramirez, 30, drove north on California 99, a tire came off his truck, crossed the north and southbound lanes, and hit Don Edwin Yarbrough, 21, of Denton, Tex., the CHP said. Yarbrough was reported dead at the scene.

*Floating: Stick (With Two Figures: To Get Various Triangles)* (details), 1972
Ten black-and-white photographs with ink; mounted on board
13⅞ x 9½ in. each (35.2 x 24.1 cm)
Emanuel Hoffmann-Stiftung, Museum für Gegenwartskunst, Basel

In 1973, the subject of violence and its turning point from fiction into reality and vice versa reappeared in *The Movie Tree Story*. Like *Rolling: Tire*, this piece focuses on an action in itself, in this case the path of a flood, a force of nature running catastrophically out of control. Baldessari has always been fascinated by natural or man-made disasters such as tornadoes, earthquakes, sinking ships, stock-market crashes, and particularly since *Rolling: Tire*, he has been intrigued by the complex phenomena of order and chaos, questioning the appearance of chaos within order, while trying to discover its hidden geometric regularity. In his book *Chaos: Making a New Science*, James Gleick writes that "chaos was the end of the reductionist program in science." For Baldessari the inclusion of chaos and randomness in his work was essential in steering him away from Minimalism. Complexity itself had to be understood: as Gleick states, "Simple systems give rise to complex behavior. Complex systems give rise to simple behavior. And most important, the laws of complexity hold universally, caring not at all for the details of a system's constituent atoms."[13] For Baldessari, civilization is only a thin veneer over a chaos that may erupt at any moment, and yet, there is his fascination with the idea that, in the words of Douglas Hofstadter, "Deep inside the chaos lurks an even eerier type of order."

*The Movie Tree Story* combines newsreel photographs of a flood with a text describing a similar disaster—this time artificially staged—that Baldessari witnessed during a visit he made with his students to Universal Studios in Los Angeles.[14] This mixture of fictional and factual events blurs the distinctions between natural and man-made, between uncontrollable and regulated chaos. On one hand, the simulation of a catastrophe suggests a ritual of enacting a tragedy in order to prevent it; on the other, the freezing of nature's forces in time and space, the reversal of their course by a Hollywood *deus ex machina*, satisfies the human desire to control one's destiny. The ill-fitting combination of verisimilitude and imagination in *The Movie Tree Story* causes real and fabricated disasters to collide. It raises the question of whether the actual photographs of disasters could have been staged; but then that may not matter, for, as the German poet Friedrich von Schiller wrote, "Deeper meaning lies in the fairy tale of my childhood than in the truth that is taught by life."[15]

At Universal Movie Studios in Los Angeles, one can take a tram tour throughout the lots. The tram goes through sets that look like London, Italy, Early America, and so on. Just after the tram goes through the Mexican town it travels down a hill and stops suddenly. The guide points to the top of the hill where gates have been opened and a flood of water comes rushing down the hill toward the tram. It is a device that is used to artificially create floods for Biblical movies. In the path of the torrent of water that comes down the hill is a giant tree. The force of the water bends the tree over slowly. It leans more and more until it appears as if it might topple over onto the tram. At the precise moment that it might crash upon the tram, its movement halts, and the tree reverses its direction and moves back to its original upright position. Like the flood it also was artificial and only a movie prop.

*The Movie Tree Story,* an artist's project, published in *Festival d'Automne à Paris: Aspects de l'art Actuel, Présentés par la Galerie Sonnabend au Musée Galliera,* catalogue, published by Centro Di, Florence, 1973

Aware of the thin line between order and chaos, construction and demolition, and always seeking a different system of symbols to serve his emotional needs, in 1982 Baldessari, while trying to come up with a piece for Documenta 7, held in Kassel in Germany, the birthplace of the Brothers Grimm, hit upon the idea of re-creating six of their fairy tales, *Little Red Cap* (Little Red Riding Hood), *Fitcher's Bird, Ashputtle* (Cinderella), *The Three Feathers, The Frog King,* and *The Story of One Who Set Out To Study Fear.*

Fairy tales as collective concoctions, handed down in their ethnographic migration by generations of traditional storytellers in a never-ending process of reflection and permutation, engender a richness of complex meaning. They seemed a perfect subject to Baldessari, despite the fact that the natural fluidity of fairy tales is counterbalanced by the restriction of unvarying, inherited patterns, without which they would suffer a loss of identity. In order to spellbind the listeners, a good storyteller must memorize, vividly and accurately, the particular sequences of incidents, connections, and metaphors that build the tale. Moreover, as Joseph Campbell points out in his introduction to Grimm's fairy tales, "It was required of every artist, no matter what his craft, that his product should show its sign of the spirit, as well as serve its mechanical end. The function of the craft of the tale, therefore, was not simply to fill the vacant hour, but to fill it with symbolic fare. And since symbolization is the characteristic pleasure of the human mind, the fascination of the tale increased in proportion to the richness of its symbolic content."[16]

In the Grimm fairy tales Baldessari found one of those instances in contemporary life in which childhood and adulthood, as well as art and life, are still interwoven. He enjoyed the simplicity of the stories' language, their inventive layering and masking of the truth behind the surface, their focus not on style but on how to tell the tale sparely yet without a loss of local color. The combination of economical form with complexity of content that lends the fairy tale its magical power reminded him of the spirituality and natural simplicity of Henri Matisse, especially of that artist's ability to bring out the "sign"—what the painter called "the briefest possible indication of the character of a thing." The Grimm fairy tales suited Baldessari so well because of their quality of being sad, troubling, but not explained. "I kept thinking of them, but had no right answers." Most of all, he was fascinated by the adventurous combination of attraction and fear in the fairy tale, which he found so like a child's reliance on his or her instincts: "Without any hesitation, a child will draw off the edge of the paper right onto the desk, while the adult, in the knowledge of boundaries, will draw within the page." It was precisely Baldessari's responsiveness to the naive quality preserved in the fairy tale that made him reluctant to concentrate solely on the cerebral game plans of the adult world, and so appreciative of Claes Oldenburg's ironic boast, "Everything I do is completely original—I made it up when I was a little kid."[17] Baldessari and Oldenburg, each in their own way, are after the child's sure aim, which releases tension, causes bewilderment, but achieves illumination, much in the way that wit does—an altogether different use of intelligence.

Catering to the child's daydream fantasies, the Grimm tales describe events in bold outlines and lend themselves well to transformation into symbolic images. Baldessari transformed key events of each tale into compositions consisting of eleven black-and-white, rectangularly cropped movie stills complemented by one color snapshot, all organized in rows of three. In each of the six works the color snapshot is set just off center and acts in the midst of the movie stills as a catalyst, with an instantaneous quality but at the same time having a summarizing function. The black-and-white stills, turned into stylized fragments through cropping, radiate meaning in many directions. They refer to their respective movies to which they once belonged in the way Roman Jakobson put it: "We can consider the perception of a film not only diachronically but also synchronically; however, the synchronic aspect of a film is not identical to an isolated image extracted from the film."[18] While, in their cropping and storyboard composition, the movie-still fragments have become integral parts of the six familiar Brothers Grimm fairy tales, enough signs are still present from their original context to make one aware of transitions from one context to another, resulting in intricate double meanings. By imparting to each tale the Hollywood glow of black-and-white movies—themselves a typologizing collective reflection on the world—the artist tapped into the stories' history of continuous re-creation. He chose to preserve their miscellaneous insights of aggregated wisdoms, and slanted their interpretation according to the fascinating insights the child psychologist Bruno Bettelheim displayed in his book *The Uses of Enchantment* about the meaning of fairy tales: "With the Grimm stories" the artist noted, "I took someone else's ideas, trying to make them workable for myself and the time I live in." But despite this emphasis on collective authorship, Baldessari also asserted his unique interest in rudimentary didactic devices: the color photographs that summarize each of the six stories like heraldic emblems; the ambivalent interpretations of the authority figure of the father in the tales; the exposure of weak links in the storylines, and the artist's own particular structural order and simplicity.

*The Story of One Who Set Out To Study Fear*, 1982
Eleven black-and-white photographs and one color photograph mounted on board, and text panel of acrylic on board
84 x 72 in. overall (213.4 x 182.9 cm)
The Sonnabend Collection

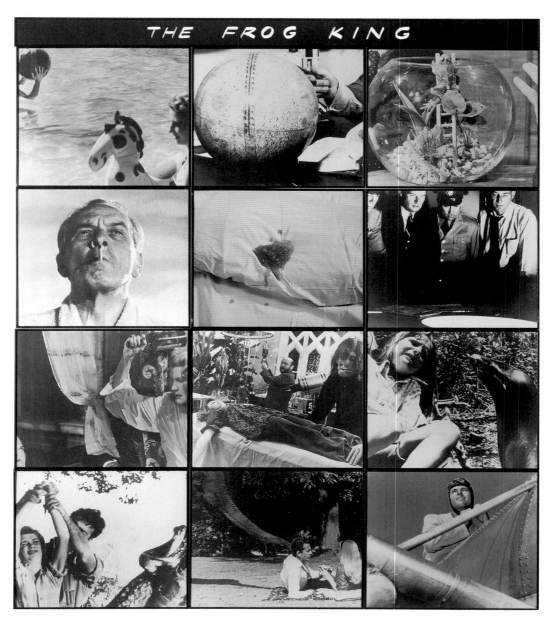

*The Frog King*, 1982
Eleven black-and-white photographs
and one color photograph mounted on
board, and text panel of acrylic on
board
84 x 72 in. overall (213.4 x 182.9 cm)
Collection of Charles and Barbara
Wright

*The Three Feathers*, 1982
Eleven black-and-white photographs
and one color photograph mounted on
board, and text panel of acrylic on
board
84 x 72 in. overall (213.4 x 182.9 cm)
Collection of Marvin and Elayne
Mordes, Baltimore, Maryland

*Ashputtle*, 1982
Eleven black-and-white photographs
and one color photograph mounted on
board, and text panel of acrylic on
board
84 x 72 in. overall (213.4 x 182.9 cm)
Whitney Museum of American Art,
New York; Purchase, with funds from
the Painting and Sculpture Committee

*Fitcher's Bird*, 1982
Eleven black-and-white photographs
and one color photograph mounted on
board, and text panel of acrylic on
board
84 x 72 in. overall (213.4 x 182.9 cm)
The Art Institute of Chicago; gift of
Auxiliary Board, 1984

223

*Little Red Cap*, 1982
Eleven black-and-white photographs
and one color photograph mounted on
board, and text panel of acrylic on
board
84 x 72 in. overall (213.4 x 182.9 cm)
Jedermann Collection, N.A.

An example is *Little Red Cap*, the well-known story of the young girl who always wore "a little cap of red velvet" her grandmother had given her. The tale is summed up in the cryptic, emblematic color snapshot that Baldessari constructed: a torn piece of red, silklike cloth caught in dense underbrush, setting a psychological tone of sexuality and violence. Bettelheim has pointed out that *Little Red Cap* takes up some crucial problems the school-age girl has to solve if oedipal attachments linger on in the unconscious, which may drive her to expose herself dangerously to the possibility of seduction."[19] Baldessari, too, takes as the theme of his story the young woman's dilemma of wavering between the pleasure and reality principles, and the threat she faces of regressing into the oceanic id symbolized by her devourment by the wolf, who turns out to be her seducer. Baldessari represents Red Cap first by the image of a young woman, then by one of a young man, an indication of the applicability of the dilemma to both sexes.

Source material for *Little Red Cap*, 1982

While the artist closely approaches and in some cases nearly paraphrases Bettelheim's interpretations of the original Brothers Grimm tales, on occasion he deviates from them, taking a far more ambivalent stand that not only blurs good and evil forces but also avoids a reduction of these stories to moralistic precautionary fables. The resulting open-endedness underscores the hermetic nature of the original tales, as well as Bettelheim's interpretation of them. In Baldessari's version of *Little Red Cap*, for instance, the wolf symbolizing the id does not confront, as the artist wrote in his notebooks, "the young woman innocently and sexually vulnerable walking along the path," but instead "the oedipal hunter/father figure" who points bow and arrow at him, ready to kill. The id force has become the defenseless one; the roles of aggressor and victim have been turned around. This idea is repeated in an image of two male hands opening up the mouth of a lion, in the artist's words a representation of "the trophy, a symbol of traditional maleness. Devourment is virtually tamed." On the other hand, the "tamed threat" is offset by a photograph of a tiger attacking a woman. Formally, this image echoes the shape of the hunter with his bow and arrow, implying an analogy with the beast. It represents ravishment by the seducer, to Baldessari, "the girl swallowed up by sexuality experienced as an act of violence." Elsewhere, primordial crocodiles slide in a river, becoming "a sea of repulsiveness, the seething, undifferentiated id."

This paradoxical ambivalence is reiterated throughout the work. Positioned next to the crocodiles is a fragment showing a man serving a plate of turkey, symbolizing the domestication of the indomitable id force into "tamed causality, sexuality made palatable." The image of the father figure "rescuing the girl from the fire of emotional life" seems in the same vein; yet the fire also symbolizes the dangers involved in the relationship of father and daughter. And the idea that the heroine herself is also not completely innocent and "pure" is supported by Baldessari's image of a man offering a ride to a girl dressed in a provocative slit skirt, representing "an invitation to seduction." In Baldessari's *Little Red Cap*, good and evil tend to reverse themselves in the character—even Grandmother is not exempt from from dark overtones. In, for example, the "innocent" scene of Grandmother cutting a roast while a young man, standing for Red Cap, looks on, along with the coziness and enticement of the mother figure, symbolizing "mature sexuality," a roast looms in the corner of the picture, symbol of "carnality." Instead of the bad wolf devouring Granny, the grandmother herself may turn out to be a wolf in sheep's clothing.

Baldessari's disclosure of ambiguous feelings about the grandmother figure recall Bettelheim's interpretation of the story:

Grandmother, too, is not free of blame. A young girl needs a strong mother figure for her own protection, and as a model to imitate. But Red Cap's grandmother is carried away by her own needs beyond what is good for the child, as we are told: "There was nothing she would not have given the child." It would not have been the first or last time that a child so spoiled by a grandmother turns into trouble in real life. Whether it is Mother or Grandmother—this mother once removed—it is fatal for the young girl if this older woman abdicates her own attractiveness to males and transfers it to the daughter by giving her a too attractive red cloak.[20]

Finally, the picture of a mountain cabin covered with snow, to Baldessari a representation of "the parental house as a refuge," and a "foil and contrast to the surrounding images of anxiety and fear," might at the same time lose its reading of "the secure and predictable," depending on whether one reads the cabin as the parental home or the grandmother's house in the woods. As Bettelheim points out, the latter connotes a quite different psychological situation: "In her own home Little Red Cap, protected by her parents, is the untroubled pubertal child who is quite competent to cope. But at the home of her grandmother, who is herself infirm, the same girl is helplessly incapacitated by the consequences of her encounter with the wolf."[21]

For child and adult alike, the fairy tale is a way to understand oneself, and to face the existential problems and inner conflicts of life. Bruno Bettelheim explains that when story elements trouble children emotionally they may spontaneously recall the story differently, by adding details, leaving out parts, or changing the original structure. "By doing this," Bettelheim writes, "the child fits unconscious content into conscious fantasies, which then enable him to deal with that content," and "the form and structure of fairy tales suggest images to the child by which he can structure his daydreams and with them give better direction to his life."[22] This procedure of changing the pattern of the fairy tale to accommodate his or her emotional needs relates to a dream Baldessari remembers using as a child to put himself to sleep. Instead of the commonly prescribed remedy of counting thousands of sheep jumping over a fence backward, as in a reversed film, he would imagine himself disassembling a bluish-silver aluminum airplane, "not a regular slender but a curvy fat one. The airplane never touched the ground, yet I don't recall it ever moving either. Looking down at the plane from a three-quarter viewpoint, in my curiosity about its smallest nut-and-bolt components, I was unable to resist the desire to dismantle it."

In retrospect, Baldessari attributes this urge to the fact that he used to build model airplanes, and often looked at "exploded" engineering drawings showing all the model's parts. However, in his dream he did not stop with the deconstruction and examination of the tiniest part of the machine, but retraced the entire process of manufacturing, following the parts back to their origin as raw aluminum in the mine. At the point at which the mineral had become reintegrated with the crust of the earth, he would start the process of building the airplane all over again. In prolonging the original childhood dream into puberty, Baldessari seems to have developed it into a recurrent daydream of sublimated masturbation, which then, through a concentration on the construction and deconstruction of the machine, shifted to a philosophical rumination on creativity, and to the opposition of life and death.

Baldessari's airplane dream may eventually be seen to contain many of the structural elements, disguises, and idiosyncratic patterns of his later activities as an artist, such as the inability to concentrate on the whole or to perceive all of one's body at once. In the works of the 1980s a blind spot or void returns in many forms, ingeniously preventing the composition from achieving completeness; this strategy aligns with Baldessari's insistence on the indissoluble connection between composition and decomposition, another element of his angle of perception detectable in the airplane dream. For him, it is the process that counts, and the end result is just one link in the constant spiraling of known and unknown. This spiral leads nowhere in particular. Thoreau stated the problem slightly differently in one of his journal entries: "The nearest approach to discovering what we are is in dreams. It is as hard to see one's self as to look backwards without turning around. And foolish are they that look in glasses with that intent."[23] Equally difficult must be the sublimation of the young adult's narcissistic dream-state into a truly creative act.

Baldessari the artist is the juggler or bricoleur: he patches, repositions, recontextualizes, and juxtaposes different components into a unit of opposites he finds palatable, until a glimpse of *his* truth emerges. Varying the original meanings of the six Grimm fairy tales according to his own insights in life, abandoning the unbearable perfection of "living happily ever after" for an imperfect but more human condition, Baldessari set up a paradox between what is imaginary and what is real. "The limitations of life can be stretched through fantasy, making it richer, while at the same time I bring in an element of reality, life as I understand it. And life being a continuous battle, I select the moment of the battle being waged. So you don't know the outcome, which is out of one's control anyway, when dumb chance comes along."

As early as 1972–73, Baldessari had set himself the impossible task of balancing order and chaos with *Throwing Four Balls in the Air to Get a Straight Line (Best of 36 Tries)* and *Throwing Three Balls in the Air to Get an Equilateral Triangle (Best of 36 Tries)*, continuing in 1974 with *Throwing Four Balls in the Air to Get a Square (Best of 36 Tries)*. In throwing curved and straight sticks in the air in the hope that they would create letterforms, or even words—he performed the ultimate exercise in wishful thinking. With the same improbability of success, Baldessari set out to juggle the open-ended images of *Little Red Cap* into one gestalt, that right configuration mirroring life. In the composite photoworks he eventually found his escape hatch by joining his Minimalist aesthetics with the styleless and gravity-defying structure of the dream. This was a powerful connection to make, since the fleeting quality of

daydreams and dreams accommodates itself well to a sense of life in flux. As Freud pointed out, the daydream of fantasy "carries in it traces both of the occasion which engendered it and of some past memory. So past, present and future are threaded, as it were, on the string of the wish that runs through them all."[24]

The series of six fairy tales anticipated the more personal and structurally sophisticated composite photoworks of the 1980s, for which Baldessari selected movie stills, dating mostly from the 1940s and 1950s, to accomplish neutrality. By making use of the magic chiaroscuro lighting of Hollywood—which in itself renders the black-and-white movie-still fragments an ideation and abstraction from real life—for Baldessari "Everything comes together in the right way. There is already a certain psychological tone. I can't express this in the right words: they are subject to rules which are not necessarily spelled out but which unite them, for instance the most favorable angle to film a person." And through their wealth of tangible, concrete detail, stereotypically mimicking reality, the fragments draw the viewer into a situation even larger than real life. Focusing not necessarily on the main action but on some unexpected chance effect in the background, Baldessari achieves a combination of convincing newsreellike reportage and fabrication, blurring truth and fiction. For him, the composite photoworks, simultaneously reverberating with subliminal personal meaning and communicating collective experience, satisfy both the Freudian pleasure principle and the reality principle of working within society. They fulfill a function, then, somewhere between dream and real life. Baldessari's method can be compared to the use of ready-made material described by Freud in his essay entitled "The Relation of the Poet to Day-Dreaming." Referring to "that class of imaginative work which must be recognized not as spontaneous production, but as a re-fashioning of ready-made material," Freud notes, "Here, too, the writer retains a certain amount of independence, which can express itself in the choice of material and in changes in the material chosen, which are often considerable. As far as it goes, this material is derived from the racial treasure-house of myths, legends and fairy tales."[25]

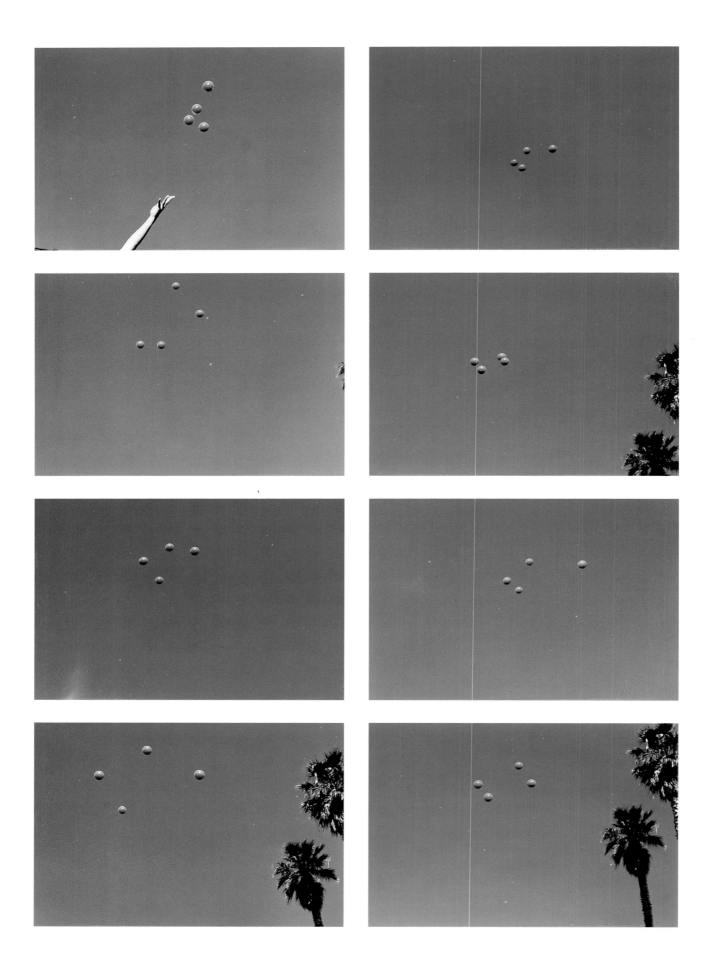

*Throwing Four Balls in the Air To Get
a Square (Best of 36 Tries)*, 1974
Eight color photographs; mounted on
board
9½ x 13¾ in. each (24.1 x 34.9 cm)
Emanuel Hoffmann-Stiftung, Museum
für Gegenwartskunst, Basel

Wilhelm Grimm, the indefatigable compiler of fairy
tales, wrote, "The mythic element resembles small
pieces of a shattered jewel which are lying strewn on
the ground all overgrown with grass and flowers, and
can only be discovered by the most far-seeing eye."[26]
Since their original sense is lost in time, such shards
of mythical hidden meaning, at once attractive and
repulsive, more often than not form the gruesome
and irrational details of the tales. And in their remote
inexplicability these shards may be compared to the
seemingly nonsensical components of dreams, which
similarly defy interpretation. The analogies between
dream images and the motifs of fairy tales connect
the latter directly to the psychoanalytic concerns of
our time, telescoping the past into the present. As
Campbell described it, "The folktale is the primer of
the picture-language of the soul."[27]

Just as the missing shards, long lost in time,
provide the fairy tales with an inexhaustible wealth
of meaning, and just as the dream defies a
reading of the whole through its displacement,
decontextualization, and alteration of specific
incidents of waking life, the composite photoworks,
subject to similar distortions, are only readable
through accidental correspondences of one
disjunctive fragment with the next. These distortions,
too, enable the artist, weary of the kind of art
"truths" that bore him in their correctness, to express
himself in allusions and hidden meanings, thus
creating the possibility of multiple interpretations.
The arbitrary, trivial details in the photographs
Baldessari inventively displays play the same role as
similar elements in dreams, distracting one from the
associations they would bear in their original
contexts, and becoming instead carriers of more
essential meanings. The dream as wish fulfillment and
the work of art that heightens sensuous aesthetic
pleasure both fulfill the function, in Freud's words,
of taking "the place of action, as elsewhere in life."[28]
Just as the dream distorts and disguises the sexual
factor of the dream-wish, making it manifest only as
latent content, the movie-still fragments allude to
erotic pleasure only through clever circumlocutions,
which Baldessari knows how to exploit.

The dream selects its elements from any and all
periods of the dreamer's life as long as it can connect
them to recent impressions through free association.
Baldessari makes similar use of "archetypal" movie
stills, both to remove himself in time and as a way to
communicate his own impressions and concerns: "I
guess I'm using images from movies, from
newspapers and so on, because there lies the
archpower of language. We can't sit down and talk in
Sanskrit, we have to talk in a language we know."
His approach recalls Freud's description of the
psychological novel: "The psychological novel in
general probably owes its peculiarities to the
tendency of modern writers to split up their ego by
self-observation into many component-egos, and in
this way to personify the conflicting trends in their
own mental life in many heroes."[29]

In the composite photoworks, John Baldessari
allows his ego to appear only in disguise and at a
distance as in a dream. He shows himself without
exposing himself, fulfilling his own wishes within a
conglomerate of motives and clues, which, even in
deciphering, inevitably lead to further interpretations.

## NOTES

1. Quoted in Hunter Drohojowska, *"No More Boring Art,"* *Artnews* 85, no. 1, January 1986, p. 67. Revised and reprinted from " 'I Will Not Make Any More Boring Art': A Profile of John Baldessari," *L.A. Weekly*, July 13–19, 1984, p. 21.
2. Ibid.
3. Quoted in *H. D. Thoreau: A Writer's Journal*, selected and edited with an introduction by Lawrence Stapleton, New York: Dover Publications, Inc., 1960, p. xii.
4. Thoreau, journal entry of April 27, 1841, in ibid., p. 6.
5. Buckminster Fuller, "The Bear Island Story," unpublished manuscript, n.d., p. 5.
6. Sigmund Freud, *The Interpretation of Dreams*, in *The Basic Writings of Sigmund Freud*, translated, edited, and with an introduction by A. A. Brill, New York: Modern Library, 1966, p. 315.
7. Ibid, pp. 345–46.
8. Charles Kligerman, *Art and the Self of the Artist*, in Arnold Goldberg, M.D., ed., *Advances in Self Psychology*, New York: International Universities Press, Inc., 1980, pp. 387–88.
9. *John Baldessari: Works 1966–1981*, Eindhoven: Van Abbemuseum, and Essen: Museum Folkwang, 1981, p. 24. Exhibition catalogue.
10. Ibid., p. 46.
11. Freud, *The Interpretation of Dreams*, trans. and ed. James Strachey, New York: Avon Books, 1965, p. 52. This section of the book is omitted in the Modern Library edition.
12. *John Baldessari: Works 1966–1981*, p. 34.
13. James Gleick, *Chaos: Making a New Science*, New York: Viking, 1987, p. 304.
14. First published in *Festival d'Automne: Aspects de l'art visuel*, catalogue for the Festival d' Automne, Florence: Editions Centro Di, September/October 1973.
15. Friedrich von Schiller, quoted in Joseph Campbell, "Folkloristic Commentary," in *The Complete Grimm's Fairy Tales*, New York: Pantheon Books, 1972, p. 835.
16. "Folkloristic Commentary," by Joseph Campbell in *The Complete Grimm's Fairy Tales*, p. 862.
17. Claes Oldenburg, quoted in *Claes Oldenburg: Skulpturer och techningar*, Stockholm: Moderna Museet, 1966, p. z (unpaginated).
18. Quoted in Claude Lévi-Strauss, *Structural Anthropology*, New York: Basic Books, Inc., 1963, p. 89.
19. Bruno Bettelheim, *The Uses of Enchantment: The Meaning and Importance of Fairy Tales*, New York: Vintage Books, 1977, p. 170.
20. Ibid., p. 173.
21. Ibid., p. 170.
22. Ibid., p. 7.
23. Thoreau, journal entry of April 27, 1841, p. 6.
24. Freud, "The Relation of the Poet to Day-Dreaming," 1908, in *Character and Culture*, New York: Collier Books, 1963, p. 38.
25. Freud, "The Relation of the Poet to Day-Dreaming," p. 42.
26. Quoted in Padraic Colum, "Introduction," in ibid., p. xiv.
27. "Folkloristic Commentary," by Joseph Campbell in *The Complete Grimm's Fairy Tales*, p. 864.
28. Freud, *The Interpretation of Dreams*, in A. A. Brill, p. 209.
29. Freud, "The Relation of the Poet to Day-Dreaming," p. 41.

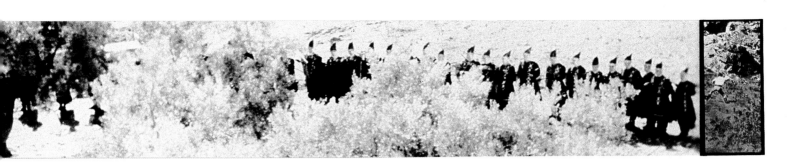

*Column (With Duelist)*, 1987
One black-and-white and two color
photographs; mounted on board and
aluminum
14 x 155⅝ in. overall (35.6 x 395.3 cm)
Olnick Organization, New York

**1931**
Born June 17, National City, California

**1949–53**
B.A., San Diego State College, California

**1954–55**
University of California at Berkeley

**1955**
University of California at Los Angeles

**1955–57**
M.A., San Diego State College, California

**1957–59**
Otis Art Institute, Los Angeles
Chouinard Art Institute, Los Angeles

# EXHIBITION HISTORY

*One- and Two-Person Exhibitions*

**1960**
Art Center in La Jolla, La Jolla, California, March 23–April 24.

**1962**
Art Works Galleries, San Diego, California, "John Baldessari: X Exhibition." June 29–July 19
Art Center in La Jolla, La Jolla, California, "Jazz at the Art Center #5." October 13. Brochure.
Southwestern College, Chula Vista, California.

**1964**
Extension Office, University of California at San Diego, La Jolla, California, "John Baldessari and Richard Allen Morris." June 22–August 14.
Southwestern College, Chula Vista, California.

**1966**
La Jolla Museum of Art, La Jolla, California, "John Baldessari: Fragments." March 30–April 24.

**1968**
Purcell Art Gallery, Chapman College, Santa Ana, California, "Wholes & A Sum of Parts." February 21–March 16.
Molly Barnes Gallery, Los Angeles, "John Baldessari: Pure Beauty." October 6–28.

**1970**
Eugenia Butler Gallery, Los Angeles, "John Baldessari." February 17–March 7.
Richard Feigen Gallery, New York. "John Baldessari: Recent Paintings." March 1–April 8.

**1971**
Nova Scotia College of Art and Design, Halifax, Nova Scotia, Canada, "John Baldessari: I Will Not Make Any More Boring Art." April 1–10.
Art & Project, Amsterdam, "John Baldessari: Art Disasters." July 3–15. Artist's project, *Bulletin 41: Art Disasters, John Baldessari, 1971*, in conjunction with exhibition.
Konrad Fischer, Düsseldorf, West Germany, "John Baldessari: Ingres and Other Parables." October 8–22.

**1972**
Galerie MTL, Brussels, Belgium, "John Baldessari: 1. Choosing: Mushrooms. 2. Xylophone (videotape)." April 4–May 15.
Jack Wendler Gallery, London, "John Baldessari: Video Tapes." April 7–21.
Galeria Franco Toselli, Milan, "John Baldessari: Choosing, Aligning, Floating." April.
Sonnabend Gallery, New York, "John Baldessari." April 28–May 12.
Galerie Sonnabend, Paris, "John Baldessari." May–June.
Galeria Schema, Florence, Italy, "John Baldessari." May 30–July 30.
Art & Project, Amsterdam, "John Baldessari: Choosing: Carrots; Asparagus." July 8–22.
Konrad Fischer, Düsseldorf, West Germany, "John Baldessari." August.
Galerie MTL, Brussels, Belgium, "John Baldessari." September.
Sperone/Fischer, Rome, "John Baldessari." October 10–November 7.

**1974**
Galeria Franco Toselli, Milan, "John Baldessari." April–May.
Jack Wendler Gallery, London, "John Baldessari." May 3–24.
Galerie MTL, Brussels, Belgium, "John Baldessari." September 2–26.
Art & Project/MTL, Antwerp, Belgium, "John Baldessari." September 17–October 19.
Galerie Skulima, Berlin, West Germany.

1975

Fine Art Gallery, University of California at Irvine, Irvine, California, "John Baldessari: Songs (1973)." January 7–February 9. Artist's book, *Throwing a Ball to Get Three Melodies and Fifteen Chords*, in conjunction with exhibition.

Samangallery, Genoa, Italy, "John Baldessari." March 21–April 8.

Felix Handschin, Basel, Switzerland, "John Baldessari." April.

The Kitchen, New York, "John Baldessari: The Italian Tape." April 8–12.

Southwestern College, Chula Vista, California, "John Baldessari." October 10–31.

Sonnabend Gallery, New York, "John Baldessari." October 4–November 12.

Stedelijk Museum, Amsterdam, "John Baldessari: Recent Work." November 22–January 4, 1976. Artist's book, *Four Events and Reactions*, in conjunction with exhibition, by Centro Di, Florence, Italy; and Galerie Sonnabend, Paris, 1975.

Galerie Sonnabend, Paris, "John Baldessari." November–December.

Lucio Amelio, Naples, Italy, "John Baldessari: Affectionate Yellow/Giallo Affezionato, Morbid Red/Rosso Morboso, Vindictive Blue/Azzurro Vendicativo." December.

Galerie MTL, Brussels, Belgium.

1976

Gallery of Fine Art, Ohio State University, Columbus, Ohio, "John Baldessari: Recent Work." February 2–14. Artist's book, *Brutus Killed Caesar*, in conjunction with exhibition and Sonnabend Gallery, New York, 1976. Traveled to Emily H. Davis Art Gallery, University of Akron, Akron, Ohio. February 23–March 12.

Whitney Museum of American Art, New York, "New American Filmmakers Series: Baldessari/Wegman." June 1–6.

George Paton Gallery, Melbourne University Union, University of Melbourne, Parkville, Victoria, Australia, "John Baldessari." June 1–8. Brochure. Traveled to Experimental Art Foundation, St. Peters, Adelaide, Australia, June 28–July 16; Undercroft Gallery, University of Western Australia, Perth, Australia, July 26–August 20; Institute of Modern Art, Brisbane, Australia, September 5–October 3; Institute of Contemporary Art, Sydney, Australia, October 11–29. (Also exhibited at Auckland City Art Gallery, Auckland, New Zealand in "1st Pan Pacific Biennele 1976: Colour Photography and Its Derivatives," see *Selected Group Exhibitions*, 1976).

James Corcoran Gallery, Los Angeles, "John Baldessari: Recent Work." September 23–October 23.

South Campus Art Gallery, Miami Dade Community College, Miami, Florida, "Bruce Boice/John Baldessari." December 6–January 19, 1977.

1977

Robert Self, London, "John Baldessari: Photographic Works." February–March.

Julian Pretto Gallery, New York, "John Baldessari." April–May.

1493 West Washington Boulevard, Los Angeles, "John Baldessari: Six Colorful Inside Jobs." October 10–15. In conjunction with "John Baldessari/Films: Six Colorful Inside Jobs, and Script," Fox Venice Theatre, Venice, California, October 29. Exhibitions organized by Foundation for Art Resources, Santa Monica, California.

Wadsworth Atheneum, Hartford, Connecticut, "John Baldessari/Matrix 32." June 7–September 18. Brochure. Text by A[ndrea] M[iller]-K[eller].

Whitney Museum of American Art, New York, "New American Filmmakers Series/Baldessari: New Films." December 27–January 1, 1978.

Galeria Massimo Valsecchi, Milan.

1978

Portland Center for the Visual Arts, Portland, Oregon, "John Baldessari: Blasted Allegories." January 20–February 19.

Artists Space, New York, "John Baldessari: Films." March 22–23.

Sonnabend Gallery, New York, "John Baldessari: Blasted Allegories." September 23–October 14.

1979

Ink. Halle für internationale neue Kunst, Zurich, "John Baldessari." August 14–September 21. Catalogue, *Dokumentation 4*. Texts by Christel Sauer, Patrick Frey, Peter Blum, John Baldessari.

1980

Galleria Locus Solus, Genoa, Italy, "John Baldessari." April 29–May 20.

Los Angeles Institute of Contemporary Art Downtown, Los Angeles, "Oasis: John Baldessari, Title." September 28.

Sonnabend Gallery, New York, "John Baldessari: Fugitive Essays." October 18–November 8.

1981

The New Museum of Contemporary Art, New York, "John Baldessari: Work 1966–1980." Part I: March 14–April 4; Part II: April 8–28. Traveled to Contemporary Arts Center, Cincinnati, Ohio, January 14–February 21, 1982; Contemporary Arts Museum, Houston, March 6–April 18, 1982. Catalogue, New York: The New Museum of Contemporary Art; and Dayton, Ohio: University Art Galleries, Wright State University, 1982. Texts by Marcia Tucker, Robert Pincus-Witten, interview by Nancy Drew.

CEPA Gallery, Buffalo, New York, "John Baldessari: Shape Derived from Subject (Snake): Used as a Framing Device to Produce New Photographs." April 3–May 17. Artist's book, *Close-Cropped Tales*, in conjunction with exhibition and Albright-Knox Art Gallery, Buffalo, New York, 1981. Traveled to Rüdiger Schöttle Gallery, Munich, West Germany, June 11–July 11; Sonnabend Gallery, New York, September 19–October 10.

Albright-Knox Art Gallery, Buffalo, New York, "John Baldessari: Selected Works." April 5–May 17. Artist's book (see CEPA Gallery, above).

Hallwalls, Buffalo, New York, "John Baldessari: Films." April 13.

Municipal Van Abbemuseum, Eindhoven, the Netherlands, "John Baldessari: Werken 1966–1981." May 22–June 21. Traveled to Museum Folkwang, Essen, West Germany, September 4–October 18. Catalogue. Texts by R[udi] H. Fuchs, John Baldessari.

Samangallery, Genoa, Italy.

1982

University Art Galleries, Wright State University, Dayton, Ohio, "John Baldessari: Art As Riddle." January 4–26. Catalogue. See *One- and Two-Person Exhibitions*, The New Museum of Contemporary Art, New York, "John Baldessari: Work 1966–1980," 1981. Traveled to Long Beach Museum of Art, Long Beach, California, May 16–June 29; Anderson Gallery, Virginia Commonwealth University, Richmond, Virginia, September 2–26.

1983

Marianne Deson Gallery, Chicago, "Baldessari/Richter." May 19– June 23.

Stampa, Basel, Switzerland, "John Baldessari: Vanitas Series: Balanced Bowling Ball, Cockroach/Cool (Short Depth of Field) Bubbles/Dandelion, Cockroach, Wire (Close Up)." June 7–July 2.

Northlight Gallery, Arizona State University, Tempe, Arizona, "John Baldessari/Robert Cumming." October 16–November 10.

### 1984
Douglas Drake Gallery, Kansas City, Missouri, "John Baldessari: Selected Works from 1974–1984." April 6–28.

Sonnabend Gallery, New York, "John Baldessari." April 7–28.

Galerie Peter Pakesch, Vienna, "John Baldessari." June 5–July 28.

Margo Leavin Gallery, Los Angeles, "John Baldessari." September 15–October 13.

Galerie Gillespie-Laage-Salomon, Paris, "John Baldessari." October 12–November 21.

### 1985
Centre d'Art Contemporain, Le Consortium, Dijon, France, "John Baldessari." March 11–April 18. Exhibition organized by Le Coin du Miroir, Dijon, France.

De Vleeshal Middelburg, Middelburg, the Netherlands, "Space Between." July 12–August 4. Brochure. Text by Anton van Gemert.

### 1986
University Art Museum, University of California at Berkeley, Berkeley, California, "John Baldessari: Matrix/Berkeley 94." March 29–May 25. Brochure. Text by Constance Lewallen.

Sonnabend Gallery, New York, "John Baldessari." April 5–26.

Santa Barbara Museum of Art, Santa Barbara, California, "John Baldessari: California Viewpoints." August 23–October 12. Catalogue. Text by Hunter Drohojowska.

Margo Leavin Gallery, Los Angeles, "John Baldessari." September 13–October 18.

Multiples, Inc., New York, "John Baldessari: Hegel's Cellar." December 9–January 3, 1987. Also exhibited at Site 311, Pacific Grove, California, October 16–November 28, 1987.

### 1987
Fotogaleria im Forum Stadtpark, Graz, Austria, "John Baldessari." February 28–March 22.

Museo d'Arte Contemporanea, Castello di Rivoli, Rivoli, Italy, "John Baldessari." May–June.

MAGASIN, Centre National d'Art Contemporain de Grenoble, Grenoble, France, "Composition for Violin and Voices (Male)." May 3–June 28. Catalogue.

Dart Gallery Alternative Space, Chicago, "John Baldessari: Recent Work." May 8–June 9.

Sonnabend Gallery, New York, "John Baldessari." November 7–28.

### 1988
Margo Leavin Gallery, Los Angeles, "John Baldessari." April 9–May 14.

Lisson Gallery, London, "John Baldessari." May 16–June 11.

Primo Piano, Rome, "John Baldessari: Opere Recenti." May–July.

Galerie Laage-Salomon, Paris, "John Baldessari." May 27–June 30.

Palais des Beaux-Arts, Brussels, Belgium, "John Baldessari: Oeuvres Récentes." September 18–November 6.

Kestner-Gesellschaft, Hanover, West Germany, "John Baldessari: Photoarbeiten." December 9–January 29, 1989. Catalogue. Texts by Carl Haenlein, Germano Celant.

Margo Leavin Gallery, Los Angeles, "John Baldessari: Laurence Sterne's The Life and Opinions of Tristram Shandy, Gentleman." November 19–December 23. Also shown at Sonnabend Gallery, New York, January 7–28, 1989.

Cirrus Gallery, Los Angeles, "John Baldessari: A Print Retrospective." December 11–January 21, 1989.

### 1989
Stephen Wirtz Gallery, San Francisco, "John Baldessari: Recent Editions." January 5–28.

Centro de Arte Reina Sofía, Madrid, "Ni por ésas/Not Even So: John Baldessari." January 11–February 20. Catalogue (Spanish and French editions). Texts by Jean-Louis Froment (French only), Guadalupe Echevarriá, Vicente Todolí, John Miller, Thomas Lawson, artist. Exhibition and catalogue by Centro de Arte Reina Sofía, Madrid; and Centre Julio González, IVAM, Instituto Valenciano de Arte Moderno, Valencia, Spain. Traveled to capc Musée d'Art Contemporain, Bordeaux, France, as "John Baldessari: Oeuvres de 1966 à 1988," March 10–April 23; Centre Julio González, IVAM, Instituto Valenciano de Arte Moderno, Valencia, Spain, May 15–July 15. Artist's book, *Lamb*, a collaboration with Meg Cranston, in conjunction with exhibition, Valencia, 1989.

Lawrence Oliver Gallery, Philadelphia, "John Baldessari." February 3–March 4. Brochure. Text by Rosetta Brooks.

Galerie Meert Rihoux, Brussels, Belgium, "John Baldessari: Recent Works." May 20–June 30.

Grossman Galery, School of the Museum of Fine Arts, Boston, "Artschwager/Baldessari." October 27–November 29.

## Selected Group Exhibitions

### 1957
Art Center in La Jolla, La Jolla, California, "Second Annual 1957 All-Media Membership Exhibition." October 5–November 6.

San Bernardino, California, "42nd National Orange Show: Painting, Photography, Sculpture."

### 1958
Exodus Gallery, San Pedro, California, "1st All Los Angeles Drawing Show." August 18–September 6.

Pasadena Museum of Art, Pasadena, California, "The 9th San Gabriel Valley Artist Exhibition." October 20–November 24.

Art Center in La Jolla, La Jolla, California, "Second Annual 1958 All-Media Membership Exhibition." November 2–December 4. Brochure. Text by Donald J. Brewer.

### 1960
Art Center in La Jolla, La Jolla, California, "Pacific Coast South; The Uncommon Denominator: Thirteen San Diego Painters." June 7–26. Catalogue. Traveled to Museum of New Mexico Art Gallery, Santa Fe, New Mexico, November 3–29.

Los Angeles County Museum, Los Angeles, "1960 Annual: Artists of Los Angeles County and Vicinity." August 17–October 7.

Los Angeles County Museum, Los Angeles, "40th.Exhibition of the California Water Color Society." October 19–November 27. Traveled to Palace of the Legion of Honor, San Francisco, California, December 12–January 17, 1961.

### 1961
San Francisco Museum of Art, San Francisco, "24th Annual Drawing, Print and Sculpture Exhibition of the San Francisco Art Association." February 2–March 5. Brochure.

Long Beach Museum of Art, Long Beach, California, "Arts of Southern California: Collage." October 1–29. Brochure.

### 1962
San Diego Fine Arts Gallery, San Diego, California, "1962: California: South" March 2–April 1. Text by Herschel B. Chipp.

San Francisco Museum of Art, San Francisco, "81st Annual Painting Exhibition of the San Francisco Art Institute." April 20–May 20. Text by George D. Culler.

Denver Art Museum, Denver, "68th Western Annual." August 12–September 23.

The Museum of Fine Arts, Houston, "The Southwest: Painting and Sculpture." December 7–January 20, 1963. Catalogue. Text by James Johnson Sweeney.

## 1963

Long Beach Museum of Art, Long Beach, California, "Arts of Southern California—XIII: Painting." June 2–June 30. Catalogue. Text by Helen Wurdemann.

i Gallery, La Jolla, California, "23 Americans." June 30–July 28.

## 1964

Southwestern College, Chula Vista, California, "Snap, Crackle and Pop: A Review of Local Pop Art." March 16–April 3.

San Diego Public Library, San Diego, California, "John Baldessari, Richard Allen Morris and Fred Cooper." July.

## 1965

Southwestern College, Chula Vista, California, "Polychrome Sculpture" January 8–February 19. Brochure. Text by John Baldessari.

La Jolla Museum of Art, La Jolla, California, "Some Aspects of California Painting and Sculpture." February 28–April 11. Catalogue. Text by Donald J. Brewer.

Long Beach Museum of Art, Long Beach, California, "3rd Annual Southern California Juried Exhibition of the Long Beach Museum of Art." April 4–25.

4040 Loma Riviera, Drive, Loma Riviera, San Diego, California, "New Art in Living Space." July 18–August 29. Brochure. Text by Louis Sander.

## 1967

Los Angeles State College, Los Angeles, "2nd Annual Small Images Competition." December 4–January 11, 1968. Catalogue. Text by Fidel A. Danielli.

## 1968

Art Gallery, University of California at San Diego, La Jolla, California, "New Work/Southern California." January 9–February 4. Catalogue. Text by James Monte.

Richard Feigen Gallery, New York, "John Baldessari, Carol Brown, David Milne, Ralph Pomeroy." October 12–November 16.

Art Gallery, University of California at San Diego, La Jolla, California, "A Few Rays of Hope." November 8–December 14.

## 1969

Long Beach Museum of Art, Long Beach, California, "Microcosm 69." January 12–February 9. Catalogue. Texts by Arthur Secunda, Jason D.

Wong. Traveled to Tom and Ann Peppers Art Center, University of Redlands, Redlands, California, March 14–April 4; College of Idaho, Caldwell, Idaho, September 9–October 4; Moorhead State College, Moorhead, Minnesota, January 8–29, 1970; Illinois State University, Normal, Illinois, October 25–November 25, 1970; Linfield College, McMinnville, Oregon, April 3–24, 1971.

Newport Harbor Art Museum, Newport Beach, California, "The Appearing Disappearing Image Object." May 11–June 28. Brochure. Text by Thomas H. Gaver.

Dwan Gallery, New York, "Language III." May 24–June 18.

Eugenia Butler Gallery, Los Angeles, "Conception—Perception." July 1–25.

Hayward Gallery, London, "Pop Art." July 9–September 3. Catalogue. Text by John Russell and Suzi Gablik. See also *Pop Art Redefined*, in *Selected General References*, 1969. Exhibition organized by Arts Council of Great Britain, London.

Seattle Art Museum Pavilion and Seattle Civic Center, Seattle, Washington, "557,087." September 5–October 5. Traveled to Vancouver Art Gallery, Vancouver, Canada, as "995,000." January 13–February 8, 1970. Catalogue. Texts by Lucy R. Lippard, projects by artists.

Städtischen Museum, Leverkusen, West Germany, "*Konzeption*—conception." October–November. Catalogue. Texts by Rolf Wedewer, Sol LeWitt, projects by artists.

Museum of Contemporary Art, Chicago, "Art by Telephone." November 1–December 14. Catalogue. Text by Jan van der Marck, projects by artists on LP record.

Whitney Museum of American Art, New York, "1969 Annual Exhibition: Contemporary American Painting." December 16–February 1, 1970. Text by John I. H. Baur.

## 1970

Allen Art Museum, Oberlin College, Oberlin, Ohio, "Art in the Mind." April 17–May 12. Catalogue. Text by Athena T. Spear, projects by artists.

Galleria Civica d'Arte Moderna, Turin, Italy, "Conceptual Art, Arte Povera, Land Art." June 6–July 12. Catalogue. Texts by Germano Celant, Lucy R. Lippard, projects by artists.

The Museum of Modern Art, New York, "Information." July 2–September 20. Text by Kynaston L. McShine, projects by artists.

The Jewish Museum, New York, "Software." September 16–November 8. Catalogue. Texts by Roy D. Chapin, Jr., Karl Katz, Jack Burnham, James A. Mahoney, Theodor H. Nelson, projects by artists.

Moore College of Art, Philadelphia, "Recorded Activities." October 16–November 19. Catalogue. Text by Lucy R. Lippard.

## 1971

Galerie nächst St. Stephan, Vienna, "Situation Concepts." March 15–April 3. Catalogue. Texts by Peter Weiermair, Ricky Comi, Joseph Kosuth, Sol LeWitt, Mel Bochner. Traveled to Galerie im Taxipalais, Innsbruck, Austria.

The Museum of Modern Art, New York, "Pier 18." June 18–August 2.

El Museo de Arte Moderno de Buenos Aires, and Centro de Arte y Comunicación, Buenos Aires, "Arte de Sistemas." July 19–August 22. Catalogue.

Städtische Kunsthalle, Düsseldorf, "Prospect '71—Projection, Film." October 8–17. Catalogue. Text by Hans Strelow. Düsseldorf: Art Press Verlag, 1971. Traveled to Louisiana Museum, Humlebaek, Denmark, as "Projektion: Udstilling på Louisiana." January 22–February 14, 1972. Catalogue. Texts by Flemming Koefoed, Robert Smithson, P. Adams Sitney, François Pluchart, Vito Acconci interviewed by Cindy Nemser, Vito Acconci, Stig Brøgger, Per Kirkeby, Dennis Oppenheim, Richard Serra.

## 1972

Venice, Italy, "La Biennale di Venezia: 36ª Esposizione Internazionale d'Arte." June 11–October 1. Catalogue. Texts by Filippo Longo, Mario Penelope, Giovanni Carandente, Giuseppe Marchiori, Renzo Salvadori, Daniela Palazzoli, Gerry Schum, Achille Bonito Oliva, Basilio Uribe, Wilfried Skreiner, F. De Lulle, Clarival do Prado Valladares, Brydon E. Smith, Jiří Hlušička, Federico Brook, Ejner Johansson, Leena Savolainen, Raoul Jean Moulin, Dieter Honisch, John Elderfield, Andrew Forge, Andreas Joannou, Jóhannes Jóhannesson, Avraham Ronen, Francesco Arcangeli, Renato Barilli, Miodrag B. Protić, Per Remfeldt, E. L. L. de Wilde, Federico Brook, A. Wojciechowski, Salah Kamel, Ion Frunzetti, Caferino Moreno Sandoval, Willy Ratzler, Lajos Vayer, Walter Hopps, Roberto Guevara, Roni Toniato.

Kunstmuseum Basel, Basel, Switzerland " 'Konzept'—Kunst." March 18–April 23. Catalogue. Texts by Zdenek Felix, Klaus Honnef, projects by artists.

Pamplona, Spain (festival), "Encuentros 1972 Pamplona." June 26–July 3. Catalogue. Texts by Santiago Amon, Antonio Agundes, Luc Ferrari, Josef Anton, Fernau Hall, Maurice Fleuret, Mauricio Kegel, Ignacio Gomez De Liaño, Gonzalo Suarez, and others. Madrid: Grupo Alea, 1972.

Museum Fridericianum, Kassel, West Germany, "Documenta 5: Befragung der Realität: Bildwelten Heute—Prozesse." June 30–October 8. Catalogue. Texts by Harald Szeemann, Jean-Christophe Ammann, Ingolf Bauer, Bazon Brock, Walter Busse, Reiner Diederich, Johannes Cladders, and others. Kassel: Documenta GmbH/Verlagsgruppe Bertelsmann/ C. Bertelsmann Verlag, 1972 (2 volumes).

Galerija 212, Belgrade, Yugoslavia, "BITEF 6: Aspekti/Aspects/Aspetti." September 14–October 8. Catalogue.

El Museo de Arte Moderno de Buenos Aires; and Centro de Arte y Comunicación, Buenos Aires, "La muestra arte de sistemas II International." September–October. Catalogue. Text by Jorge Glusberg.

Contemporary Arts Museum, Houston, "John Baldessari, Frances Barth, Richard Jackson, Barbara Munger, Gary Stephan." September 8–November 16. Catalogue. Text by Jay Belloli.

Pasadena Art Museum, Pasadena, California, "Southern California Attitudes '72." September 19–November 5. Catalogue. Text by Barbara Haskell.

De Saisset Art Gallery and Museum, University of Santa Clara, Santa Clara, California, "Twelfth Annual October St. Jude Invitational: Videotapes." October 3–29. Traveled to Everson Museum of Art, Syracuse, New York, November 1–19.

1973

Whitney Museum of American Art, New York, "1973 Biennial Exhibition." January 10–March 18. Catalogue. Text by John I. H. Baur.

Galleria Civica d'Arte Moderna, Turin, Italy, "Combattimento per un'immagine: Fotografi e Pittori." February 28–April. Catalogue. Texts by Daniela Palazzoli and Luigi Carluccio.

John Gibson Gallery, New York, "Story." April 7–May 3.

Everson Museum of Art, Syracuse, New York, "Circuit: A Video Invitational." April 17–May 18. Catalogue. Text by David Ross. Catalogue published as "Circuit: A Video Invitational." *Radical Software* (New York) 2, no. 5 (1973). Traveled to Henry Art Gallery, University of Washington, Seattle, Washington, April 26–May 27; Cranbrook Academy of Art Museum, Bloomfield Hills, Michigan, May 1–20; Los Angeles County Museum of Art, Los Angeles, October 30–November 25; School of the Museum of Fine Arts Gallery, School of the Museum of Fine Arts, Boston, January 7–February 3, 1974.

Galerija Savremene Umjetnosti, Zagreb, Yugoslavia, "Tendencies 5." June 1–July 1. Catalogue. Text by Marijan Susovski. Exhibition organized by Galerija Grada Zagreb, Zagreb, Yugoslavia.

Galleriaforma, Genoa, Italy, "Indice." June–July.

Museum Dhondt-Dhaenens, Deurle, Belgium, "Deurle 11/7/73." July 11–August 8. Catalogue. Texts by artists. Exhibition organized by Galerie MTL, Brussels, Belgium.

Musée Galliera, Paris, "Festival d'Automne: Aspects de l'art actuel." September 14–October 27. Catalogue. Projects by artists. Florence, Italy: Centro Di, 1973. Exhibition organized by Galerie Sonnabend, Paris.

Kunsthalle, Düsseldorf, "Prospect '73: Painting." September 28–October 7.

Newspace, Los Angeles, "Baldessari, Burden, McCarthy, Smith: Videotapes." November.

Parcheggio di Villa Borghese, Rome, "Contemporanea." November 28–February, 1974. Catalogue. Text by Filiberto Menna. Exhibition organized by Incontri Internazionali d'Arte, Rome.

1974

Sonnabend Gallery, New York, "Films: Vito Acconci, John Baldessari, David Haxton, David Shulman." January 8–12.

National Gallery of Victoria, Melbourne, Australia, "Some Recent American Art." February 12–March 10. Traveled to Art Gallery of New South Wales, Sydney, Australia, April 5–May 5; Art Gallery of South Australia, Adelaide, Australia, May 31–June 30; West Australian Art Gallery, Perth, Australia, July 26–August 21; City of Auckland Art Gallery, Auckland, New Zealand, October 14–November 17. Catalogue. Texts by Gordon Thomson, Waldo Rasmussen, Jennifer Licht. Melbourne:

National Gallery of Victoria with permission of The Museum of Modern Art, New York, 1973. Exhibition organized by the International Council of The Museum of Modern Art, New York.

Heidelberger Kunstverein, Heidelberg, West Germany, "Demonstrative Fotografie." February 24–March 31. Catalogue. Texts by Hans Gercke.

The Art Institute of Chicago, Chicago, "Idea and Image in Recent Art." March 23–May 5. Catalogue. Texts by Anne Rorimer, A. James Speyer, artists.

Kölnischer Kunstverein, Cologne, West Germany, "Video Tapes." July 6–August 8. Catalogue. Text by Wulf Herzogenrath.

Kunsthalle Obergeschoss, Cologne, West Germany, "Kunst bleibt Kunst—Projekt '74—Aspekte internationaler Kunst am Anfang der 70er Jahre." July 6–September 8. Catalogue. Texts by Dieter Ronte, Evelyn Weiss, Manfred Schneckenburger, Albert Schug, Marlis Grüterich, Wulf Herzogenrath, David A. Ross, Birgit Hein, projects by artists.

Cannaviello Studio d'Arte, Rome, "Narrative Art." November. Text by Filiberto Menna.

A.R.C.2/Musée d'Art Moderne de la Ville de Paris, Paris, "Art Video/Confrontation 74." November 8–December 8. Catalogue. Texts by Michel Fansten, Suzanne Pagé, Donald A. Foresta, Dominique Belloir, Yann Pavie.

Diagramma/Luciano Inga-Pin, Milan, "Narrative Art." December–January 1975. Catalogue. Texts by Achille Bonito Oliva, Filiberto Menna, artists.

1975

Institute of Contemporary Art, University of Pennsylvania, Philadelphia, "Video Art." January 17–February 28. Catalogue. Texts by David Antin, Lizzie Borden, Jack Burnham, John McHale. Traveled to Contemporary Arts Center, Cincinnati, Ohio, March 22–May 30; Museum of Contemporary Art, Chicago, June 28–August 31; Wadsworth Atheneum, Hartford, Connecticut, September 17–November 2.

The Museum of Modern Art, New York, "Projects: Video III." February 1–April 30.

Museo Progressivo d'Arte Contemporanea, Livorno, Italy, "Narrative Art." March. Catalogue. Texts by Renato Barilli, Achille Bonito Oliva, Vittorio Fagone, Lara-Vinca Masini, Filiberto Menna.

238

Malmö Konsthall, Malmö, Sweden, "New Media 1." March 22–May 19. Catalogue. Text by Günter Metken.

Serpentine Gallery, London, "The Video Show." May 1–26. Catalogue. Texts by Sue Grayson, John Howkins. London: Arts Council of Great Britain, 1975.

Paula Cooper, New York, group show. December 13–January 14, 1976.

1976

Whitney Museum of American Art, New York, "New American Filmmakers Series: Text and Image." February 11–17.

University Art Museum, Berkeley, University of California at Berkeley, California, "Commissioned Video Works." March 2–28. Brochure. Text by James Melchert.

Galleria Comunale d'Arte Moderna, Parma, Italy, "Foto & Idea." April–May. Catalogue. Text by Ilaria Bignamini.

P.S. 1/Institute for Art and Urban Resources, Long Island City, Queens, New York, "Rooms P.S. 1." June 9–26. Catalogue. Texts by Alanna Heiss, Linda Blumberg, artists, others. New York, 1977.

Israel Museum, Jerusalem, "The Artist and the Photograph (II): 2nd Triennale of Photography." September–November. Catalogue. Text by Yona Fischer.

A.R.C.2/Musée d'Art Moderne de la Ville de Paris, Paris, "Boîtes." December 16–January 30, 1977. Catalogue. Texts by Francoise Chatel, Suzanne Pagé, Boris Vian, Sigmund Freud, Hélène Cixous, Michel Bernard, Claudine Romeo, Jean Clair. Traveled to Le Grand Huit, Maison de la Culture, Rennes, France, February 3–March 2, 1977.

1977

Whitney Museum of American Art, New York, "1977 Biennial Exhibition." February 15–April 3. Catalogue. Texts by Tom Armstrong; Barbara Haskell, Marcia Tucker, and Patterson Sims.

Whitney Museum of American Art Downtown Branch, New York, "Words: A Look at the Use of Language in Art, 1967–1977." March 9–April 13. Catalogue. Unattributed text.

Happy New Art Gallery, Students' Cultural Centre, Belgrade, Yugoslavia, "umetnost, ironija itd . . . / art, irony etc . . . " April 1–8.

Castelli Uptown, New York, "Some Color Photographs." June 4–July 2.

Museum of Contemporary Art, Chicago, "A View of a Decade." September 10–November 10. Catalogue. Texts by Martin Friedman, Robert Pincus-Witten, Peter Gay.

The Museum of Fine Arts, Houston, "Contemporary American Photographic Works." November 4–December 31. Catalogue. Texts by William C. Agee, Lewis Baltz, John Upton.

Contemporary Arts Museum, Houston, "American Narrative/Story Art: 1967–1977." December 17–February 25, 1978. Texts by James Harithas, Paul Schimmel, Marc Freidus, Alan Sondheim, audio works by artists on LP record. Houston, 1978. Traveled to University Art Museum, University of California at Berkeley, Berkeley, California, September 3–October 22, 1978; Art Museum, University of California at Santa Barbara, Santa Barbara, January 3–February 4, 1978.

Institute of Contemporary Art, Boston, "Wit and Wisdom: Works by Baldessari, Hudson, Levine and Oppenheim." December 21–February 5, 1978.

1978

Julian Pretto Gallery, New York, "A Selection of Conceptual Works by Eight Americans." February 5–March 15.

Institute of Contemporary Art, Boston, "Narration." April 18–June 18. Catalogue. Text by Michael Leja.

Whitney Museum of American Art, New York, "Art About Art." July 19–September 24. Catalogue. Text by Leo Steinberg, Jean Lipman, Richard Marshall. Traveled to North Carolina Museum of Art, Raleigh, North Carolina, October 15–November 26; Frederick Wight Art Gallery, University of California at Los Angeles, Los Angeles, December 19–February 11, 1979; Portland Art Museum, Portland, Oregon, March 6–April 15, 1979.

Castelli/Sonnabend Tapes & Films, Leo Castelli Gallery, New York, "Film/Video Works 1976–1978." December 2–20.

1979

Museum Bochum, Bochum, West Germany, "Words." January 27–March 11. Traveled to Genoa, Italy, Palazzo Ducale, March 28–May 4. Catalogue. Text by Dorine Mignot.

Whitney Museum of American Art, New York, "1979 Whitney Biennial." February 6–April 8. Catalogue. Texts by Tom Armstrong; John G. Hanhardt, Barbara Haskell, Richard Marshall, Mark Segal, and Patterson Sims.

Heidelberger Kunstverein, Heidelberg, West Germany, "Text—Foto—Geschichten: Story Art/Narrative Art." June 30–August 5. Traveled to Bonner Kunstverein, Bonn, West Germany, August 17–September 30; Krefelder Kunstverein, Krefeld, West Germany, October 7–November 3. Catalogue. Texts by Margarethe Jochimsen, Hans Gercke, Georg Jappe, Annelie Pohlen, Marlis Grüterich. Catalogue published as Kunstforum International (Mainz, West Germany), no. 33 (3/1979). Exhibition organized by Bonner Kunstverein, Bonn, West Germany.

1980

High Museum of Art, Atlanta, "Contemporary Art in Southern California." April 26–June 8. Catalogue. Texts by Gudmund Vigtel, Clark V. Poling.

Hayward Gallery, London, "Pier + Ocean: Construction in the Art of the Seventies." May 8–June 22. Traveled to Rijksmuseum Kröller-Müller, Otterlo, the Netherlands, July 13–September 8. Texts by Joanna Drew and Andrew Dempsey, Gerhard von Graevenitz. London: Arts Council of Great Britain, 1980. Exhibition organized by the Arts Council of Great Britain, London.

Mappin Art Gallery, Sheffield, England, "Artist and Camera." October 25–November 23. Traveled to City Museum & Art Gallery, Stoke-On-Trent, England, November 29–January 3, 1981; Durham Light Infantry Museum and Arts Centre, Durham, England, January 10–February 8, 1981; Cartwright Hall, Bradford, England, February 14–March 29, 1981. Catalogue. Texts by Joanna Drew, Miranda Strickland-Constable. London: Arts Council of Great Britain, 1980. Exhibition organized by the Arts Council of Great Britain, London.

1981

Museen der Stadt Köln, Cologne, West Germany, "Westkunst." May 30–August 16. Catalogue. Texts by Hugo Borger, Laszlo Glozer, Kaspar Koenig, Karl Ruhrberg. Cologne: DuMont Buchverlag, 1981.

Los Angeles County Museum of Art, Los Angeles, "Art in Los Angeles: The Museum as Site: Sixteen Artists." July 21–October 4. Catalogue. Text by Stephanie Barron.

Neuberger Museum, State University of New York at Purchase, Purchase, "Soundings." September 20–December 23. Catalogue. Texts by Suzanne Delehanty, Dore Ashton, Germano Celant, Lucy Fischer.

Nordiska Kompaniet, Stockholm, "US Art Now: Aktuella tendenser i amerikansk konst." October 20–November 7. Catalogue. Texts by Jan Eric Löwenadler, Lars Peder Hedberg. Traveled to Konsthallen, Götaplatsen, Göteborg, Sweden, January 9–31, 1982.

Wiener Secession, Vienna, "5th Vienna International Biennale: Erweiterte Fotographie." October 22–November 22. Catalogue.

Stedelijk Museum, Amsterdam, "Instant fotografie." December 4–January 17, 1982. Catalogue. Texts by Els Barents.

1982

Museum of Art, Rhode Island School of Design, Providence, Rhode Island, "California Photography." January 8–February 9. Catalogue. Text by Deborah J. Johnson; symposium statements by John Baldessari, Judy Dater, Andy Grundberg, Leland Rice, Arthur Taussig, Gary Metz.

Art Gallery of New South Wales; Power Gallery of Contemporary Art, University of Sydney; Ivan Dougherty Gallery; City Art Institute; Australian Centre for Photography; Gallery A Courtyard Space; Roslyn Oxley Gallery, Sydney, Australia, "The 4th Biennale of Sydney: Vision in Disbelief." April 7–May 23. Catalogue. Texts by William Wright, Paula Latos-Vailer, Elwyn Lynn.

The Art Institute of Chicago, Chicago, "74th American Exhibition." June 12–August 1. Catalogue. Texts by A. James Speyer, Anne Rorimer.

Museum Friedericianum, Kassel, West Germany, "Documenta 7." June 19–September 28. Catalogue. Texts by Rudi Fuchs, Coosje van Bruggen, Germano Celant, Johannes Gachnang, Saskia Bos, Gerhard Storck, Walter Nikkels. Kassel: D + V Paul Dierchs GmbH, 1982 (2 volumes).

Groninger Museum, Groningen, the Netherlands, "Peter Blum Edition, New York." September 4–October 10. Also shown at: Multiples, Inc., New York, as "Three Portfolios: John Baldessari, Jonathan Borofsky, Francesco Clemente," December 3–December 31; Roger Ramsay Gallery, Chicago, as "3 Portfolios," January 15–February 13, 1983. Catalogue. Texts by Bice Curiger, Peter Blum. New York: Peter Blum Edition, 1984

1983

Whitney Museum of American Art, New York, "1983 Biennial Exhibition." March 24–May 22. Catalogue. Texts by Tom Armstrong; John G. Hanhardt, Barbara Haskell, Richard Marshall, and Patterson Sims.

National Museum of Modern Art, Tokyo, "Photography in Contemporary Art." October 7–December 4. Catalogue. Texts by Kenji Adachi and Michiaki Kawakita; Hisae Fujii; Yukio Kondo; Tohru Matsumoto. Traveled to National Museum of Modern Art, Kyoto, Japan, December 13–January 22, 1984.

The New Museum of Contemporary Art, New York, "Language, Drama, Source & Vision." October 8–November 27.

1984

Tanja Grunert; and Rüdiger Schöttle, Stuttgart, West Germany, "Idea." March 9–April 30. Catalogue. Text by Tanja Grunert.

The Queens Museum, Flushing, New York, "Verbally Charged Images." April 28–June 10. Traveled to University of South Florida Art Galleries, University of South Florida, Tampa, Florida, September 21–November 2; University Art Gallery, San Diego State University, February 2–March 2, 1985; University Art Gallery, California State College at San Bernardino, San Bernardino, California, April 10–May 8, 1985; Blanden Memorial Art Museum, Fort Dodge, Iowa, September 26–November 13, 1985. Catalogue. Texts by Susan Solins, Nina Felshin. New York: Independent Curators Incorporated, 1984; reprinted in *WhiteWalls* (New York), no. 10/11 (Spring/Summer 1984). Exhibition organized by Independent Curators Incorporated, New York.

Whitney Museum of American Art, New York, "New American Video Art: A Historical Survey, 1967–1980." June 13–July 1. Brochure. Text John G. Hanhardt. Traveled to Video Culture Canada, Toronto, November 2–4; Mandeville Gallery, University of California at San Diego, La Jolla, California, January 4–February 3, 1985; Institute of North American Studies, Barcelona, Spain, January 15–31, 1985; Blaffer Gallery, University of Houston, Houston, Texas, March 5–31, 1985; Arvada Center for the Arts and Humanities, Arvada, Colorado, June 7–July 5, 1985; Williams College, Williamstown, Massachusetts, September 11–October 9, 1985; University Art Gallery, University of California at Riverside, Riverside, California, January 6–27, 1986.

Hirshhorn Museum and Sculpture Garden, Washington, D.C., "Content: A Contemporary Focus, 1975–1984." October 4–January 6, 1985. Catalogue. Texts by Abram Lerner, Howard N. Fox, Miranda McClintic.

Cable Gallery, New York, "Sex." December 8–January 14, 1985.

1985

Whitney Museum of American Art, New York, "1985 Biennial Exhibition." March 13–June 9. Catalogue. Texts by Tom Armstrong; Richard Armstrong, John G. Hanhardt, Barbara Haskell, Richard Marshall, Lisa Phillips, and Patterson Sims.

La Grande Halle du Parc de la Villette, Paris, "La Nouvelle Biennale de Paris." March 21–May 21. Catalogue. Texts by Bernard Blistene, Georges Boudaille, Pierre Courcelles, Jean-Pierre Faye, Alanna Heiss, Achille Bonito Oliva, Marie-Luise Syring, Gérald Gassiot-Talabot, artists. Paris: Electa Moniteur, 1985.

Edith C. Blum Art Institute, Bard College, Annandale-on-Hudson, New York, "The Maximal Implications of The Minimal Line." March 24–May 5. Catalogue. Texts by Linda Weintraub, Donald Kuspit, Phyllis Tuchman.

Film in the Cities & First Banks, Minneapolis, Minnesota, "ArtSide Out." May 31–August 31. Catalogue. Texts by Ricardo Block, Lynne Sowder, and Richard Weise. In conjunction with First Bank Atrium, Pilsbury Center, Minneapolis, Minnesota, "An Exhibition of Photography by the Eight Commissioned Artists," May 31–June 28.

San Francisco Museum of Modern Art, San Francisco, "Extending the Perimeter of Twentieth Century Photography." August 2–October 6. Catalogue. Text by Dorothy Vandersteel.

Carnegie Institute, Museum of Art, Pittsburgh, "1985 Carnegie International." November 9–January 5, 1986. Catalogue. Texts by John R. Lane; John R. Lane and John Caldwell; Rudi H. Fuchs, Jannis Kounellis, Germano Celant, Per Kirkeby, Johannes Gachnang, Bazon Brock, Achille Bonito Oliva, Nicholas Serota, Benjamin H. D. Buchloh, Hal Foster, Donald B. Kuspit, Mark Rosenthal, Peter Schjeldahl, Thomas McEvilley, Hilton Kramer, artists.

1986

Museum of Art, Fort Lauderdale, Florida, "An American Renaissance: Painting and Sculpture Since 1940." January 12–March 30. Catalogue. Texts by Sam Hunter, Malcolm R.

Daniel, Harry F. Gaugh, Karen Koehler, Kim Levin, Robert C. Morgan, Richard Sarnoff. New York: Abbeville Press, 1986.

The Queens Museum, Flushing, New York, "The Real Big Picture." January 17–March 19. Catalogue. Text by Janet Schneider.

Stadtmuseum Graz, Graz, Austria, "Die Wahlverwandtschaften—Zitate." September 21–November 20. Catalogue. Texts by Peter Pakesch, Denys Zacharopoulos, August Ruhs, Johannes von Schlebrügge, Alberto Boatto, Elisabeth Wiesmayr-Schlebrügge.

The Museum of Contemporary Art, Los Angeles, "Individuals: A Selected History of Contemporary Art 1945–1986." December 10–January 10, 1988. Texts by Germano Celant, Hal Foster, Donald Kuspit, Kate Linker, Achille Bonito Oliva, Ronald J. Onorato, John C. Welchman, Thomas Lawson. New York: Abbeville Press; and Los Angeles: The Museum of Contemporary Art, 1986.

1987

Los Angeles Contemporary Exhibitions, Los Angeles, "Surveillance." February 27–April 12. Catalogue. Texts by Banba Miller, Gerry T. Marx, Deborah Irmas, artists.

John and Mable Ringling Museum of Art, Sarasota, Florida, "This is Not a Photograph: 20 Years of Large-Scale Photography, 1966–1986." March 7–May 31. Catalogue. Texts by Laurence J. Ruggiero, Gordon Lewis, Joseph Jacobs, Marvin Heiferman. Traveled to Akron Art Museum, Akron, Ohio, October 31–January 10, 1988; Chrysler Museum, Norfolk, Virginia, February 26–May 1, 1988.

University Art Museum, University of California at Berkeley, Berkeley, California, "Made in U.S.A." April 4–June 21. Catalogue. Texts by Sidra Stich, James E. B. Breslin, Thomas Schaub, Ben H. Bagdikian. Berkeley, University of California Press, 1987. Traveled to The Nelson-Atkins Museum of Art, Kansas City, Missouri, July 25–September 6; Virginia Museum of Fine Arts, Richmond, Virginia, October 7–December 7.

Marian Goodman Gallery, New York, "John Baldessari, Christian Boltanski, James Coleman, Dan Grahm, Rebecca Horn, Sol LeWitt, Giulio Paolini, Lawrence Weiner." April 7–May 4.

Los Angeles County Museum of Art, Los Angeles, "Avant-Garde In the '80s." April 23–July 12. Catalogue. Text by Howard Fox.

Los Angeles County Museum of Art, Los Angeles, "Photography and Art: Interaction Since 1946." June 4–August 30. Traveled to Museum of Art, Fort Lauderdale, Florida, October 15–January 24, 1988; The Queens Museum, Flushing, New York, February 16–April 3, 1988; Des Moines Art Center, Des Moines, Iowa, May 6–June 26, 1988.

Wolff Gallery New York, "Real Pictures." June 4–27.

Toyama Museum of Modern Art, Toyama, Japan, "Toyama Now '87." July 4–September 3. Catalogue. Texts by Masataka Ogawa, Jo-Anne Birnie Danzker, Kyung-Sung Lee, Richard Koshalek, Kenji Otsubo, artists.

Hoffman/Borman Gallery, Santa Monica, California, "The New Who's Who." July 30–August 30. Brochure. Text by Marvin Heiferman.

Centre International d'Art Contemporain de Montréal, Montreal, "Stations." August 1–November 1. Catalogue. Texts by M. Jacques, E. Lefebvre, Claude Gosselin, Roger Bellemare, Roland Schaer, James D. Campbell, Barnett Newman. Montreal, 1988.

Galleria Schema, Florence, "Conceptual Languages." September–October.

Centro de Arte Reina Sofía, Madrid, "25 años de selección y de actividad: Colección Sonnabend." October 30–February 15, 1988. Catalogue (Spanish edition). Texts by Jean-Louis Froment, Michel Bourel, Michel Ragon, Robert Pincus-Witten, Edi de Wilde, Harald Szeemann, Peter Ludwig, Giuseppe Panza, Yvon Lambert, Grégoire Müller, Michel Guy, Sarkis, Germano Celant, Achille Bonito Oliva. Madrid: Ministerio de Cultura, 1987. Traveled to capc Musée d'Art Contemporain, Bordeaux, France, as "25 Années de choix et d'activités d'Ileana et Michael Sonnabend: Collection Sonnabend." May 6–August 21. Catalogue (French edition). Bordeaux, 1988; Hamburger Bahnhof, West Berlin, West Germany, as "Museum der Avantgarde Die Sammlung Sonnabend New York," December 7–February 26, 1989. Catalogue (German edition). Milan: Electa, 1988; Galleria Nazionale d'Arte Moderna Rome, as "La Collezione Sonnabend. Dalla Pop Art in poi." April 14–October 2, 1989. Catalogue (Italian edition). Milan: Electa, 1989. Exhibition organized by capc Musée d'Art Contemporain, Bordeaux, France.

Bank of Boston Art Center, Boston, "L.A. Hot and Cool: Pioneers." November 23–January 15, 1988. Cat-

alogue. Texts by Dana Friss-Hansen; Christopher Knight and Howard Singerman. Cambridge: List Visual Arts Center, 1987. Exhibition organized by List Visual Arts Center, Massachusetts Institute of Technology, Cambridge, Massachusetts, as part of "L.A. Hot and Cool."

Stichting de Appel, Amsterdam, the Netherlands, "Nightfire." December 20–January 31, 1988. Catalogue. Texts by Saskia Bos, Edna van Duyn, Leonardo da Vinci, Marlene Dumas, Abramović/Ulay, Niek Kemps, De Vier Evangelisten, Pieter Laurens Mol, J.C.J. van der Heyden, Tom Puckey, Fortuyn/O'Brien.

1988

Marian Goodman Gallery, New York, "As Far As the Eye Can See." January 13–February 6.

Padiglione d'Arte Contemporanea di Milano, Milan, "Presi per Incantamento." June 1–July 18. Texts by Gregorio Magnani, Daniela Salvioni, Giorgio Verzotti. Milan: Giancarlo Politi Editore, 1988.

R. C. Harris Water Filtration Plant, Toronto, "WaterWorks." June 22–September 30. Catalogue. Texts by Fred Gaysek, Hennie L. Wolff, George Baird, Patricia C. Phillips. Published as ArtViews (Toronto) 14, no. 2/3 (Spring/Summer 1988). Exhibition organized by Visual Arts Ontario, Toronto.

Henry Art Gallery, University of Washington, Seattle, Washington, "Life Stories: Myth, Fiction and History in Contemporary Art." September 16–November 6. Catalogue. Texts by Richard Andrews, Chris Bruce.

Cleveland Center for Contemporary Art, Cleveland, Ohio, "The Turning Point: Art and Politics in Nineteen Sixty-Eight." September 9–October 26. Catalogue. Texts by Nina Castelli Sundell and Marjorie Talalay, Anita D. Cosgrove, Leonard Lief, Nina Castelli Sundell, Irwin Unger. Traveled to Lehman College Art Gallery, Lehman College, City University of New York, Bronx, New York, November 10–January 14, 1989.

Observatoire de Paris, Paris, "L'Observatoire." November 30–January 14, 1989. Catalogue. Texts by Alice Huei-Zu Yang, Francois Gundbacher. New York and Paris: Farideh Cadot Gallery, Inc., 1988. Exhibition organized by Farideh Cadot Gallery, New York; and Galerie Farideh Cadot, Paris.

Whitney Museum of American Art Downtown at Federal Reserve Plaza, New York, "Identity: Representations of the Self." December 14–February 10, 1989. Catalogue. Unattributed text.

1989

Germans Van Eck, New York, "Five Themes In Photography 1920's–1980's." January 14–February 8.

Michael Kohn Gallery, Los Angeles, "300 Years of Still Life." January 20–February 25.

Tony Shafrazi Gallery, New York, "Words." January 21–February 18.

G.H. Dalsheimer Gallery, Baltimore, Maryland, "Photography Expanded." January 24–February 23. Brochure. Text by George H. Dalsheimer.

Paula Cooper, New York, "Richard Artschwager, John Baldessari, Jonathan Borofsky, Robert Gober, Peter Halley, Nancy Shaver." January 28–February 25.

Edith C. Blum Art Institute, Bard College, Annandale-on-Hudson, New York, "Sequence (con)Sequence: (sub)Versions of Photography in the 80s." February 10–April 15. Catalogue. Texts by Linda Weintraub, Julia Ballerini, William S. Wilson, Lori Zippay. New York: Aperture Foundation, Inc., 1989.

Karsten Schubert Ltd, London, "A Brave New World." March 14–April 15. Text by Colin Gardner.

Wight Art Gallery, University of California at Los Angeles, Los Angeles, "Forty Years of California Assemblage." April 4–May 21. Catalogue. Texts by Henry Hopkins, Anne Ayres, Peter Boswell, Phillip Brookman, Verni Greenfield. Los Angeles: Regents of the University of California, 1989. Traveled to San Jose Museum of Art, San Jose, California, June 9–August 13; Fresno Art Museum, Fresno, California, September 8–November 12; Joslyn Art Museum, Omaha, Nebraska, December 15–February 4, 1990.

Museum Ludwig in den Rheinhallen der Kölner Messe, Cologne, West Germany, "Bilderstreit: Widerspruch, Einheit und Fragment in der Kunst seit 1960." April 8–June 28. Catalogue. Texts by Hans Belting, Michael Compton, Siegfried Gohr, René Denizot, Per Kirkeby, Rudi H. Fuchs, Luciano Fabro, Wilfried Dickhoff, Kay Heymer, Piet de Jonge, Walter Seitter, Christiane Meyer-Thoss, Dieter Schwarz, Antje von Graevenitz, Jole de Sanna, Johannes Gachnang, Rudolf Schmitz, André Berne-Joffroy, Emile Cioran, Mathias Schreiber, Georges Teyssot, Walter Nikkels, Eduard Trier, Reiner Speck. Cologne: DuMont Buchverlag, 1989.

Newport Harbor Art Museum, Newport Beach, California, "L.A. Pop in the Sixties." April 20–July 9. Catalogue. Text by Anne Ayres, Jay Beloli, Frances Colpitt, Judi Freeman, Marilu Knode, Andrea Liss, Robert L. Pincus, Karen Tsujimoto. Traveled to Henry Art Gallery, University of Washington, Seattle, Washington, September 20–November 5; Palm Springs Desert Museum, Palm Springs, California, November 17–January 14, 1990; Neuberger Museum, State University of New York at Purchase, Purchase, New York, April 8–June 17, 1990; Phoenix Art Museum, Phoenix, Arizona, July 9–August 19.

National Gallery of Art, Washington, D.C., "On the Art of Fixing a Shadow: 150 Years of Photography." May 7–July 30. Catalogue. Texts by Joel Snyder, Sarah Greenough, David Travis, Colin Westerbeck. Washington, D.C., 1989. Traveled to The Art Institute of Chicago, Chicago, September 16–November 26; Los Angeles County Museum of Art, Los Angeles, December 21–February 25, 1990.

Marian Goodman Gallery, New York, "A Photo Show." May 16–June 10.

Centre Georges Pompidou; and La Grande Halle du Parc de la Villette, Paris, "Magiciens de la Terre." May 18–August 14. Catalogue. Texts by Jean-Hubert Martin, Aline Luque, Mark Francis, André Magnin, Pierre Gaudibert, Thomas McEvilley, Homi Bhabha, Jacques Souillou, Bernard Marcadé.

The Metropolitan Museum of Art, New York, "Invention and Continuity in Contemporary Photographs." June 13–October 8. Brochure. Unattributed text.

The Museum of Modern Art, New York, "California Photography: Remaking Make-Believe." June 28–August 22. Catalogue. Text by Susan Kismaric.

Cooper Union School of Art, Cooper Union for the Advancement of Science and Art, New York, "Symbolism." October 30–November 20.

Hirschl & Adler Modern, New York, "Departures: Photography 1924–1989." November 2–December 2. Catalogue. Texts by Donald McKinney, Simon Watney.

Whitney Museum of American Art, New York, "Image World." November 8–February 18, 1990. Catalogue. Texts by Marvin Heiferman, Lisa Phillips, John G. Hanhardt.

# BIBLIOGRAPHY

## Interviews with the Artist

**1976**

Hugunin, James. "A Talk With John Baldessari." *The Dumb Ox* (Northridge, California) 1, no. 2 (Fall): 11–12.

**1977**

Spodarek, Diane. "Feature Interview: John Baldessari." *Detroit Artists' Monthly* (Detroit) 2, no. 6 (June): 1–6.

**1978**

Rubinfien, Leo. "Through Western Eyes." *Art in America* (New York) 66, no. 5 (September/October): 75–83.

**1980**

McMullin, Daniel. "Interview: John Baldessari." *Artists' News* (Topanga, California) 3, no. 5 (October/November): 6–10.

**1983**

Poling, Clark. "New Boundaries & Black Dice: An Interview with John Baldessari." *Art Papers* (Atlanta) 7, no. 6 (November/December): 2–3.

**1984**

Guenther, Joan, and Sheila Skjeie. "Art For People to Live With." *State of the Arts* (California Arts Council, Sacramento, California), no. 50 (November/December): 4–5.

Kraft, Barbara. "An Interview With John Baldessari." *Articles* (California Institute of the Arts, Valencia, California) 1, no. 2 (December/January): 11–13.

**1985**

"Talking Back to the Media." *Stichting de Appel* (Amsterdam), no. 3/4 (November): text published on microfiche.

**1987**

Selwyn, Marc. "John Baldessari." *Flash Art* (Milan), no. 135 (Summer): 62–64.

**1988**

Bakargiev, Carolyn Christov. "La foto non è soltanto foto." *II Sole—24 Ore* (Rome), June 12.

Berkson, Bill. "Conversations: John Baldessari." *Shift* (San Francisco) 2, no. 3: 36–39.

Braet, Jan. "Surrogaten voor woorden." *Knack Magazine* (Brussels, Belgium), no. 39 (September 28): 187–194.

Davis, Susan A. "For the Record." *C Magazine* (Toronto, Canada), no. 17 (Spring): 34–37.

Siegel, Jeanne. "John Baldessari: Recalling Ideas." *Arts Magazine* (New York) 62, no. 8 (April): 86–89.

———. "John Baldessari: Recalling Ideas." *Artwords 2: Discourse on the Early 80s*. Ann Arbor, Michigan: UMI Research Press, 1988 (revised from *Arts Magazine* 62, no. 8 (April): 86–89.

**1989**

Cranston, Meg. "John Baldessari: Part One." *Journal of Contemporary Art* (New York) 2, no. 1 (Spring/Summer): 41–49.

Cranston, Meg. "John Baldessari: Part Two." *Journal of Contemporary Art* (New York) 2, no. 2 (Fall/Winter 1989/90): 51–58.

## Selected Articles and Reviews

**1957**

Langsner, Jules. "Art News From Los Angeles." *ARTnews* (New York) 56, no. 2 (April): 20.

**1962**

Kietzmann, Armin. "Signs of Controversy: Baldessari Comes to Defense of X Exhibits." *San Diego Union* (San Diego, California), July 22.

**1963**

R.[euschel], J.[ohn]. Review. *Artforum* (San Francisco) 2, no. 3 (September): 17.

**1964**

Kietzmann, Armin. "Pop Gets Snap, Crackle." *San Diego Union* (San Diego, California), March 1.

———. "At Library: An Intimate Pop." *San Diego Union* (San Diego, California), July 19.

**1966**

Hagberg, Marilyn. "Neglected, Underrated, Intellectual Baldessari." *San Diego Magazine* (San Diego, California) 18, no. 3 (January): 66–68.

———. Review. *Artforum* (Los Angeles) 4, no. 9 (May): 18.

Kietzmann, Armin. "Baldessari: Knowledge is Fragmentary." *San Diego Union* (San Diego, California), April 10.

**1968**

L.[ast], M.[artin]. Review. *ARTnews* (New York) 67, no. 8 (December): 14, 17.

Livingston, Jane. Review. *Artforum* (New York) 7, no. 4 (December): 66.

Perreault, John. Review. *Village Voice* (New York), November 7.

W[ilson], W[illiam]. Review. *Los Angeles Times*, October 11.

**1969**

Pomeroy, Ralph. "New York: Moving Out." *Art and Artists* (London) 3, no. 10 (January): 55.

**1970**

A.[cconci], V.[ito] H. Review. *ARTnews* (New York) 69, no. 3 (May): 27.

Baker, Naomi. "Cremated Art by Baldessari to Form Exhibit." *Evening Tribune* (San Diego, California), September 8.

Forman, Nessa. "It's All on the Record But What Does it Add?" *The Sunday Bulletin* (Philadelphia), October 25.

Goldsmith, Barbara. "Where is The Art?" *Harper's Bazaar* (New York), no. 3102 (May): 144–147.

H.[ess], T.[homas] B. "Editorial: Burning Issues." *ARTnews* (New York) 69, no. 4 (Summer): 27.

Hotaling, Ed. "Los Angeles." *ARTnews* (New York) 69, no. 1 (March): 24.

O'Connor, John J. "The Gallery: Gerbils and Wheelchairs." *Wall Street Journal* (New York), November 4.

Perreault, John. "The Action." *Village Voice* (New York), March 26.

———. "Information." *Village Voice* (New York), July 16.

Plagens, Peter. Review. *Artforum* (New York) 8, no. 9 (May): 82–83.

Sharp, Willoughby. "Outsiders: Baldessari, Jackson, O'Shea, Ruppersberg." *Arts Magazine* (New York) 44, no. 8 (Summer): 42–43.

Strelow, Hans. "Der Computer oder das falsche Denken: 'Software' und Konzepte in einer New Yorker Ausstellung." *Frankfurter Allegemeine Zeitung* (Frankfurt, West Germany), October 5.

Vinklers, Bitite. "Art and Information: 'Software' at the Jewish Museum." *Arts Magazine* (New York) 45, no. 1 (September/October): 46–49.

Young, Joseph E. Review. *Studio International* (London) 14, no. 6 (Summer): 110–111.

**1971**

Baker, Elizabeth C. "Los Angeles, 1971." *ARTnews* (New York) 70, no. 5 (September): 27–39.

Frankenstein, Alfred. "Pier 18 Conceptual Project of Artists." *San Francisco Examiner & Chronicle*, July 4.

Genauer, Emily. "Art and the Artist." *New York Post*, January 2.

Meehan, Thomas. " 'Non-Art,' 'Anti-Art,' 'Non-Art' and 'Anti-Art Art' Are Useless. If Someone Says His Work Is Art, It's Art." *Horizon* (New York) 13, no. 4 (Autumn): 5–15.

Restany, Pierre. "Notes de Voyage: Houston—New York." *Domus* (Milan), no. 498 (May): 45–50.

**1972**

Butler, Susan L. "Art Circles." *Houston Chronicle* (Houston, Texas), September 17.

Freed, Eleanor. "The Contemporary Arts Quintet." *Houston Post* (Houston, Texas), September 17.

Tisdall, Caroline. "Arts Guardian: John Baldessari." *The Guardian* (London), April 15.

**1973**

Collins, James. Review. *Artforum* (New York) 12, no. 1 (September): 83–87.

———. "Pointing, Hybrids and Romanticism: John Baldessari." *Artforum* (New York) 12, no. 2 (October): cover, 53–58.

Frank, Peter. Review. *ARTnews* (New York) 72, no. 6 (Summer): 96.

Plagens, Peter. Review. *Artforum* (New York) 11, no. 6 (February): 89–91.

Wilson, William. Review. *Los Angeles Times*, November 2.

Winer, Helene. "Scenarios/Documents/Images I." *Art in America* (New York) 61, no. 2 (March/April): 42–47.

———. "Art News." *Los Angeles Times Calendar*, April 29.

**1974**

Brett, Guy. "The Changing Face of Chinese Art" [review including John Baldessari's work]. *The Times* (London), May 21.

Brooks, Rosetta. Review. *Studio International* (London) 187, no. 967 (June): Review 13–Review 14.

Collins, James. Review. *Artforum* (New York) 13, no. 1 (September): 75–78.

Denegri, J. "Tretman fotografije u konceptualnom radu Johna Baldessarija." *Spot* (Yugoslavia), no. 4: 48.

Gwinn, Carol. "Television Is an Art Form to Guest Artist Baldessari." *The University Daily Kansan* (University of Kansas, Lawrence, Kansas), January 29.

Jochimsen, Margarethe. "Story Art: Text-Foto-Synthesen." *Magazin Kunst* (West Berlin) 14, no. 4: 43–73.

del Renzio, Toni. Review. *Art and Artists* (London) 9, no. 5, no. 101 (August): 39.

Wilson, William. "Yes, They Call This Art." *Los Angeles Times*, March 23.

**1975**

Bourdon, David. "What Develops When Painters Pick Up Cameras." *Village Voice* (New York), October 20.

Collins, Tara. "John Baldessari." *Arts Magazine* (New York) 50, no. 4 (December): 6.

van Garrel, Betty. "Een Onderzoek in Kijken." *Hollands Diep* (Amsterdam), December 6.

Von Graevenitz, Antje. "Akkorde aus Aktion und Reaktion: John Baldessari im Amsterdamer Stedelijk-Museum." *Süddeutsche Zeitung* (Munich), December 27–28.

Kozloff, Max. "Pygmalion Reversed." *Artforum* (New York) 14, no. 3 (November): 30–37.

"Prints & Photographs Published." *Print Collector's Newsletter* (New York) 6, no. 5 (November/December): 135.

Welling, Jim. Book review. *Artweek* (Oakland, California) 6, no. 9 (March 1): 13–14.

**1976**

Auping, Michael. "Recent Work by John Baldessari." *Artweek* (Oakland, California) 7, no. 36 (October 23): 1.

Burke, Janine. Review. *Melbourne Times* (Melbourne, Australia), June 9.

Foote, Nancy. Review. *Artforum* (New York) 14, no. 5 (January): 63–65.

Gilchrist, Maureen. "A Californian Shows Some Amusing Work." *Age* (Melbourne, Australia), June 2.

Knott, Laurie. "Artist has a Talent 'to See.'" *The Sunday Times* (Perth, Australia), August 1.

Mason, Murray. Review. *The Western Australian* (Perth, Australia), July 31.

O'Connor, John. "TV: Video at Whitney." *The New York Times*, June 3.

Robinson, Walter and Edit deAk. "Thematic Anthology." *Art-Rite* (New York), no. 14 (Winter 1976/77): 16–31.

Wortz, Melinda. "Special Prints Section: New Editions." *ARTnews* (New York) 75, no. 7 (September): 68.

**1977**

Chrissmas, Dwight. "Reviews: Two Cherries and a Lemon." *The Dumb Ox* (Northridge, California) 1, no. 3 (Winter): 20–22.

Forgey, Benjamin. "The Whitney Biennial." *ARTnews* (New York) 76, no. 4 (April): 120–21.

Frank, Peter. Review. *ARTnews* (New York) 76, no. 8 (October 1977): 136.

Kingsley, April. "Pictures and Picture Books." *Soho Weekly News* (New York), April 7.

"Multiples & Objects & Artists' Books." *Print Collector's Newsletter* (New York) 8, no. 3 (July/August): 80.

Perrone, Jeff. Review. *Artforum* (New York) 16, no. 1 (September): 81.

Weinbren, Grahame. "John Baldessari on 'Work.'" *Artweek* (Oakland, California) 8, no. 39 (November): 1.

Wiegand, Ingrid. "Biennial Sleepers and Early Classics." *Soho Weekly News* (New York), March 17.

**1978**

Anderson, Alexandra. "John Baldessari." *Village Voice* (New York), October 16.

Bell, Jane. Review. *ARTnews* (New York) 77, no. 9 (November): 184.

Carroll, Noel. "Obsession." *Soho Weekly News* (New York), January 5.

Failing, Patricia. "John Baldessari: Taking Visual Notes." *Sunday Oregonian Northwest Magazine* (Portland, Oregon), February 5.

Garrett, Robert. "Offspring of 'Dada' Duchamp Misbehave Esthetically in Current ICA Exhibit." *Boston Herald*, January 15.

Larsen, Susan C. "Los Angeles: Inside Jobs." *ARTnews* (New York) 77, no. 1 (January): 110.

McDarrah, Fred. "Voice Choices: Photo." *Village Voice* (New York), October 16.

Montague, Kyra. "Color Photo Exhibit May be Too Ambitious." *Boston Ledger*, January 13.

Schmidt, Dan. "Ambivalent Images Make A Strong Show." *Sunday Oregonian Northwest Magazine* (Portland, Oregon), February 5.

Sutinen, Paul. "Baldessari Cleaver, Weak and Uneven." *Williamette Week* (Portland, Oregon), February 7.

Taylor, Robert. "Cerialism—Spread the Word." *Boston Globe*, January 8.

Thomas, Kevin. "Two by Baldessari at the Vanguard." *Los Angeles Times*, March 28.

**1979**

Foster, Hal. "John Baldessari's 'Blasted Allegories.'" *Artforum* (New York) 18, no. 2 (October): 52–55.

Pohlen, Annelie. Review. *Kunstforum* (Mainz, West Germany), no. 5 (1979): 200–201.

Stimson, Paul. Review. *Art in America* (New York) 67, no. 2 (March/April): 155–56.

**1980**

Lifson, Ben. "Well Hung." *Village Voice* (New York), November 5.

Poling, Clark. "John Baldessari." *Atlanta Art Papers* (Atlanta) 4, no. 3 (May/June): 18.

Talley, Dan R. Review. *Atlanta Art Papers* (Atlanta) 4, no. 4 (July/August): 9–10.

**1981**

Bannon, Anthony. "Baldessari Is Maverick Conceptualist." *Buffalo Evening News* (Buffalo, New York), April 7.

———. "Baldessari and a New Book: The Art of Language." *Buffalo Evening News* (Buffalo, New York), May 2.

Casademont, Joan. Review. *Artforum* (New York) 19, no. 5 (January): 73–74.

Cavaliere, Barbara. Review. *Arts Magazine* (New York) 55, no. 5 (January): 35.

Groot, Paul. "Kunst van Baldessari grenst aan banaliteit." *NRC Handelsblad* (Rotterdam), July 12.

Heynen, Pieter. "Fotowerk Baldessari rijk aan associaties." *De Volkskrant* (Amsterdam), June 17.

Huntington, Richard. "Baldessari Asks Embarrassing Question: What Is Art?" *Buffalo Courier Express* (Buffalo, New York), April 12.

Knight, Christopher. "Baldessari Artful 'Pointlessness' on View in New York Retrospective." *Los Angeles Herald Examiner*, April 1.

Larson, Kay. "Minds and Hearts." *New York Magazine*, April 27: 72.

Levin, Kim. "Get the Big Picture?" *Village Voice* (New York), April 22.

Morgan, Robert C. "Conceptual Art and Photographic Installations: The Recent Outlook." *Afterimage* (Rochester, New York) 9, no. 5 (December): 8–11.

Owens, Craig. "Telling Stories." *Art in America* (New York) 69, no. 5 (May): cover, 129–35.

P.[eters], Ph.[ilip]. "Bekijk't maar." *De Tijd* (Amsterdam), June 12.

Perreault, John. "Storyville." *Soho Weekly News* (New York), April 15.

Peters, Philip. "Baldessari's Visuele Satire." *Kunstbeeld* (Amsterdam), 5, no. 8 (May): 11.

Pohlen, Annelie. "Spiele mit der Kunstwirklichkeit: Arbeiten von John Baldessari im Folkwang-MuseumEssen." *Süddeutsche Zeitung* (Munich), September 18.

**1982**

Crossley, Mimi. " 'John Baldessari.' " *Houston Post* (Houston, Texas), March 28.

Johnson, Patricia C. "Works of John Baldessari Challenge What Art Is Through Wit And Humor." *Houston Chronicle* (Houston, Texas), March 13.

Knaff, Deborah L. "Modern Art that Means Something in the Context of Art." *Rice Thresher* (Rice University, Houston Texas), March 12.

Muchnic, Suzanne. "Mind Games Over Matter." *Los Angeles Times*, June 9.

Owens, Craig. "Bayreuth '82." *Art in America* (New York) 70, no. 8 (September): 132–39.

Vance, Lynn. "John Baldessari: Artist as Artist." *Dialogue: The Ohio Arts Journal* (Columbus, Ohio) 4, no. 3 (January/February): 34–39.

Zutter, J.[örg]. "Neuer Subjektivismus in Malerei, Skulptur und Fotografie." *Kunstforum* (Mainz, West Germany), no. 2 (February/March): 180–84.

**1983**

Dellabough, Robin. "High/low/roll." *CalArts Today* (California Institute of the Arts, Valencia, California) 8, no. 4 (March): 1, 6–7.

Knight, Christopher. "The Winner in the Olympics Poster Sweepstakes." *Los Angeles Herald Examiner*, January 12.

Moser, Charlotte. "Ellen Lanyon Fuses Nature Images and Fantasy." *Chicago Sun-Times*, June 12.

"Prints & Photographs Published." *Print Collector's Newsletter* (New York) 13, no. 6 (January/February): 216.

**1984**

Drohojowska, Hunter. "I Will Not Make Any More Boring Art." *L.A. Weekly* (Los Angeles), July 13.

Drohojowska, Hunter. "Pick of the Week." *L.A. Weekly* (Los Angeles), September 21.

Fisher, Jean. Review. *Artforum* (New York) 23, no. 3 (November): 99–100.

Gardner, Colin. "Signs in Search of a Subject." *Reader* (Los Angeles), October 5.

Geyrhofer, Friedrich. "Kreuzwort-Rätsel der Sinne." *Wiener* (Vienna), vol. 6 (June): 126–27.

Hoffmann, Donald. " 'Intimate' Introduction to the Work of Some Area Artists." *Kansas City Star* (Kansas City, Missouri), April 15.

Hugo, Joan. "Parables and Parodies." *Artweek* (Oakland, California) 15, no. 33 (October 6): 11.

"John Baldessari: maudites allégories!" *Art Press* (Paris), no. 87 (December): 9.

Kraft, Barbara. "Art Is What Artists Do." *Articles* (California Institute of the Arts, Valencia, California) 1, no. 2 (December 1984/January 1985): 8–9.

Knight, Christopher. "Playful, Profound Baldessari." *Los Angeles Herald Examiner*, October 10.

Lichtenstein, Therese. Review. *Arts Magazine* (New York) 58, no. 10 (June): 44.

Pincus, Robert L. Review. *Los Angeles Times*, September 21.

Prodhon, Françoise-Claire. Review. *Flash Art* [French edition] (Milan), no. 6 (Winter 1984/1985): 55.

Simon, Richard. "Parking Lot Gives Way to a Sculpture Garden." *Sacramento Union* (Sacramento, California), June 19.

Zelevansky, Lynn. Review. *ARTnews* (New York) 83, no. 9 (November): 174.

**1985**

Honnef, Klaus. "Nouvelle Biennale de Paris." *Kunstforum* (Mainz, West Germany) no. 2 (May/June): 216–32.

**1986**

Drohojowska, Hunter. "No More Boring Art." *ARTnews* (New York) 85, no. 1 (January 1986): 62–69.

Gardner, Colin. Review. *Artforum* (New York) 25, no. 4 (December 1986): 122–23.

Haus, Mary Ellen. Review. *ARTnews* (New York) 85, no. 7 (September): 115.

Honnef, Klaus. "Die Welt als Entwurf: Baldessari." *Kunstforum International* (Mainz, West Germany), no. 84 (June/July/August): 118–19.

Isenberg, Barbara. "John Baldessari: The Artist As Conduit." *Los Angeles Times Calendar*, December 21. (Also published in *Mexico City News* (Mexico City), December 28, as "Artist Baldessari Consumes the Written Word.")

Knight, Christoper. "Debut LACE Exhibition Explores Television as a Canvas for Our Times." *Los Angeles Herald Examiner*, March 2.

———. "Unveiling the State of L.A.'s Art." *Los Angeles Herald Examiner*, September 21.

———. "Exhibit of Work by Raul Guerrero Borders on Being Retrospective." *Los Angeles Herald Examiner*, October 5.

Lewallen, Constance. "New Photographic Works by John Baldessari." *University Art Museum Calendar* (University Art Museum, University of California at Berkeley, Berkeley, California) 8, no. 10 (April): 3.

Lichtenstein, Therese. Review. *Flash Art* (Milan), no. 129 (Summer): 68.

Lufkin, Liz. "Through the Aperture: Witty and Punk." *San Francisco Chronicle*, April 27.

Muchnic, Suzanne. Review. *Los Angeles Times*, October 10.

"Prints & Photographs Published." *Print Collector's Newsletter* (New York) 17, no. 5 (November/December): 181.

Relyea, Lane. "Pick of the Week." *L.A. Weekly* (Los Angeles), September 26.

Russell, John. Review. *The New York Times*, April 18.

Rychlik, Otmar. "Zwischen Photographien: John Baldessari in der Galerie Pakesch." *Die Presse* (Vienna), December 10.

Tamblyn, Christine. "Ambiguities and Associations." *Artweek* (Oakland, California) 17, no. 17 (May 3): 15–16.

Welish, Marjorie. Review. *Artscribe International* (London), no. 59 (September/October): 75–76.

### 1987

Aletti, [Vince]. Review. *Village Voice* (New York), November 24.

Artner, Alan G. "Artist's Fresh Look Revitalizes Familiar Scenes." *Chicago Tribune*, May 4.

B., H. "L'Effet divers Baldessari." *Lyon Libération* (Lyons, France), no. 203 (May 2–3): 31–32.

Dagbert, Anne. Review. *Art Press* (Paris), no. 116 (July/August): 72–73.

Dobbels, Daniel. "On Trouve Tout au CNAN." *Lyon Libération* (Lyons, France), May 27.

Dragone, Angelo. "Sotto le antiche travi minsteri di parole e segni." *La Stampa Torino Sette* (Turin, Italy), July 3.

Drohojowska, Hunter. "The Artists Who Matter: L.A.'s New Scene Makes History." *Antiques & Fine Art* 4, no. 4 (May/June): 48–55.

Shapiro, David. "John Baldessari: Le Dernier des Symbolistes." *Galeries Magazine* (Paris), no. 19 (June/July): 70–73.

Smith, Roberta. Review. *The New York Times*, November 27.

### 1988

Archer, Michael. " 'Staffa Project'; Imants Tillers; John Baldessari." *Art Monthly* (London), no. 117 (June): 24–25.

Breslauer, Jan. "Collage Industry." *L.A. Weekly* (Los Angeles), May 6.

C.[urtis], C.[athy]. Review. *Los Angeles Times*, November 25.

Caley, Shaun. Review. *Flash Art* (Milan), no. 139 (March/April): 109.

Crogan, Jim. "Another Art Attack." *L.A. Weekly* (Los Angeles), June 24.

Fisher, Jennifer and Beth Seaton. "Waterworks." *Parachute* (Montreal), no. 52 (September/October/November): 57–61.

Gourmelon, Mo. "Dynamiser un espace: Entretien avec John Baldessari." *Artefactum* (Antwerp, Belgium) 5, no. 23 (April/May): 16–19.

Knight, Christopher. "A Prophet Without Honor in California." *Los Angeles Herald Examiner*, April 10.

"Making Art." *Life* (New York) 11, no. 10 (Fall): 62–68.

Miller, John. Review. *Artforum* (New York) 26, no. 7 (March): 135.

Roberts, John. Review. *Artscribe International* (London), no. 71 (September/October): 75.

Tuchman, Laura J. "Baldessari's Multilayered Images Mirror Today's Multilayered World." *Orange County Register* (Santa Ana, California), July 20.

Wilson, William. Review. *Los Angeles Times*, April 15.

### 1989

Clothier, Peter. "John Baldessari: Talking Pictures." *Angeles* (Los Angeles), July 1989: 32–35.

Costa, J. M. "John Baldessari: La ironía es necesaria para describir la complejidad de la vida." *ABC* (Madrid), January 11.

Donohoe, Victoria. "Art that Focuses on Photographs." *The Philadelphia Inquirer*, February 11.

Frizot, Michel. "John Baldessari." *Beaux-Arts Review* (Paris), no. 67 (April): 107.

Gardner, Colin. "A Systematic Bewildering." *Artforum* (New York) 28, no. 4 (December 1989): 106–12.

"Goya y las nuevas tendencias artísticas, referencias de la exposición del californiano John Baldessari." *Ya* (Madrid), January 11.

Gracia, Fernando. " 'Me impresiona la gran profusión de enanos y de brujas en el arte español', dice John Baldessari." *Diario 16* (Madrid), January 12.

Grundberg, Andy. "Further Developments in the California State of Mind." *The New York Times*, July 23.

Lambrecht, Luk. Review. *Flash Art* (Milan), no. 145 (March/April): 126–27.

Miller, John. "The Deepest Cut: John Baldessari." *Artscribe International* (London), no. 75 (May): 52–56.

Muchnic, Suzanne. "Remaking Make-Believe in California." *Los Angeles Times*, July 21.

"Multiples & Objects & Books." *The Print Collector's Newsletter* (New York) 19, no. 6 (January–February): 230.

Pérez, Luis Francisco. "John Baldessari." *Contemporanea* (New York) 2, no. 3 (May): 90.

Real, Olga. "John Baldessari: Oto nivel de percepción." *Levante* (Valencia, Spain), May 19.

Salvioni, Daniela. "Letter from France." *Arts Magazine* (New York) 63, no. 10 (Summer): 105–106.

Serraller, F.[rancisco] Calvo. "Reconstruir la mirada: John Baldessari frente a Goya." *El Pais* (Madrid), January 7.

Serraller, Francisco Calvo. "Un planteamiento original y excitante." *El Pais* (Madrid), January 12.

Spector, Buzz. "Folio." *Artforum* (New York) 27, no. 9 (May): 13.

Squiers, Carol. "California Conceptualism." *Elle* (New York) 4, no. 11 (Summer): 30.

Torres, Rosana. "John Baldessari: 'El arte es cuestión de fe; si no, todo seria irrelevante.' " *El Pais* (Madrid), January 12.

Trenas, Miguel Ángel. "John Baldessari, la foto como pincel." *La Vanguardia* (Madrid), January 12.

Woodward, Richard B. "Novel Ideas." *ARTnews* (New York) 88, no. 4 (April): 127.

## Selected General References

### 1969

Gablik, Suzi, and John Russell. *Pop Art Redefined*. New York: Frederick A. Praeger Publishers, p. 53

### 1970

Goldin, Amy. "Words in Pictures." *Narrative Art: Art News Annual XXVI*. New York: Newsweek, Inc., pp. 61–71.

### 1971

Meyer, Ursula. *Conceptual Art*. New York: E. P. Dutton, pp. 32–33.

Tuchman, Maurice and Jane Livingston. *A & T: A Report on the Art and Technology Program of the Los Angeles County Museum of Art 1967–1971*. Los Angeles: Los Angeles County Museum of Art, p. 53.

### 1972

Lippard, Lucy R., ed. *Six Years: The Dematerialization of the Art Object from 1966 to 1972*. New York: Frederick A. Praeger Publishers, pp. 58, 113, 243, 254.

Price, Jonathan. *Video-Visions: A Medium Discovers Itself*. New York: The New American Library, Plume Books, pp. 163–67.

### 1973

Kahmen, Volker. *Art History of Photography*. New York: Viking Press, pp. 34, 209.

de Wilde, Edy. *De collectie van het Stedelijk Museum 1963–1973*. Amsterdam: Stedelijk Museum, p. 176.

### 1976

*Art Actuel: Skira Annuel '76*. Geneva: Skira, p. 174-A.

Gottlieb, Carla. *Beyond Modern Art*. New York: E. P. Dutton, pp. 364, 368–369.

Korot, Beryl and Ira Schneider, eds. *Video Art*. New York: Harcourt, Brace, Jovanovich, p. 18.

1977
Battcock, Gregory. *Why Art?*. New York: E. P. Dutton, pp. 8, 13, 14.
Crimp, Douglas. *Pictures*. New York: Artists Space, pp. 8–10.

1980
*Art Actuel: Skira Annuel Numéro Spécial 1970–1980*. Geneva: Skira, pp. 104–105.

1982
Herzogenrath, Wulf. *Videokunst In Deutschland 1963–1982*. Cologne: Kölnischer Kunstverein, pp. 53, 74.

1983
Gruber, Bettina, and Maria Vedder. *Kunst und Video: Internationale Entwicklung und Künstler*. Cologne: DuMont Buchverlag, pp. 79–81.

1984
Green, Jonathan. *American Photography: A Critical History 1945 to the Present*. New York: Harry N. Abrams, pp. 222–26.

1985
Phillpot, Clive. "Some Contemporary Artists and Their Books." In *Artists' Books: A Critical Anthology and Sourcebook*. Joan Lyons, ed. Rochester, New York: Visual Studies Workshop Press, pp. 117–19.

1986
Cameron, Dan. *Art and Its Double*. Barcelona, Spain: Centre Cultural de la Fundació Caixa de Pensions, p. 20.
Zutter, Jörg. *John Baldessari*. Basel: Museum für Gegenwartskunst Basel (Museum brochure with essay).

1987
*Collection 1987*. Lyons, France: Ville de Lyon, Musée Saint Pierre, Art Contemporain Lyon, pp. 68–79.

1988
Sandler, Irving. *American Art of the 1960s*. New York: Harper & Row, pp. 138, 294, 349, 350.

### Artist's Books

1972
*Ingres and Other Parables*. Texts in English, French, German, and Italian. London: Studio International Publications.
*Choosing: Green Beans*. Milan: Edizioni Toselli.

1973
*Throwing Three Balls in the Air to Get a Straight Line (Best of Thirty-Six Attempts)*. Milan: Giampaolo Prearo Editore S.r.L.; and Galleria Toselli.

1975
*Four Events and Reactions*. Florence: Centro Di; and Paris: Galerie Sonnabend.
*Throwing a Ball Once to Get Three Melodies and Fifteen Chords*. Berkeley, California: Regents of the University of California; and Irvine, California: Art Gallery, University of California at Irvine.

1976
*Brutus Killed Caesar*. Akron, Ohio: Emily H. Davis Art Gallery, University of Akron, Ohio; in cooperation with Sonnabend Gallery, New York, and Ohio State University, Columbus, Ohio.

1977
*A Sentence of Thirteen Parts (With Twelve Alternate Verbs) Ending in FABLE*. Hamburg, West Germany: Anatol AV und Filmproduktion.

1981
*Close-Cropped Tales*. Buffalo: CEPA Gallery and Albright-Knox Art Gallery.

1988
*The Telephone Book (With Pearls)*. Ghent, Belgium: Imschoot, Uitgevers for IC.

1989
*Lamb*. Collaboration with Meg Cranston. Valencia, Spain: Centre Julio González. IVAM, Instituto Valenciano de Arte Moderno.

### Published Writings by the Artist

1974
"TV Like 1. A Pencil 2 Won't Bite Your Leg." *Art-Rite* (New York), no. 7 (Autumn): 22–23. (Reprinted in *Essays, Statements, and Videotapes Based on "Open Circuits: An International Conference on the Future of Television"*. Cambridge, Massachusetts: MIT Press, 1977.)

1977
Untitled statement in "White in Art is White?" *Print Collectors Newsletter* (New York) 8, no. 1 (March/April): 2.

1978
Untitled statement in "Ask Not What Our Country Can Do For Us, But When Will We Realize That We Are The Country—Or—What's On the Menu." *Umbrella* (Glendale, California) 1, no. 5 (September): 100–102.

1982
Untitled statement. *Dialogue: The Ohio Arts Journal* (Columbus, Ohio) 4, no. 3 (January/February): 38–39.

1984
"John Baldessari: maudites allégories!" *Art Press* (Paris), no. 87 (December 1984): 9–14.

1985
"Black Dice." *Aperture* (New York), no. 100 (Fall 1985): 22–25.
Untitled lecture notes. *Camera Austria* (Graz, Austria), no. 19/20 (1985/1986): 4–15.

1986
"An Exhibition About TV and Art—Have Any Artists Withstood It? Perhaps A Counter/Parallel Show of Such Artists? The Numbers Would Be Few." Also "Notebook Entries to Myself for Work That is Not Yet." *TV Generations*. Los Angeles: Los Angeles Contemporary Exhibitions.

1987
Untitled statements. "John Baldessari." *Artfinder* (New York), April/June: 66–67.
Untitled statement. *Artsreview* (National Endowment for The Arts, Washington, D.C.) 4, no. 3 (Spring): 41–42.
"A Text by John Baldessari." *Spazio Umano/Human Space* (Milan), no. 1/87 (January): 68.
"My Files of Movie Stills." *Blasted Allegories: An Anthology of Writings by Contemporary Artists*. New York: The New Museum of Contemporary Art; and Cambridge, Massachusetts: MIT Press. (Reprinted from *1985 Carnegie International*. Pittsburgh, Carnegie Institute, 1985.)
Untitled statement. *Flash Art News* (Flash Art Supplement) (Milan), no. 142 (October): 15.

1989
Untitled statement in McKenna, Kristine. "You're a Pop Artist—The Museum Says So." *Los Angeles Times Calendar*, April 23.
Untitled statement in "The State of California." *Artcoast* (Los Angeles) 1, no. 2 (May/June): 34–35.

### Projects for Periodicals and Books by the Artist

1970
"Affidavit." *San Diego Union* (San Diego, California) August 10.
"Boundary." *Interfunktionen* (Cologne), no. 5: 30.
"John Baldessari." *Studio International* (London) 180, no. 924 (July/August): 3.

1971
"Informationen." *Interfunktionen* (Cologne), no. 8: 105–108.

**1972**

"Two Artists." *Artweek* (Oakland, California) 3, no. 42 (December 9): 16. (Reprinted from *Ingres and Other Parables*. London: Studio International Publications Ltd., 1972.)

"John Baldessari: Parabole." *Data* (Milan), no. 4 (May): 47–50. (Reprinted from *Ingres and Other Parables*. London: Studio International Publications Ltd., 1972.)

"Story Art." *Interfunktionen* (Cologne), no. 9: 66–73. (Reprinted from *Ingres and Other Parables*. London: Studio International Publications Ltd., 1972.)

"Art Disasters" in *Third Assembling: A Collection of Otherwise Unpublishable Manuscripts*. Richard Kostelanetz, Henry Korn, and Mike Metz, eds. New York: Assembling Press, pp. 15–16.

**1973**

"Choosing .71." *Interfunktionen* (Cologne), no. 10: 126–30.

"Police Portraits" in *Breakthrough Fictioneers*. Richard Kostelanetz, ed. West Glover, Vermont: 336.

**1974**

Cover illustration. *Stooge* (Oconomowoca Lake, Wisconsin), no. 11.

"John Baldessari: 'Easel Painting' 1972–73" in *Il Corpo Come Linguaggio (La "Body-Art" e storie simili)*. Lea Verigine, ed. Milan: Giampaolo Prearo Editore, four pages (unpaginated).

**1975**

"I Will Not Make Any More Boring Art" in *Essaying Essays: Alternative Forms of Exposition*. Richard Kostelanetz, ed. Out of London Press: New York, September, p. 177.

"Boxed Thinking." *Journal of Los Angeles Institute of Contemporary Art* (Los Angeles), no. 6 (June/July): 11.

"Retouch Portrait." *Tri-Quarterly* (Northwestern University, Evanston, Illinois) no. 32 (Winter): two pages (unpaginated).

"Three Ways to Measure Los Angeles." *AQ* (Dudweiler, West Germany), no. 15: cover, four pages (unpaginated).

**1976**

"The Bra Story." *Unmuzzled Ox* (New York) 4, no. 1, no. 13: 25.

"Sentence 1. Sentence 2. Sentence 3." *Transit*. Beuningen, Holland: Stichting Brummense Uitgeverei. pp. 233–35.

**1977**

"I Suppose So." *LAICA Journal* (Los Angeles), no. 16 (October/November): cover.

**1978**

"Attempts to Throw a Straight Line With 3 Balls." *Domus* (Milan), no. 583 (June): 48. [Reprinted from *Throwing Three Balls in the Air to Get a Straight Line (Best of Thirty-Six Attempts)*.] Milan: Giampaolo Prearo Editore S.r.L.; and Galleria Toselli.)

**1979**

"Make Sense. I Too Have Sinned. I'll Do It For Money..." in *1970–1979*. Melody Sumner, ed. Oakland, California: Burning Books.

"Artist/Saw/Legs..." *Unmuzzled Ox* (New York) 4, no. 4, vol. 5: 129–94.

"L Three Leers / W Three Whys." *Journal: A Southern California Art Magazine* (Los Angeles), no. 23 (June/July): 48–49.

**1982**

"A Four-Sided Story—Part One: A Four Sided Story—Part Two." *Views Beside....* Berlin, West Germany: Ed Vogelsang.

"Learn to Read, Learn to Write." *Art Journal* (New York) 42, no. 2 (Summer): 134–36.

**1985**

"Two Crowds With Shape of Reason Missing." *Journal: A Contemporary Art Magazine* (Los Angeles) 5, no. 42 (Fall): cover, 47.

"The reason why are no more because." *Stichting de Appel* (Amsterdam), no. 3/4 (November): loose postcard.

**1986**

" 'Yellow, (With On Lookers)'; 'Spaces Between (One Risky).' " *Bomb* (New York), no. 16 (Summer): 32–33.

"Crowds With Shape of Reason Missing." *Zone* (New York), no. 1/2: 32–39.

**1987**

"Two Men (One With Vertical Lines; One With Radiating Lines.)" *Picture This: Films Chosen by Artists*. Ed. by Steve Gallagher. Buffalo, New York: Hallwalls.

"Athletes (Study for Olympic Poster Design)." *New Observations* (New York), no. 46 (March): 13.

"Back To Back Is Not The Same As Side By Side." *Parkett* (Zurich), no. 7: insert.

"If Not About Money, It's Not About Much." *Artists' Statements*. Richard Kriesche, ed. Graz, Austria: Richard Kriesche.

"Disneyworld In France." *Lyon Libération* (Lyons, France), no. 203 (May 2–3): 32.

**1988**

"Two Viewpoints (Blue) On Red Horizon." *C Magazine* (Toronto, Canada), no. 17 (Spring): 38–43.

"2 Smiles." *MAG Magazine* (Santa Monica, California) 1, no. 1 (April): cover.

"Return of the Hero." *Aperture* (New York), no. 110 (Spring): 9–15.

**1989**

"Special Project for Tema Celeste: *Two Elephants (from pink to blue with conflict between)*, 1989." *Tema Celeste* (Siracusa, Italy), no. 22–23 (October–December): 58–61.

### Films

*Isocephaly*, 1968
Super-8, color
3 minutes

*What To Leave Out*, 1968
Super-8, color
3 minutes

*Cremation*, 1970
16mm, black-and-white
10 minutes

*New York City Art History*, 1971
Super-8, color
3 minutes

*New York City Postcard Painting*, 1971
Super-8, color
3 minutes

*Waterline*, 1971
Super-8, black-and-white
3 minutes

*Dance*, 1971
Super-8, color
3 minutes

*Minimalism*, 1971
Super-8, black-and-white
3 minutes

*Tabula Rasa*, 1971
Super-8, black-and-white
3 minutes

*Black-Out*, 1971
Super-8, black-and-white
3 minutes

*Easel Painting*, 1972–73
Super-8 film loop (originally in 16mm), color
34 seconds

*Time—Temperature*, 1972–73
Super-8 film loop (originally in 16mm), color
4 minutes, 56 seconds

*Water to Wine to Water*, 1972–73
Super-8 film loop (originally in 16mm), color
36 seconds

*The Hollywood Film*, 1972–73
Super-8 film loop (originally in
16mm), color
66 seconds

*Title*, 1973
16mm, black-and-white and color,
sound
25 minutes

*Throwing Leaves Back at Tree*, 1973
Super-8 film loop, color
3 minutes

*Ice Cubes Sliding*, 1974
Super-8 film loop, color
3 minutes

*Taking a Slate: Ilene and David (#1)*,
1974
Super-8 film loop (originally 16mm),
black-and-white
20 seconds

*Taking a Slate: Ilene and David (#2)*,
974
Super-8 film loop (originally 16mm),
color
3 minutes

*Taking a Slate: David*, 1974
Super-8 film loop (originally 16mm),
black-and-white
48 seconds

*Ted's Christmas Card*, 1974
Super-8 film loop, color
3 minutes

*Script*, 1973–77
16mm, black-and-white and color,
sound
25 minutes

*Six Colorful Inside Jobs*, 1977
16mm, color
35 minutes

## *Videotapes*

*Folding Hat: Version 1*, 1970
Black-and-white, sound
30 minutes

*Folding Hat*, 1970
Black-and-white, sound
30 minutes

*Black Painting*, 1970
Black-and-white
15 minutes

*Black Curtain*, 1970
Black-and-white, sound
15 minutes

*Life Drawing*, 1970
Black-and-white
30 minutes

*I Will Not Make Any More Boring Art*,
1971
Black-and-white
30 minutes

*Walking Forward—Running Past*, 1971
Color
20 minutes

*I Am Making Art*, 1971
Black-and-white, sound
19 minutes

*Art Disasters*, 1971
Black-and-white
30 minutes

*Police Drawing*, 1971
Black-and-white, sound
30 minutes

*Xylophone*, 1972
Black-and-white, sound
5 minutes

*Baldessari Sings LeWitt*, 1972
Black-and-white, sound
19 minutes

*Inventory*, 1972
Black-and-white, sound
24 minutes

*Teaching a Plant the Alphabet*, 1972
Black-and-white, sound
19 minutes

*Ed Henderson Reconstructs Movie
Scenarios*, 1973
Black-and-white, sound
25 minutes

*How We Do Art Now*, 1973
Black-and-white, sound
Segments:
*How Various People Spit Out Beans*
*Comparing Two Sounds*
*A 20′ Tape*
*The Eye Does Not Naturally Pan*
*Cigar Lexicon*
*On Making a Masterpiece*
30 minutes (overall)

*Haste Makes Waste*, 1973
Black-and-white, video loop
2 minutes

*Practice Makes Perfect*, 1973
Black-and-white, video loop
2 minutes

*Three Feathers and Other Fairy Tales*,
1973
Black-and-white, sound
30 minutes

*The Way We Do Art Now and Other
Sacred Tales [The Birth of Art and
Other Sacred Tales]*, 1973
Black-and-white, sound
Segments:
*Some Words I Mispronounce*
*You Tell Me What I Do*
*Anna Names Animals She Has Never
Seen*
*Taping a Stick; Lifting It from the
Other End*
*No Dice*
*Talking with One Knee to Another*

*Examining Three 8d Nails*
*What Follows Is What He Liked To Do
Best*
*For Sylvia Plath*
*A Riddle*
*Insincerely Promising a Cat a Carrot*
*A Sentence with Hidden Meaning*
*For Marcel Proust*
*Close-up*
*Flight Bag (This is a kind of interesting
object . . . )*
*It is Cruel To Put a Dog on a Mirror*
*The Way We Do Art Now (The Birth of
Abstract Art)*
30 minutes (overall)

*The Sound Made by Kicking a Bottle*,
1973
Black-and-white, sound
3 minutes

*Ed Henderson Suggests Sound Tracks
for Photographs*, 1974
Black-and-white, sound
28 minutes

*The Italian Tape*, 1974
Black-and-white, sound
8 minutes

*Six Colorful Stories: From the
Emotional Spectrum (Women)*, 1977
Color, sound
17 minutes

*Two Colorful Melodies*, 1977
Color, sound
6 minutes

# CHECKLIST OF THE EXHIBITION

All of the following works appear at the exhibition held at The Museum of Contemporary Art, Los Angeles. The works preceded by an asterisk do not appear at all venues on the exhibition's tour.

*Wrong, 1967
Acrylic and photoemulsion on canvas
59 x 45 in. (149.9 x 114.3 cm)
Los Angeles County Museum of Art; Contemporary Art Council, New Talent Purchase Award

An Artist Is Not Merely the Slavish Announcer..., 1967–68
Acrylic and photoemulsion on canvas
59 x 45 in. (149.9 x 114.3 cm)
Private collection, courtesy of Sonnabend Gallery, New York

*Econ-O-Wash..., 1967–68
Acrylic and photoemulsion on canvas
59 x 45 in. (149.9 x 114.3 cm)
Collection of the artist

Painting for Kubler, 1967–68
Acrylic on canvas
68 x 56½ in. (172.7 x 143.5 cm)
Collection of Judy and Stuart Spence, South Pasadena, California

Pure Beauty, 1967–68
Acrylic on canvas
45⅜ x 45⅜ in. (115.3 x 115.3 cm)
Collection of Ed and Nancy Kienholz

*Quality Material—..., 1967–68
Acrylic on canvas
68 x 56½ in. (172.7 x 143.5 cm)
Collection of Robert Shapazian, Los Angeles

*Tips for Artists Who Want To Sell, 1967–68
Acrylic on canvas
68 x 56½ in. (172.7 x 143.5 cm)
Collection of Robert Shapazian, Los Angeles

A Work with Only One Property., 1967–68
Acrylic on canvas
45 x 45 in. (114.3 x 114.3 cm)
The Grinstein Family, Los Angeles

This Is Not To Be Looked At., 1968
Acrylic and photoemulsion on canvas
59 x 45 in. (149.9 x 114.3 cm)
Collection of Councilman Joel Wachs, Los Angeles

A 1968 Painting, 1968
Acrylic and photoemulsion on canvas
59 x 45 in. (149.9 x 114.3 cm)
Courtesy of Sonnabend Gallery, New York

Lighted Moving Message: Viewpoint..., 1968
Commercial lighted moving message unit with formica-laminated plywood base
54 x 56 x 7½ in. (137.2 x 142.2 x 19.5 cm)
Collection of the artist

*Semi-Close-Up of Girl by Geranium (Soft View), 1968
Acrylic on canvas
68 x 56½ in. (172.7 x 143.5 cm)
Emanuel Hoffmann-Stiftung, Museum für Gegenwartskunst, Basel

A Painting That Is Its Own Documentation, 1968–present
Acrylic on canvas
102 x 56½ in. overall
(259.1 x 143.5 cm)
Original canvas: 68 x 56½ in.
(172.7 x 143.5 cm)
Additional canvas: 34 x 56½ in.
(86.4 x 143.5 cm)
Collection of Molly Barnes, Los Angeles

California Map Project, Part I: California, 1969
Eleven Type-R prints and typewritten sheet; mounted on board
Prints: 8 x 10 in. each (20.3 x 25.4 cm); text: 8½ x 11 in. (21.6 x 27.9 cm)
Collection of Hubert Burda, Munich

Commissioned Paintings, 1969
Fourteen paintings: oil or acrylic on canvas
59¼ x 45½ in. each (150.5 x 115.6 cm)
Private collection, courtesy of Sonnabend Gallery, New York (except ...A Painting by Sam Jacoby, location unknown)

Cremation Project, 1970
Bronze plaque and urn, box of ashes, six color photographs mounted on board
Plaque: 9⅛ x 16⅛ in. (23.2 x 40.9 cm); urn: 10 x 8¼ x 3⅜ in. (25.4 x 20.9 x 8.5 cm); box of ashes: 3½ x 6¼ x 9½ in. (8.8 x 15.8 x 24.1 cm); photographs: 20¼ x 24¼ in each (51.4 x 61.5 cm)
Courtesy of Sonnabend Gallery, New York

Ingres and Other Parables, 1971
Ten black-and-white photographs and ten typewritten sheets
Photographs: 8 x 10 in. each; text: 11 x 8½ in. each (20.3 x 25.4; 27.9 x 21.6 cm)
Collection of Angelo Baldassarre, Bari, Italy

Choosing (A Game for Two Players): Rhubarb, 1972
Seven Type-R prints and one typewritten sheet; mounted on board
Prints: 14 x 11 in. each; text: 11 x 8½ in. (35.6 x 27.9 cm; 27.9 x 21.6 cm)
Collection of Angelo Baldassarre, Bari, Italy

Floating: Color, 1972
Six Type-C prints; mounted on board
11 x 14 in. each (27.9 x 35.6 cm)
Collection of Mario Bertolini, Breno, Italy

Cigar Smoke To Match Clouds That Are Different (By Sight—Side View), 1972–73
Three Type-C prints; mounted on board
14 x 9½ in. each (35.6 x 24.1 cm)
Courtesy of Sonnabend Gallery, New York

*Color Corrected Studio (With Window), 1972–73
Three color photographs on board with paint and colored pencil on board
31½ x 14¾ in. overall (80 x 37.5 cm)
Collection of Susan and Lewis Manilow

A Different Kind of Order (The Thelonious Monk Story), 1972–73
Five black-and-white photographs and one typewritten sheet; mounted on board; arrangement variable
Six panels: 11⅝ x 14¹¹⁄₁₆ in. each (29.5 x 37.3 cm)
The Museum of Fine Arts, Houston; Museum Purchase with partial funding provided by the National Endowment for the Arts

Goodbye to Boats (Sailing Out), 1972–73
Twelve Type-C prints; mounted on board
9¹⁵⁄₁₆ x 6¾ in. each (25.2 x 17.1 cm)
Private collection, courtesy of Sonnabend Gallery, New York

If It Is A.M.; If It Is P.M., 1972–73
Three panels, each with graph paper, one black-and-white photograph, and ink
14 x 10¼ in. each (35.6 x 26 cm)
Courtesy of Sonnabend Gallery, New York

The Mondrian Story, 1972–73
Two Type-C prints; mounted on board
13 x 20 in. each (33 x 50.8 cm)
Collection of Ida Gianelli, Milan

*A Movie: Directional Piece Where People Are Looking*, 1972–73
Twenty-eight black-and-white photographs with acrylic; mounted on board
3½ x 5 in. each (9 x 12.7 cm)
Installation dimensions variable
Jedermann Collection, N.A.

*The Pencil Story*, 1972–73
Two Type-R prints on board with colored pencil
22 x 27¼ in. overall (55.9 x 69.2 cm)
Collection of Mr. and Mrs. Nicola Bulgari, New York

*Binary Code Series: Lily (Yes/No)*, 1974
Two Type-C prints; mounted on board
10¾ x 14 in. each (27.3 x 35.6 cm)
Courtesy of Sonnabend Gallery, New York

**Binary Code Series: Orange Peel and Ties (Female/Female Male/Male Female/Male Male/Female)*, 1974
Eight Type-C prints; mounted on board
6⅞ x 10 in. each (17.5 x 25.4 cm);
Courtesy of Sonnabend Gallery, New York

*Embed Series: Cigar Dreams (Seeing Is Believing)*, 1974
Three black-and-white photographs (retouched); mounted on board
20 x 16 in. each (50.8 x 40.6 cm)
International Museum of Photography at George Eastman House, Rochester, New York

*Embed Series: Oiled Arm (Sinking Boat and Palms)*, 1974
Two black-and-white photographs (retouched); mounted on board
16¾ x 23⅝ in. each (42.5 x 60 cm)
Collection of Susan and Lewis Manilow

*Extended Corner: Bruegel (Peasant Wedding, circa 1565)*, 1974; remade 1989 (original work lost)
Color photograph and tape
Photograph: 11 x 14¼ in. (27.9 x 36.2 cm); 44⅞ x 64 in. overall (114 x 162.6 cm)
Courtesy of the artist

*Movie Storyboard: Norma's Story*, 1974
Six panels of black-and-white photographs and ink on storyboard layout paper
Five panels: 8½ x 29⅞ in. each (21.6 x 75.9 cm); one panel: 8½ x 20¾ in. (21.6 x 52.7 cm)
Courtesy of Sonnabend Gallery, New York

**Throwing Four Balls in the Air To Get a Square (Best of 36 Tries)*, 1974
Eight color photographs; mounted on board
9½ x 13¾ in. each (24.1 x 34.9 cm)
Emanuel Hoffmann-Stiftung Museum für Gegenwartskunst, Basel

*Action Reaction (Synchronized): Finger Touching Cactus*, 1975
Twelve black-and-white photographs; mounted on board
5 x 7 in. each (12.7 x 17.8 cm)
Collection of the artist

*Alignment Series: Arrows Fly Like This, Flowers Grow Like This, Airplanes Park Like This*, 1975
Twenty-four black-and-white photographs; mounted on board
3½ x 5 in. each (8.9 x 12.7 cm)
Installation dimensions variable
Collection of Massimo Valsecchi, Milan

**Alignment Series: Palm Tree (For Charlemagne)*, 1975
Type-C prints, black-and-white photograph, and postcards on board with colored pencil
40 x 26 in. overall (101.6 x 66 cm)
Cincinnati Art Museum, Ohio; gift of RSM Co.

*Alignment Series: Things in My Studio (By Height)*, 1975
Eleven black-and-white photographs with ink; mounted on board
3½ x 5 in. each (8.9 x 12.7 cm)
Courtesy of Sonnabend Gallery, New York

*Kissing Series: Simone Palm Trees (Near)*, 1975
Two color photographs; mounted on board
10 x 8 in. each (25.4 x 20.3 cm)
Courtesy of Sonnabend Gallery, New York

*Pathetic Fallacy Series: Venial Tongue; Venal Tongue*, 1975
Two black-and-white photographs; mounted on board
16 x 20 in. each (40.6 x 50.8 cm)
Collection of Dr. Jack E. Chachkes, New York

*Strobe Series/Futurist: Trying To Get a Straight Line with a Finger*, 1975
Four black-and-white photographs; mounted on board
16 x 20 in. each (40.6 x 50.8 cm)
Courtesy of Sonnabend Gallery, New York

*Thaumatrope Series: Two Gangsters (One with Leather Suit)*, 1975
Three black-and-white photographs; mounted on board
One photograph: 5 x 7 in. (12.7 x 17.8 cm); two photographs: 11 x 14 in. each (27.9 x 35.6 cm)
Courtesy of Sonnabend Gallery, New York

*Word Chain: Sunglasses (Ilene's Story)*, 1975
Sixty-two 35mm black-and-white contact prints, one color contact print on grid paper, and typewritten sheet
Grid paper: 33 x 27 in. (83.8 x 68.6 cm); text: 11 x 8½ in. (27.9 x 21.6 cm)
Collection of Massimo Valsecchi, Milan

*Concerning Diachronic/Synchronic Time: Above, On, Under (With Mermaid)*, 1976
Six black-and-white photographs; mounted on board
28¾ x 27¾ in. overall (73 x 70.5 cm)
Courtesy of Sonnabend Gallery, New York

**Pangram Series: Pack My Box with Five Dozen Liquor Jugs*, 1976
Thirty-two black-and-white photographs; mounted on board
8 x 10 in. each (20.3 x 25.4 cm);
8 x 390 in. overall (20.3 x 990.6 cm)
Private collection, courtesy of Sonnabend Gallery, New York

*Repair Retouch Series: An Allegory About Wholeness (Plate and Man with Crutches)*, 1976
Four black-and-white photographs; mounted on board
15 x 24 in. overall (38.1 x 61 cm)
Collection of Gilbert and Lila Silverman, Detroit

*Violent Space Series: Five Vignetted Portraits of Stress Situations*, 1976
Five black-and-white photographs; mounted on board
11 x 13⅞ in. each (27.9 x 35.2 cm)
Collection of Mr. and Mrs. Bing Wright

*Violent Space Series: Nine Feet (Of Victim and Crowd) Arranged by Position in Scene*, 1976
Black-and-white photographs; mounted on board
24⅜ x 36 1½ in. overall (61.9 x 92.7 cm)
Collection of Robert H. Halff

*Violent Space Series: Story Outline (A Story That Ends Up Mostly in Bed)*, 1976
Eight black-and-white contact prints with ink; mounted on board
8¼ x 5½ in. (21 x 14 cm)
Courtesy of Sonnabend Gallery, New York

*Violent Space Series: Two Stares Making a Point but Blocked by a Plane (For Malevich)*, 1976
Black-and-white photograph with collage; mounted on board
24⅛ x 36 in. (61.3 x 91.4 cm)
Collection of James Corcoran, Los Angeles

*Blasted Allegories (Colorful Sentence): Stern Stoic Streak (Y.O.R.V.B.G.).*, 1978
Six Type-C prints and six black-and-white photographs on board with colored pencil
30½ x 40 in. (77.5 x 101.6 cm)
Lowe Art Museum, The University of Miami, Coral Gables, Florida; Museum Purchase through a grant from the National Endowment for the Arts and Matching Funds

*Blasted Allegories (Colorful Sentence): Yellow Weigh* ..., 1978
Five Type-C prints and one Polaroid print on board with colored pencil, tape, and stickers
27¾ x 40 in. (70.5 x 101.6 cm)
Continental Insurance Companies, courtesy of Douglas Drake Gallery, New York

*Blasted Allegories (Colorful Sentence): Through (≠ True) Blue to AGOG...*, 1978
Color photographs on board with colored pencil
30¾ x 40 inches (78.1 x 101.6 cm)
Courtesy of Sonnabend Gallery, New York, and Monika Sprüth Galerie, Cologne, West Germany

*Baudelaire Meets Poe*, 1980
Two black-and-white photographs and one Type-C print; mounted on board
114 x 114 in. overall (289.6 x 289.6 cm)
Courtesy of Sonnabend Gallery, New York

*Shape Derived from Subject (Snake): Used as a Framing Device to Produce New Photographs*, 1981
Nine black-and-white photographs; mounted on board
56 x 44 in. each (142.2 x 111.8 cm)
Installation dimensions variable
Courtesy of Sonnabend Gallery, New York

*Little Red Cap*, 1982
Eleven black-and-white photographs and one color photograph mounted on board, and text panel of acrylic on board
84 x 72 in. overall (213.4 x 182.9 cm)
Jedermann Collection, N.A.

*Black and White Decision*, 1984
Four black-and-white photographs; mounted on board
64 x 72¾ in. overall (162.6 x 184.8 cm)
The Eli Broad Family Foundation

*Emma and Freud*, 1984
Two black-and-white photographs and acrylic on acetate
24 x 16 in. overall (61 x 40.6 cm)
Courtesy of Galerie Peter Pakesch, Vienna

*\*Horizontal Men*, 1984
Black-and-white photographs; mounted on board
97¼ x 48⅝ in. overall (247 x 123.5 cm)
Frederick R. Weisman Art Foundation

*Knife/Dive*, 1984
Two black-and-white photographs; mounted on board
60 x 36 in. overall (152.4 x 91.4 cm)
Collection of Peter Blum, New York

*\*Lizards to Pianist (With Gold Sphere)*, 1984
Black-and-white photographs and color photograph; mounted on board
108 x 65 in. overall (274.3 x 165.1 cm)
Centro Cultural/Arte Contemporaneo, Mexico City

*Man and Woman with Bridge*, 1984
Collage of black-and-white photographs; mounted on board
14½ x 48 in. overall (36.8 x 121.9 cm)
Collection of Elisabeth and Ealan Wingate

*Pelican in Desert*, 1984
Black-and-white photograph; mounted on board
24 x 30 in. (61 x 76.2 cm)
Collection of Claes Oldenburg and Coosje van Bruggen, New York

*Starry Night Balanced on Triangulated Trouble*, 1984
Black-and-white photographs with oil tint; mounted on board
50¾ x 40 in. overall (128.9 x 101.6 cm)
Collection of Beatrice and Philip Gersh

*Three Tires with Chinese Man*, 1984
Black-and-white photographs; mounted on board
55¼ x 45½ in. overall (140.3 x 115.6 cm)
Courtesy of Margo Leavin Gallery, Los Angeles

*Two Crowds (With Shape of Reason Missing)*, 1984
Two black-and-white photographs and board; mounted on board
48 x 30 in. overall (121.9 x 76.2 cm)
Jedermann Collection, N.A.

*Civic Piece*, 1986
Black-and-white photographs with oil tint and gouache; mounted on board
106¾ x 72½ in. overall (271.2 x 184.2 cm)
Collection of Lenore S. and Bernard A. Greenberg

*\*Elephant Weight (Blue)*, 1986
Black-and-white photographs with oil tint; mounted on board
64¾ x 73½ in. overall (164.5 x 186.7 cm)
Collection of Isabella del Frate Rayburn, New York

*\*Heel*, 1986
Black-and-white photographs with vinyl paint and oil tint, and one black-and-white photograph printed on metallic paper; mounted on board
106½ x 87 in. overall (270.5 x 220.9 cm)
Los Angeles County Museum of Art; Modern and Contemporary Art Council Fund

*Letter*, 1986
Black-and-white photographs with vinyl paint and board; mounted on board
107½ x 48½ in. overall (273 x 123.2 cm)
Courtesy of Margo Leavin Gallery, Los Angeles

*\*Life's Balance*, 1986
Black-and-white photographs and board; mounted on board
97¾ x 68¾ in. overall (248.2 x 174.6 cm)
Collection of Brooke and Carolyn Alexander, New York

*Some Rooms*, 1986
Black-and-white photographs with gouache; mounted on board
96½ x 109½ in. overall (245.1 x 278.1 cm)
The Museum of Contemporary Art, Los Angeles; gift of The Eli Broad Family Foundation

*Upward Fall*, 1986
Black-and-white photographs with oil tint and black-and-white photographs printed on metallic paper; mounted on board
95 x 68 in. overall (241.3 x 172.7 cm)
Fried, Frank, Harris, Shriver & Jacobson Art Collection, Los Angeles

*Ancient Wisdom (With Repairs), 1987
Three black-and-white photographs
with vinyl paint and oil tint; mounted
on board
84 x 30 in. overall (213.4 x 76.2 cm)
Courtesy of Sonnabend Gallery,
New York

Bloody Sundae, 1987
Black-and-white photographs
with vinyl paint; mounted on board
93 x 65½ in. overall
(236.2 x 166.4 cm)
Collection of Joseph Rank

Column (With Duelist), 1987
One black-and-white and two color
photographs; mounted on board and
aluminum
14 x 155⅝ in. overall (35.6 x 395.3 cm)
Olnick Organization, New York

Helmsman (With Flaw), 1987
Black-and-white photographs;
mounted on aluminum
81 x 98 in. overall (205.7 x 248.9 cm)
Collection of Vijak Mahdavi and
Bernardo Nadal-Ginard, Boston

Inventory, 1987
Black-and-white and color
photographs with vinyl paint;
mounted on board and masonite
97 x 97½ in. overall (246.4 x 247.7 cm)
Collection of the artist

Planets (Chairs, Observer, White
Paper), 1987
Color and black-and-white
photographs with oil tint, vinyl paint,
and board; mounted on board and
aluminum
100 x 105½ in. overall (254 x 268 cm)
Private collection, Los Angeles

Sailing and Tennis, 1987
Color and black-and-white
photographs; mounted on board and
aluminum
90 x 96 in. overall (228.6 x 243.8 cm)
Private collection, courtesy of
Sonnabend Gallery, New York

Two Stories, 1987
Black-and-white and color
photographs with oil tint and vinyl
paint; mounted on board and
aluminum
96 x 50⅞ in. overall (243.8 x 129.2 cm)
Collection of Dakis Joannou, Athens

Yellow Harmonica (With Turn), 1987
Black-and-white photographs with
vinyl paint and board; mounted
on board
94½ x 107 in. overall (240 x 271.8 cm)
The Rivendell Collection

Banquet, 1988
Black-and-white photographs with
vinyl paint; mounted on board
73¼ x 144½ in. overall (186.1 x 367 cm)
Courtesy of Brooke Alexander,
New York

Double Landscape, 1988
Two black-and-white photographs
with oil tint; mounted on board
26¾ x 98 in. overall (67.9 x 248.9 cm)
Collection of Emily Fisher Landau

Double Man and Seal, 1988
Black-and-white photographs;
mounted on board
48 x 110¾ in. overall (121.9 x 281.3 cm)
Collection of Bob and Linda Gersh, Los
Angeles

*Fish and Ram, 1988
Black-and-white and color
photographs with vinyl paint;
mounted on board
109¾ x 144¼ in. overall (278.8 x
366.4 cm)
Museum of Contemporary Art,
Chicago; Museum Purchase with
funds from Gerald S. Elliott and the
National Endowment for the Arts

*If This Then That, 1988
Black-and-white photographs with
vinyl paint; mounted on board and
plastic
80¼ x 67 in. overall (203.8 x 170.2 cm)
PaineWebber Group, Inc., New York

Mountain Climber, 1988
Black-and-white photographs with oil
tint; mounted on board
Top: 25⅞ x 19⅛ in. (65.7 x 48.6 cm);
bottom: 69¼ x 91½ in. (175.9 x 232.4 cm)
Collection of James and Linda
Burrows, Los Angeles

*Sphinx, 1988
Black-and-white photographs with
vinyl paint; mounted on board
96⅜ x 89 in. overall
(244.8 x 226.1 cm)
The Capital Group, Inc., Los Angeles

Three Red Paintings, 1988
Black-and-white photographs with
vinyl paint; mounted on board
94¼ x 128¼ in. overall (239.4 x
325.8 cm)
Lannan Foundation

*Two Languages (Begin), 1989
Black-and-white photographs with
vinyl paint; mounted on board and
plastic
109 x 115 in. overall (276.9 x 292.1 cm)
Collection of Emily Fisher Landau

# LENDERS TO THE EXHIBITION

Brooke Alexander, New York
Brooke and Carolyn Alexander, New York
Angelo Baldassarre, Bari, Italy
Molly Barnes, Los Angeles
Mario Bertolini, Breno, Italy
Peter Blum, New York
The Eli Broad Family Foundation
Mr. and Mrs. Nicola Bulgari, New York
Hubert Burda, Munich
James and Linda Burrows, Los Angeles
The Capital Group, Inc., Los Angeles
Centro Cultural/Arte Contemporaneo, Mexico City
Dr. Jack E. Chachkes, New York
Cincinnati Art Museum, Ohio
Continental Insurance Companies, New York
James Corcoran, Los Angeles
Fried, Frank, Harris, Shriver & Jacobson Art
    Collection, Los Angeles
Bob and Linda Gersh, Los Angeles
Beatrice and Philip Gersh
Lenore S. and Bernard A. Greenberg
The Grinstein Family, Los Angeles
Robert H. Halff
Emanuel Hoffmann-Stiftung, Museum für
    Gegenwartskunst, Basel
International Museum of Photography at George
    Eastman House, Rochester, New York
Jedermann Collection, N.A.
Dakis Joannou, Athens
Ed and Nancy Kienholz

Emily Fisher Landau
Lannan Foundation
Margo Leavin Gallery, Los Angeles
Los Angeles County Museum of Art
Lowe Art Museum, The University of Miami, Coral
    Gables, Florida
Vijak Mahdavi and Bernardo Nadal-Ginard, Boston
Susan and Lewis Manilow
Museum of Contemporary Art, Chicago
The Museum of Contemporary Art, Los Angeles
The Museum of Fine Arts, Houston
Claes Oldenburg and Coosje van Bruggen, New York
Olnick Organization, New York
Galerie Peter Pakesch, Vienna
PaineWebber Group, Inc., New York
Private collection
Private collection, Los Angeles
Joseph Rank
Isabella del Frate Rayburn, New York
The Rivendell Collection
Robert Shapazian, Los Angeles
Gilbert and Lila Silverman, Detroit
Sonnabend Gallery, New York
Judy and Stuart Spence, South Pasadena, California
Monika Sprüth Galerie, Cologne, West Germany
Massimo Valsecchi, Milan
Councilman Joel Wachs, Los Angeles
Frederick R. Weisman Art Foundation
Elisabeth and Ealan Wingate
Mr. and Mrs. Bing Wright

# INDEX

Page numbers in italics indicate illustrations

A Cigar Is a Good Smoke, 25, 26
A Different Kind of Order (The Thelonious Monk Story), 80–81, 82–83
A Movie: Directional Piece Where People Are Looking, 84, 85, 198
A 1968 Painting, 33
A Painting That Is Its Own Documentation, 43
A Sentence of Thirteen Parts (With Twelve Alternative Verbs) Ending in FABLE, 100–1, 102, 103, 108
A Sentence with Hidden Meaning, 131, 132
A Two-Dimensional Surface..., 28
A Work with Only One Property., 42
Acconci, Vito, 57
Action/Reaction (Synchronized): Finger Touching Cactus, 142, 145
Aligning Balls, 170, 170–71, 173
Alignment Series: Arrows Fly Like This, Flowers Grow Like This, Airplanes Park Like This, 53, 53
Alignment Series: Palm Tree (For Charlemagne), 31, 31
Alignment Series: Things in My Studio (By Height), 62
Altoon, John, 11
An Artist Is Not Merely the Slavish Announcer..., 36, 37, 38
Ancient Wisdom (With Repairs), 177, 179
Andre, Carl, 57
Antin, David, 38–39, 41, 47
Apple, 19
Apollinaire, 25
Art Lesson(s), 22, 23, 24, 25, 26, 30
Ashputtle, 218, 222
Atkinson, Terry, 40

Baldessari, Antonio, 11, 212
Baldwin, Michael, 41
Banquet, 190, 191
Molly Barnes Gallery, 39, 40, 41
Barry, Robert, 41, 57
Baudelaire, Charles, 115, 118
Baudelaire Meets Poe, 114, 115, 115, 118
Bell, Larry, 12
Bellamy, Richard, 41
Bengston, Billy Al, 12
Berman, Wallace, 12
Bettelheim, Bruno, 218, 226
Beuys, Joseph, 80
Binary Code Series: Lily (Yes/No), 154
Black and White Decision, 176, 176
Black Dice, 16, 17, 18–19
Blasted Allegories, 19, 108, 139
Blasted Allegories (Colorful Equation): Intertwined with Green Offshoot Intersecting at Pressure Point, 113
Blasted Allegories (Colorful Sentence and Purple Patch): Starting With Red Father..., 108, 109

Blasted Allegories (Colorful Sentence): Stern Stoic Streak (Y.O.R.V.B.G.), 113
Blasted Allegories (Colorful Sentence): Through (≠ True) Blue to AGOG..., 108, 112
Blasted Allegories (Colorful Sentence): Yellow Weigh ..., 112
Bloody Sundae, 132, 139, 140
Boat and Ship, 153, 155
Bochner, Mel, 41
Bowl (With Two Voices), 206, 209
Brach, Paul, 38, 57
Braque, Georges, 13
Brutus Killed Caesar, 97, 98–99, 100, 108, 118
Buildings = Guns = People: Desire, Knowledge, and Hope (With Smog), 185, 186–87
Buren, Daniel, 17
Eugenia Butler Gallery, 40

Cage, John, 75, 78, 93
California Institute of the Arts, 57, 75–76, 83, 91, 215
California Map Project, Part I: California, 44, 44–45
California Map Project— Sacramento, September 15, 1969, 46, 46
California—Mexico Boundary Project, 46, 46
Campbell, Joseph, 218, 219
Canetti, Elias, 163
Car Color Series: All Cars Parked on the West Side of Main Street, Between Bay and Bicknell Streets, Santa Monica, at 1:15 P.M., September 1, 1976, 64–65
Cézanne, Paul, 11, 41, 97, 118
Choosing (A Game for Two Players): Rhubarb, 47, 52, 53, 79
Chouinard Art Institute, 11
Cigar Smoke to Match Clouds That Are Different (By Sight— Side View), 25, 25
Cigar Smoke To Match Clouds That Are Different (By Memory—Front View), 25
Civic Piece, 188, 189, 191
Close-Cropped Tales, 119, 120, 121, 122, 142
Color Corrected Studio (With Window), 61
Column (With Duelist), 230–31
Columns and Grillwork, 163, 166
Commissioned Paintings, 47, 48–51, 54, 91
Composing on a Canvas., 43
Composition for Violin and Voices (Male), 192, 195, 195, 196–97
Concerning Diachronic/ Synchronic Time: Above, On, Under (With Mermaid), 35, 35
Couple, 153, 157
Cremation Project, 54, 56, 57
Crowds (With Shape of Reason Missing), 180
Cubism, 13

Dada, 11, 25, 38
De Maria, Walter, 46–47
"Documenta 7" exhibition, 218
Double Landscape, 153, 156
Double Man and Seal, 180, 183
Duchamp, Marcel, 41, 80
Eagle/Rodent, 153, 155
Earthquake, 132, 137
Econ-O-Wash..., 29, 30
Ed Henderson Suggests Sound Tracks for Photographs, 78, 79

Elephant, 153, 156
Elephant Weight (Blue), 202, 203, 206, 212
Eluard, Paul, 24, 25
Embed Series, 26
Embed Series: Cigar Dreams (Seeing is Believing), 27
Embed Series: Oiled Arm (Sinking Boat and Palms), 27
Emma and Freud, 130
Ernst, Max, 24, 25 ("L'Invention")
Eruption with Clouds Arranged by Color, 167
Everything Is Purged..., 40, 40
Evidence, 57, 59
Examining Pictures, 39
Exterior Views, 198, 201

Ferus Gallery, 11, 57
Finger Pointing at Objects, 51
Konrad Fischer Gallery, 41, 69
Fish and Ram, 203, 205, 206, 212
Fitcher's Bird, 218, 223
Floating Color, 104, 105
Floating: Stick (Two Figures: Two Choices, One Framing), 215, 216
Floating: Stick (With Two Figures: To Get Various Triangles), 215
Fluxus, 38
Folding Hat: Version 1, 121, 121
Four Events and Reactions, 142
4 Types of Chaos / 4 Types of Order, 153, 159
Fragment Series, 13–14, 19, 21, 21; "Fragments" poster, 22
Francis, Sam, 29
Freud, Sigmund, 108, 121, 130, 131, 149, 150, 180, 188, 203, 227, 229
Fugitive Essays, 131
Fugitive Essays (With Caterpillar), 116–17, 118
Fuller, Buckminster, 146
Futurism, 53, 55

Gavel, 153, 158
Ghetto Boundary Project, 44, 45, 46
Gift, 132
Giraffe Weight, 203, 204, 206, 212
Godard, Jean–Luc, 91
Goodbye to Boats (Sailing In), 84, 84, 173
Goodbye to Boats (Sailing Out), 84, 172–73, 173
Goya, Francisco, 32, 176
Graham, Dan, 41, 57
Griffith, D.W., 32, 76
Brothers Grimm, 216, 226, 229

Haacke, Hans, 57
Harrison, Newton, 38
Hawthorne, Nathaniel, 108
Heel, 163, 164, 165, 191
Held, Al, 47
Helmsman (With Flaw), 142, 145
Higgins, Dick, 38
High Flight, 148, 149, 150
Hogarth, William, 53
Hopps, Walter, 11
How Various People Spit Out Beans, 126
Huebler, Douglas, 41, 47, 57
Hunter College, 57
Huston, John, 83

I Will Not Make Any More Boring Art, 58, 58; lithograph, 58
If It Is A.M.; If It Is P.M., 90, 91

If This Then That, 144
Imagine This Woman..., 100, 100–1
Ingres and Other Parables, 69–70, 72, 73, 74, 75, 166
Inventory, 212, 213
Inverse (Brackets), 206, 209

Jakobson, Roman, 218
Jazz at the Art Center #5, 12–13, 12; slide show, 13
Jensen, Hedvig, 11
Judd, Donald, 122

Kaprow, Alan, 38, 83
Kauffman, Craig, 11
Kawara, On, 41
Kienholz, Edward, 11
Kiss/Panic, 165, 165
Kissing Series: Simone Palm Trees (Near), 31
Knife/Dive, 153, 153
"Konzeption—conception" exhibition, 41, 54
de Kooning, Willem, 104
Kosuth, Joseph, 40–41, 57
Kubler, George, 32, 33

Landscape, 153, 157
Langer, Susanne K., 97
Lebrun, Rico, 11
Letter, 162, 163
Lévi-Strauss, Claude, 57, 108
LeWitt, Sol, 57
Life's Balance, 180, 181
Light and Dark, 177, 177
Lighted Moving Message: Isocephaly..., 39, 40
Lighted Moving Message: Viewpoint..., 39, 40
Lighthouse, 206, 208
Line of Force, 55
Little Red Cap, 218, 224, 225, 225, 226–27
Livingston, Jane, 40–41
Lizards to Pianist (With Gold Sphere), 70, 71
Looking East on 4th and C..., 29, 30

Maciunas, George, 38
Magritte, René, 25, 192
Malevich, Kazimir, 96
Man and Woman with Bridge, 198, 200; Installation, 200
Man Ray, 25
Mary, 206, 210
Matisse, Henri, 11, 57, 218
Measurement Series: Measuring A Chair With a Coffee Cup (Top-Bottom), 63
Minerva (With Old and New Truths), 206, 208
Morris, Richard Allen, 93
Moses, Ed, 12
Mountain Climber, 150, 152
Movie Storyboard: Norma's Story, 19, 84, 93, 94, 95, 96, 97
Mullican, Matt, 215

Nauman, Bruce, 39, 41, 80
Newman, Barnett, 122
Nicolaides, George, 44, 46, 47
Nietzsche, 118–19, 131

Oldenburg, Claes, 47, 80, 218
"Op losse Schroeven" exhibition, 41
Oppenheim, Dennis, 46, 47 Time Line
Otis Art Institute, 11
Ozenfant, Amédée, 121

Paik, Nam June, 83
*Painting for Kubler*, 32, *33*
*Pathetic Fallacy Series*, 191
*Pathetic Fallacy Series:*
  *Glowering Hair*, 191, *192*
*Pathetic Fallacy Series: Happy*
  *Landscape: Sad Landscape*,
  191, *192*
*Pathetic Fallacy: Injured Yellow*,
  191, *193*
*Pathetic Fallacy: Stoic Peach*, 191,
  *193*
*Pathetic Fallacy: Venial Tongue;*
  *Venal Tongue*, 191, *193*
*Pelican in Desert*, 180, *180*
Phototext canvases, 29, 36, 38,
  41, 47
Picabia, Francis, 90
Picasso, Pablo, 13 139, *141* (*Glass*
  *of Absinthe*)
*Pier 18*, 119, *119*
*Place a Book in a Strong*
  *Light . . .* , 32, *33*
*Planets (Chairs, Observer, White*
  *Paper)* 142–43, *143*, 146, 149
Poe, Edgar Allan, 115, 118
*Police Drawing*, 57, *59*
Pollock, Jackson, 76, 180
Post-studio Art, 57
Pound, Ezra, 68, 76
*Pure Beauty*, 38

*Quality Material—. . .* , 36

Rauschenberg, Robert, 29, 30
Read, Herbert, 97
Reise, Barbara, 32
*Repair/Retouch Series: An*
  *Allegory About Wholeness (Plate*
  *and Man with Crutches)*, 184,
  *185*
Resnais, Alain, 168
*Ribbon*, 206, *207*
*Roller Coaster*, 153, 160, *160*
*Rolling Tire*, 214, *214–15*, 216
Ruscha, Edward, 12, *28*, 29, 47
  (*Standard Station 10¢ Western*
  *Being Torn in Half*)
*Ryan Oldsmobile*, 30, *30*

*Sailing*, 177, *178*
*Sailing and Tennis*, 166, 168, *168*,
  *169*, 170, 191
San Diego State College, 11
Schapiro, Miriam, 38

*Script*, 91, *92*, *93*
*Semi-Close-Up of Girl by*
  *Geranium (Soft View)*, 32, *34*,
  35, *76*
*Shape Derived from Subject*
  *(Snake): Used as a Framing*
  *Device to Produce New*
  *Photographs*, 122, *123*, *124*, *125*
*Six Colorful Inside Jobs*, 104–5,
  *106–7*
*Six Colorful Stories: From the*
  *Emotional Spectrum (Women)*,
  101, *104*, 108, 192
*Small Landscape*, 153, *158*
Smith, Hassell, 11
Smithson, Robert, 47, 57
"Software" exhibition, 57
*Some Rooms*, 37, *37*
*Songs: 1 Sky / Sea / Sand*
  *2 Sky / Iceplant / Grass*, 131,
  *136*, *136*, 192
Southwestern Junior College, 69
*Space Between (24 Photographs*
  *of Middleburg Residents)*, 199,
  *199*

*Spaces Between*, 198
*Spaces Between (One Risky)*, 198
*Sphinx*, 166, *167*
*Stain*, 174, *175*
*Stalk (With Tire)*, 132
*Standard Hand*, 16
*Starry Night Balanced on*
  *Triangulated Trouble*, 146, *147*
Stella, Frank, 32, 105
Stieglitz, Alfred, 25
*Story with 24 Versions*, 93, *93*
*Strobe Series/Futurist: Girl with*
  *Flowers Falling from Her*
  *Mouth (For Botticelli) #1*, *34*,
  35
*Strobe Series/Futurist: Trying to*
  *Get a Straight Line with a*
  *Finger*, 53, *54–55*
*Stroll*, 206, *206*
*Suppose It is True After All? What*
  *Then?*, 24, 26
Surrealism, 11, 25, 38
Symbolism, 25

*Teaching a Plant the Alphabet*,
  78, *80*
*Team*, 132, *133*
Text canvases, 27, 28, 36, 38, 41,
  *93*

*That Is*, 206, *207*
*Thaumatrope Series*, 184
*Thaumatrope Series: Two*
  *Gangsters (One with Scar and*
  *Gun)*, 184, *184*
*The Back of All the Trucks Passed*
  *While Driving from Los Angeles*
  *to Santa Barbara, California.*
  *Sunday 20 January 1963*, 13,
  *14–15*
*The Frog King*, 218, *220*
*The Mondrian Story*, 76, *78*, 96
*The Movie Tree Story*, 216, *217*
*The Pencil Story*, 80, *81*, 191
*The Soul Returns to the Body*,
  153, *154*
*The Spectator is Compelled . . .*,
  *32*, 32
*The Story of One Who Set Out to*
  *Study Fear*, 218, *219*
*The Three Feathers*, 218, *221*
*The Way We Do Art Now and*
  *Other Sacred Tales*, 131, *132*
*This Is Not To Be Looked At.*, 19,
  *20*, 32
Thoreau, Henry David, 122, 146,
  220
*Three Feathers and Other Fairy*
  *Tales*, 77–78, *78*
*Three Red Paintings*, 139, *141*
*Three Tires with Chinese Man*,
  19, *20*
*Three Types of Light*, 177, *179*
*Throwing Four Balls in the Air to*
  *Get a Square (Best of 36 Tries)*,
  227, *228*
*Throwing Four Balls in the Air to*
  *Get a Straight Line (Best of 36*
  *Tries)*, 227
*Throwing Three Balls in the Air*
  *To Get an Equilateral Triangle*
  *(Best of 36 Tries)*, 173, *174–5*,
  227
*Tips for Artists Who Want to Sell*,
  42
*Title*, 84, 86, *88*, *89*, 91, *172*, *173*
*(Two Chests) For Example*, 19
*Two Crowds (With Shape of*
  *Reason Missing)*, 180, *182*
*Two Crowds: Trouble*
  *(Excluded); Watching*
  *(Included)*, 177
*Two Fish*, 206, *211*
*Two Languages (Begin)*, 194, *195*
*Two Stories*, 75, 77, 84

*Untitled*, 1962, *16*
*Untitled*, 1967, 27, *28*
*Upward Fall*, 149, 150, *151*, 180
*US Mall Marks the X*, 14

*Vanitas Series*, 131, 134, 191
*Vanitas Series: Warm (Short*
  *Depth of Field) Bubbles*
  *Descending, Wine Glass / Key,*
  *Watch Skull*, 70, *134*
*Violent Space Series: Five*
  *Vignetted Portraits of Stress*
  *Situations*, 192, *198*
*Violent Space Series: Nine Feet*
  *(Of Victim and Crowd)*
  *Arranged by Position in Scene*,
  188, *188*
*Violent Space Series: Six*
  *Situations with Guns Aligned*
  *(Guns Sequenced Small to*
  *Large)*, 84, *87*
*Violent Space Series: Six*
  *Vignetted Portraits of Guns*
  *Aligned and Equipoised*
  *(Violet)*, 84, *86–87*
*Violent Space Series: Story*
  *Outline (A Story That Ends Up*
  *Mostly in Bed)*, 111
*Violent Space Series: Two Stares*
  *Making a Point but Blocked by*
  *a Plane (For Malevich)*, 96, *96*
*Virtues and Vices (for Giotto)*,
  131, *135*

Warhol, Andy, 29
Weiner, Lawrence, 41, 57
*What This Painting Aims To Do.*,
  39
"When Attitudes Become Form"
  exhibition, 41
*White Shape*, 180, *183*
Wilder, Nicholas, 41
Williams, Emmett, 38, 83
Wittgenstein, Ludwig, 57, 75
Wixom, Carol, 30
*Word Chain: Sunglasses (Ilene's*
  *Story)*, 110, 108
*Wrong*, 30, *30*, *31*, 31, 32

*Yellow (With Kiss)*, 132
*Yellow (With Onlookers)*, 132,
  *138*
*Yellow Harmonica (With Turn)*,
  153, *161*, 163, 191

# PHOTOGRAPH CREDITS

Photographs have been supplied in many instances by the owners named in the captions. Those for which an additional credit is due are listed below.

Jon Abbott, courtesy of Sonnabend Gallery, New York, 36 right, 40 bottom, 116–17, 145 top, 179 left, 180, 193 top, 198, 200 top; the artist, 13, 16, 20 top left, 21, 22, 24 bottom and top right, 28 top, 44–45 top, 46 top and center, 52, 60, 78 bottom, 79, 80, 98–99, 102, 105, 121, 126, 200 bottom; Quentin Bertoux, courtesy of MAGASIN, Centre National d'Art Contemporain, Grenoble, 195; Courtesy Blum Edition, New York, 17; courtesy of the Carnegie Museum of Art, Pittsburgh, 186–87; Sheldan C. Collins, courtesy of Whitney Museum of American Art, New York, 222; Colorphoto Hinz, 228; Peter Cox, courtesy of Van Abbemuseum, Eindhoven, the Netherlands, 135 bottom; Bevan Davies, courtesy of Sonnabend Gallery, 35, 55 bottom; D. James Dee, courtesy of Douglas Drake Gallery, New York, 112 top; Al Elai, 202; Ken Feingold, 58 bottom, 94, 95; IVAM, Instituto Valenciano de Arte Moderno, Valencia, Spain, 87, 144, 221; Salvatore Licitra, courtesy of Massimo Valsecchi, Milan, 53, 110; William Nettles, courtesy of Margo Leavin Gallery, Los Angeles, 176; George Nicolaides, 59 top

four images, 214–15; Douglas M. Parker Studio, courtesy of Margo Leavin Gallery, Los Angeles, 137, 141 bottom, 148, 151, 152, 155 bottom, 156 top, 158 right, 159, 160, 162, 164, 166, 167 top, 181, 183, 189, 190, 201, 204, 205, 206, 207, 208 left, 209 bottom, 211; David Platzker, courtesy of the artist, 104, 132; Friedrich Rosenstiel, courtesy of Sonnabend Gallery, New York, 39 left and right; courtesy of Ed Ruscha, 28 bottom; Fred Scruton, courtesy of Sonnabend Gallery, New York, 31 top left and right, 48, 49 top left and bottom left and right, 50, 51 top left and right, 54, 55 top left and right, 62, 71, 77, 81, 85, 86–87 top, 93, 100–1, 113 bottom, 114, 115, 123, 124, 125, 133, 134, 138, 140, 143, 145 bottom, 154, 155 top, 156 bottom, 157 bottom, 158 left, 161, 169, 175, 179 right, 192, 194, 208 right, 209 top, 210, 213, 219, 220, 224, 230–31; Nick Sheidy, courtesy of Sonnabend Gallery, New York, 63, 90, 111, 184, 185; courtesy of Harry Shunk, 119; Jim Strong, 24 top left; John Thomas, courtesy of the artist, 32, 33 bottom left, 34 bottom, 42 right, 49 top right, 56, 136; John F. Thomson, 188; Michael Tropea, Chicago, 109; Wolfgang Woessner, courtesy of Galerie Peter Pakesch, Vienna, 157 top, 177, 178; Zindman/Fremont, courtesy of Sonnabend Gallery, New York, 37.